THE TWENTIETH-CENTURY HUMANIST CRITICS:
FROM SPITZER TO FRYE

The Twentieth-Century Humanist Critics revisits the work and place of eight scholars roughly contemporary with Anglo-American New Criticism: Leo Spitzer, Ernst Robert Curtius, Erich Auerbach, Albert Béguin, Jean Rousset, C.S. Lewis, F.O. Matthiessen, and Northrop Frye. First, William Calin considers the achievements of each critic, examining their methodologies and basic presuppositions as well as the critiques marshalled against them. Calin then explores their relation to history, to canon-formation, and to current theoretical debates. He goes on to show how these eight scholars form a current in the history of criticism, a current that is related to both humanism and modernism.

Underscoring the international, cosmopolitan aspects of literary scholarship in the last century, *The Twentieth-Century Humanist Critics* discusses humanist critical traditions from Europe, the United Kingdom, and North America, and reveals the surprising extent to which, across various languages and academic systems, critics posed similar questions and arrived at a wealth of complementary responses.

WILLIAM CALIN is a graduate research professor in the Department of Romance Languages at the University of Florida.

The Twentieth-Century Humanist Critics: From Spitzer to Frye

WILLIAM CALIN

UNIVERSITY OF TORONTO PRESS
Toronto Buffalo London

© University of Toronto Press Incorporated 2007
Toronto Buffalo London
Printed in Canada

ISBN 978-0-8020-9283-0 (cloth)
ISBN 978-0-8020-9475-9 (paper)

Printed on acid-free paper

Library and Archives Canada Cataloguing in Publication

Calin, Wiliam
The twentieth-century humanist critics: from Spitzer to Frye / William Calin.

Includes bibliographical references and index.
ISBN 978-0-8020-9283-0 (bound) – ISBN 978-0-8020-9475-9 (pbk.)

1. Criticism – History – 20th century. 2. Critics. 3. Humanism – History –
20th century. I. Title.

PN94.C35 2007   801'.950904   C2007-904953-2

University of Toronto Press acknowledges the financial assistance to its publishing
program of the Canada Council for the Arts and the Ontario Arts Council.

Contents

vi Contents

Acknowledgments

I wish to thank friends and colleagues who, over the years, offered encouragement and support for this book. They are medievalists, *vingtiémistes* including those active in the International Colloquia on Twentieth and Twenty-first Century French Studies, the pioneers in the International Society for Studies in Medievalism, and comrades from all over. The list is long yet terribly incomplete: Thelma Fenster, who gave me the idea, and Ron Akehurst, Alex Alberro, Nora Alter, Barbara Altmann, Andrés Avellaneda, Philip Bennett, Françoise Calin, Frédéric Canovas, Bill Cloonan, Frank Collins, Steve Durrant, David Ellison, Franz Futterknecht, Martine Guyot, Pat Henry, Otto Johnston, Sarah Kay, Dragan Kujundzic, Brian Merrilees, Gwen Morgan, Geraldine Nichols, Rupert Pickens, Gina Psaki, Peter Schakel, Helen Solterer, David Staines, Richard Utz, Kathleen Verduin, Timmie Vitz, Mary Watt, and the late, great Leslie Workman.

In 2000 I was a Fellow at the Northrop Frye Centre, University of Toronto, and in 2004–5 a Fellow at the Centre for Reformation and Renaissance Studies, also University of Toronto. Those two centres and the University of Florida Research Foundation contributed enormously to the elaboration of this project.

I wish to express gratitude to the anonymous readers for the University of Toronto Press, to my editors at the Press – Ron Schoeffel, Jill McConkey, and Barb Porter – and to Ruth Pincoe, who copyedited, read proof, and made the index. And special thanks to my graduate student research assistants Rachel Hart, Kate Hunter, Jaime O'Dell, Barbara Petrosky, and Giovanna Summerfield.

THE TWENTIETH-CENTURY HUMANIST CRITICS:
FROM SPITZER TO FRYE

Introduction

In the course of our culture wars there appear, from time to time, statements repudiating earlier approaches to literary study, approaches that preceded the advent of theory and the postmodernist outlook. The repudiation often refers directly to the New Criticism, denouncing the New Critics for elitism, for proclaiming one and only one acceptable method of reading, for isolating literary texts from history and denying their ideological content and context, and for imposing a narrow literary canon of conservative writers, the leading critics themselves being men of the Right. There is a tiny kernel of truth to the accusations, although the generalizations are excessive, there are numerous exceptions to the rule, and New Criticism, like any critical school worth its salt, was made up of divergent currents and divergent individuals.

The purpose of this book is to cast a wider net, to bring together for consideration a greater range of scholar-critics roughly contemporary with the New Criticism – some from the Continent and some from the English-speaking countries. I chose the three leading figures of the German school of Romance studies, two of whom found refuge in the United States and played a role in the maturation of the American university; two of the leading figures in the Geneva school or critics of consciousness, the most important current in the French *nouvelle critique*; and three anglophones, one each from England, the United States, and Canada, two of whom reacted against the New Criticism and two of whom are regularly attacked by some postmodernists as if they were New Critics.

Who are they? Leo Spitzer (1887–1960), famous for his stylistic close reading of books in all the Romance languages, was an Austrian who taught in Germany, was forced into exile under the Third Reich, and ended his distinguished career at Johns Hopkins University. Ernst Robert Curtius (1886–1956), best known for *European Literature and the Latin Middle Ages*, his book on the dominant role of rhetoric, figures of speech, and topoi in the construction of Western literature, was a professor at Heidelberg and Bonn, living the 'inner emigration' during the Hitler years. Erich Auerbach (1892–1957) is celebrated for *Mimesis*, his study of the representation of reality in literature from Homer to Proust. Like Spitzer, he was a professor in Germany forced into exile. He followed Spitzer to Turkey, as the successor to Spitzer's chair, and then to America, ending his career at Yale. Albert Béguin (1901–57), professor at Basel and, later, public intellectual in Paris, is recognized above all for *L'âme romantique et le rêve* with its thesis that the writers of German romanticism are the direct predecessors and originators of European modernism. Jean Rousset (1910–2002), a long-standing professor at Geneva, is respected for his structuralist studies of narrative but, above all, for his path-breaking volume on the baroque – as literature and as culture – in France. C.S. Lewis (1898–1963), the religious apologist and Oxford and Cambridge don, is best known in academic circles for *The Allegory of Love* and its rehabilitation of chivalry, courtly love, erotic allegory, and high courtly language in medieval and postmedieval literature. F.O. Matthiessen (1902–50) of Harvard wrote *American Renaissance* to claim a usable past for American culture, a generation of American classics that expressed the ideals and endured the pain of the American experience. Last of all, Northrop Frye (1912–91), who spent his career at the University of Toronto, is famous because of *Anatomy of Criticism*, his attempt at a universal study of literature, its rules, its parameters, and its structures.

These eight critics share a number of traits. Like the New Critics, they all rebelled against the then-dominant academic orthodoxy of philology and literary history; on the contrary, they insisted on the autonomy of literature and of criticism, the necessity of reading literary texts in only literary terms and not as autobiography, history, or anthropology. Thus, they practised the close reading of texts and what we call practical criticism. Unlike many New Critics they were solid scholars, they knew their history, and they accepted the role of intuition, sympathy, *Erlebnis*, and *présence* in their work. They reshaped but also enlarged the canon rather than narrowing it; eschewing narrow specialization, they worked on several literatures, or on several literary periods, or both. Each contributed a personal, path-breaking new vision of literature and of its history. Their visions were often something like totalizing systems that made sense of *longue durée* and offered an insight into the mental structures of the past – and of the present. For they insisted on the value of our cultural past allied to the present, and the value of the present preserving and branching out from the past.

I shall discuss the question of humanism in chapter 9. Suffice it to say here that these eight can legitimately be called humanists, more in the Renaissance (*umanisti*) and German romantic (*Humanismus*) terms than would be, perhaps, the case today. They were schoolteachers (university professors); they dealt, often, with old texts, rehabilitating and renewing old classics; they relished the study of literary language and style; they believed, implicitly or explicitly, in *Bildung*, in a book-oriented culture that will expand our horizons and bring us strength and joy; and they had the sense of high European culture, descended from Homer and Virgil or from the Bible, a totality of culture that forms our history and explains what we are.

How did I choose these eight and not eight others? In part, for subjective reasons. All eight, at one time or another, played a role in shaping my life and my own vision of literature. This is especially true for Auerbach, Lewis, and Frye, yet is not limited to them. All eight have the 'grand design,' a totalizing grasp of the Western tradition taken as a whole. Some critics whom I admire did not, it appears to me, have the design, or were narrower in their interests, or made a lesser contribution. Others are closer and can be more properly assimilated to New Criticism (F.R. Leavis), or the postmodern turn (Roland Barthes), or the non-academic tradition of journalism and cultural critique (Edmund Wilson). My choices are partially subjective yet also, I am convinced, representative of one of the major thrusts or directions in literary studies – that of scholars from a pretheory world who dominated their age and have now given way to new thrusts and directions. It is also true that, in my analyses, I will perhaps be guilty of overemphasizing the French and the medieval. These are two areas of my greater expertise. Given this, I do not think that I betray the letter or the spirit of the humanist critics. Auerbach was accused of similar distortion. He was my teacher, and I am trying to follow his example.

The structure of this book is quite simple. The first eight chapters (part 1) are devoted to the eight critics: Spitzer, Curtius, Auerbach, Béguin, Rousset, Lewis, Matthiessen, and Frye. In each chapter I examine the achievement of one figure, explicating his work and also scrutinizing his methodology and basic presuppositions, and the critiques, including my own, marshalled against him. A much longer chapter 9 (part 2), entitled 'Discussion,' offers a synthesis: first, arguing that the eight can be brought together and identified as forming a current in the history of criticism, and illustrating how and why they do so, and second, relating them to humanism and to the two dominant mindsets or period styles of our century: modernism and postmodernism. In particular, I will make a case for their modernism – as a reaction against modernity and for the autonomy of art, because of their cultural role in expanding the canon and establishing a tradition of great writing, and because of their innovative work as students and even champions of modernist writing. This discussion will, throughout, address the question of history: how the humanist critics reflect, are shaped by, and react to the history of their age, and what kind of history, if any, they themselves author(ize). In the final section I speak, in my own voice, on the literary canon – what should we read, teach, and research? – perhaps the central and most divisive issue in our culture wars. I address this question from my own perspective as an heir to the humanist critics, employing some of their arguments yet, at the same time, sympathetic to more recent approaches and seeking to negotiate between the two. In other words, I hope to bridge the gap between the opposing camps by offering moderate, reasoned answers to often vexing and passionately stated problems.

Two questions. First, why do I devote so much space to exposition? Because I am addressing a readership of faculty from a wide spectrum of languages and centuries as well as students in the various literature departments. Academic specialization has proceeded much farther today than when Spitzer and Curtius began their careers. No critique on my part is meant to accompany the observation that the majority of Anglicists will be unacquainted with some of the names on my list and have a more or less sketchy acquaintance with others. Although the names are changed, the same is also true for scholars in foreign language departments. The same is true for students. In addition, people who have read a major book by one of the eight may well be unaware of his other equally important contributions. Here I am thinking of Curtius on twentieth-century French writers, Béguin on twentieth-century Catholic writers, Rousset on narrative technique (the I-novel and the narratee), Lewis on the English sixteenth century and Milton, and Frye on English writers from the Renaissance to the twentieth century, Canadian writers, and the Bible.

Second, where is my introductory theoretical chapter? Or chapters? Given the realities of academic specialization, given the fact that, for most of my readers, some of the critics will be *terrae incognitae,* I felt that I had to make a place for exposition and that the meat of the book, so to speak, had to come before the theory, that an inductive rather than a deductive approach was called for. This introduction, nevertheless, includes a statement of my own beliefs and ideological stance, contextualized in terms of the current debate.

By consulting the notes to the individual chapters and the bibliography, the reader will see that considerable scholarship has been devoted to these eight critics. In addition to articles, article collections, and conference proceedings, there are full-length studies in the various languages. There are books on Spitzer in English, on Curtius in French and German, on Auerbach in English and German, on Béguin in French, German, and Italian, on Rousset in French, on Lewis in several languages, on Matthiessen in English, and on Frye in several languages. There are also general studies of the German Romance scholars and of the Geneva school. Yet no one study treats them all.

This volume – in some ways an introduction and in other ways a synthesis – is the first to bring together, under the same umbrella and from one vantage point, humanist critical traditions from Germany, Switzerland, Great Britain, and North America. I want to underscore the international, cosmopolitan aspect of literary scholarship in the twentieth century, and the extent to which, in the various language areas and academic systems, critics were posing similar questions and offering a gamut of similar responses.

I argue that the humanist critics, for all their inevitable divergences, come together on a number of issues and make a significant contribution to the history of our modernism and modernity. They offer global visions of both literature and civilization and of their historical evolution – of culture taken in the many senses of the term's current semantic field. Their grand designs are also meaningful to us as one emancipatory element in the European tradition. Theirs is not a reading for evil but a *critique des beautés* (Spitzer's term) that gives value to our past and binds it to our present and our future. From a strictly cultural studies perspective their work offers fascinating insights into the history of academe and the mental structures of one current in high modernism.

In addition, not only do the critics anticipate many of today's theoretical approaches, but because they do so from a humanist vantage point they can contribute to a reconsideration of current disputes over the role and function of humanism in literary studies. Instead of the usual rather narrow parameters within which humanism is discussed and which cause it to be situated outside the modernism/postmodernism purview, a broader perspective will enable me to argue that the newer approaches which reject humanism are often themselves forms of humanism and, therefore, that the clash of humanisms may well prove to be central to our concerns.

The history of criticism has undergone a series of mutations over the past few centuries. Criticism as rhetoric and the adherence to models – *imitatio* and *amplificatio* – from the Middle Ages and Renaissance yielded, in the eighteenth century, to an impressionistic belles-lettres response to texts; which yielded, late in the nineteenth century, to literary scholarship as an academic subject, objective and scientific – *Philologie* and *Literaturwissenschaft*; which yielded, in the twentieth century, to criticism as we know it, as practiced by the Russian Formalists, New Critics, myth critics, *nouveaux critiques*, structuralists, and other schools; which, since the 1970s, has yielded to the postmodern turn, with emphasis on theory, deconstruction, the new historicism, postcolonialism, cultural studies, feminism, and queer theory.

Yet the neat, clear schema of succeeding schools and modes is inaccurate and will always lead to distortion and error. In thirteenth-century France feudal epics, courtly romances, allegories of love, and anticourtly texts were written, side by side, for the same literary public. Similarly, in France and England from 1550 to 1650, we find, side by side, works that can be labelled Renaissance, mannerist, baroque, and classical. On our campuses today, in departments of English and foreign languages, we can find, working side by side, philologists, literary historians, traditional humanist critics, and new postmodernist critics and theoreticians. Impressionist belles-lettres survives outside the academy.

The coexistence of multiple approaches is one reason why this book is not meant to be an assault on or a denial of contemporary critical practices. I do not have nostalgia for a bygone past, nor would I wish to return to it, were it possible – which, of course, it is not. I do believe that the humanist critics remain one voice among many in our cacophonous oratorio and one model among many for what to do and how to do it. One purpose of this book is to serve as a dialogue among the many voices or, perhaps, the prolegomena to such a dialogue.

This said, given the ferocity of our cultural wars and given the fact that to claim an ideologically neutral stance when one is not and cannot be neutral would be in itself ideologically charged and an instance of false consciousness, it is important that I state my own beliefs here in the introduction.

I have enormous respect for the eight critics studied in this book. I admire their scholarship and erudition, their superb close reading of texts, their revisions of the canon, their visions of the Western tradition taken as a whole, and their ties to the world around them, including high modernism. I am committed to privileging the great books and to aesthetic humanism, that is to a high culture of literature, art, architecture, music, philosophy, and theology over the centuries, from the earliest times to our twenty-first century. This stance requires the recognition of an aesthetic sense in mankind as universal and as essential to our common humanity as the ethical, the epistemological, and the metaphysical. In my case it includes also some sense of a Neoplatonic connection between the true, the beautiful, and the good. And it is grounded in or gives rise to a vision of history as a totality, cyclical rather than linear, disdaining neither the past nor the present. Finally, I uphold certain concepts attributed to the Enlightenment: reason, logic, aesthetic value, the rights of the individual, freedom, and transcendence although a number of these can be ascribed, with equal cogency, to European romanticism.

Does this stance, do these convictions, constitute an ideology? Yes, if by ideology we mean an all-encompassing view of the world, or a system of complex cultural symbols or structures, or the ideas and beliefs that represent or are the outward expression of the aggregate of a person's life experiences. But perhaps not, if we define ideology in the more common contemporary sense as a set of false beliefs that function to ensure privileges for a ruling class or as cultural expressions which, by means of concealment and distortion, rationalize and legitimate the hegemony of the ruling class. Admittedly, ideological implications arise from the privileging of aesthetic criteria, the literariness of literature, and the history of great authors and great works. At the same time it is obvious that high culture is not a governing-class conspiracy. If in the past it may have contributed to ruling-class hegemony as the embodiment or manifestation of certain skills, Pierre Bourdieu's 'cultural capital,' that the Establishment insisted upon for people to accede to positions of authority, such has ceased to be the case, especially in the United States. In the nineteenth and twentieth centuries reading English at Johns Hopkins never led to the corridors of power.

Although high culture may at one time have been construed as such cultural capital, I submit that it is not elitist. The great Marxist critics – Pierre Barbéris, Lucien Goldmann, György Lukács, and Hans Mayer, to name a few – revered the classics of world literature and sincerely believed that one mission of a socialist society would be to bring them to the people. Similarly, the great twentieth-century writers in the European minority literatures – Breton, Catalan, Occitan, and Scots – sought neither to flaunt their ethnicity nor to seek popular acclaim by exploiting a sentimental folk culture from the past but instead to partake of and contribute to European literature on its terms, for they believed that cultural freedom is to be attained only by entry into pan-European modernism.

Is such an ideology bourgeois? Of course it is and has been since the age of Voltaire. On the other hand, the cultured intellectual bourgeoisie has been replaced, in North America at least, by the new technological-managerial class. In today's climate love of the great books, fine art, and classical music proclaims one to be a member of the intelligentsia (formerly a clerisy) and of a small fringe group within it. For the most part this fringe group rebels against modernity and envisages great works of art as emancipatory, as in Theodor Adorno's negative dialectics or Northrop Frye's myth of freedom.

Is it not possible to recognize how the social and the political contribute to and help determine all mental structures, whether we call them world views, mindsets, or ideologies, and thus to be aware of one's own assumptions and presuppositions, yet also to believe in them and to justify them intellectually on their own terms? Can we not be historically aware and aesthetically sensitive at the same time? To do so, however, we have to resist two lures: embracing a distorted, nostalgic vision of the past and embracing a no less distorted, tyrannical vision from the present.

Now, at the beginning of a new millennium, for a number of reasons – some technological, some philosophical and ideological – for the first time in history we have within reach the great literature, art, architecture, music, philosophy, and theology from all the centuries and from all over the world. We can appreciate the high civilizations of classical China, Japan, and India, of the Arab world, Persia, and Turkey, and of our Western tradition – all are within reach and at our command. We also have the rich, unique traditions of sub-Saharan Africa and of the First Peoples in the Americas. Finally, we have within reach and at our command all the schools and approaches of literary studies, whether they are called criticism, scholarship, or theory. No one can practice them all. Yet we can benefit from them and also from the myriad interdisciplinary and pluridisciplinary approaches in their wake. Now is the most exciting time – certainly in my lifetime and perhaps in the history of the discipline – to do literary studies.

Literary studies have emerged as one battlefield on which our culture wars are fought. The tenor of our work, whether lauded or scorned, counts for something on the outside. We ought not to resent this development. During the 1960s when I was moving through the ranks at Stanford, a number of my colleagues were outraged that their carefully hoarded research time and their elegantly honed research topics were tarnished by the student protests which compelled us to face questions such as student rights, the Vietnam War, the class system around us, what we teach, and what we write. I was overjoyed. For the first time since Joan of Arc, I mused, the university is at the centre of public 'affairs; what we do and say is meaningful to society as a whole. Maybe this time we can get it right.

PART ONE

1 Leo Spitzer; or, How to Read a Text

Leo Spitzer, Ernst Robert Curtius, Erich Auerbach, Karl Vossler, and Helmut Hatzfeld form a circle or current of German-language academic criticism that was the finest in their day and, many believe, is comparably important today. This generation of German and Austrian scholars combined vast scholarship and historical knowledge with a rare literary sensitivity and imagination; they specialized in all three major Romance literatures, from the Middle Ages to the twentieth century; and they authored a rich, extensive corpus of original critical scholarship. Spitzer, whose career spanned some fifty years and who reached the summit of his profession first in Marburg and Cologne, then, when the world changed, at Johns Hopkins, is the epitome of his generation's French-oriented German humanism. This is the francophilia embodied in a number of German and Austrian writers – among the latter, Rainer Maria Rilke, Joseph Roth, Arthur Schnitzler, and Stefan Zweig – who felt closer to Paris than to Berlin and who admired the loser of the Franco-Prussian War for its older and richer high culture and for its avant-garde in contrast to the more conservative Wilhelmine *Kultur.* France remained a beacon for the arts during the tempest-tossed decades following the First World War. Yet, in many ways, Spitzer stands apart from the others. Spitzer is, in a sense, unique. I should like to explore aspects of his uniqueness that help to explain his extraordinary accomplishments and, at the same time, the limits without which these accomplishments would not have been possible.

Spitzer's uniqueness lies in the fact that he was a philologist – a historical linguist – in addition to being a literary scholar or critic. According to the MLA Spitzer Bibliography,[1] he published 572 essays in linguistics (many were notes) and another seventeen essays in 'stylistics,' although one could maintain that everything he wrote, without exception, was *Stilforschung*, that is, research into and analysis of literary style and creative variation in language. He also published, it would appear, forty-three articles concerned with the topic 'Miscellany'; I would have assigned most of them also to linguistics. In point of fact, throughout his life Spitzer was an active publishing linguist, especially concerned with historical semantics, etymology, and lexicology; he was fascinated by the words on the page, by individual words and their arrangement in phrases and clauses. Thus he bridged the gap between linguistics and literature. Both as a linguist and as a student of literature, he focused on the creative and/or deviant use of language, linguistic innovation, the break from a norm. He preferred always such creativity, the creativity of a great writer, over the ordinary speech of ordinary people. In this, David Bellos observes, Spitzer resembles the Russian Formalists.[2]

From this fascination for language the master accounted for his method as the 'philological circle.'[3] The philological circle describes a movement back and forth from one or more observable linguistic or stylistic features that breaks literary conventions to larger patterns such as the author's lived experience (*Erlebnis*), repressed complexes in the author's psyche, his creative soul (today we would say perhaps 'mindset'), the work's poetic structure, central symbol, or total form (*Gestalt*), or a culture's way of viewing the world. Spitzer considered the process to be both inductive and deductive, as he related the microdetail to the megastructure and vice versa:

> What he [a scholar] must be asked to do, however, is, I believe, to work from the surface to the 'inward life-center' of the work of art: first observing details about the superficial appearance of the particular work (and the 'ideas' expressed by a poet are, also, only one of the superficial traits in a work of art); then, grouping these details and seeking to integrate them into a creative principle which may have been present in the soul of the artist; and, finally, making the return trip to all the other groups of observations in order to find whether the 'inward form' one has tentatively constructed gives an account of the whole ... Our to-and-fro voyage from certain outward details to the inner centre and back again to other series of details is only an application of the principle of the 'philological circle' ... My personal way has been from the observed detail to ever broadening units which rest, to an increasing degree, on speculation. It is, I think, the philological, the inductive way, which seeks to show significance in the apparently futile, in contrast to the deductive procedure which begins with

units assumed as given – and which is rather the way followed by the theologians ... or by the mathematicians.[4]

This can be called a phenomenological approach because it begins – chronologically and ontologically – with and is always grounded in the style and texture of a particular book and ever refers back to it, burrowing and worrying at it. The process is, first and foremost, text oriented and is often presented as an *explication de texte*. In this respect Spitzer resembles the New Critics, except that he knew so much more than they did and delved deeper than they ever could. Spitzer's extraordinary literary sensitivity and imaginative empathy also enabled him to say so much about a particular book – for example, *El libro de buen amor*, François Villon's *Testament*, *El Buscón*, *Phèdre*, *La vie de Marianne*, and *I Malavoglia* – and, at the same time, because of the very nature of the unique style and texture of the book, to limit himself to it.

It should also be said (Spitzer neglected proclaiming this aspect of his method) that he often was launched onto a brilliant reading of a text by (dixit Spitzer) someone else's botched misreading. Quite often, especially in his later years, he would compose a superb, definitive fifty-page article, of which perhaps only the first half was devoted to destroying the wretch who had committed the botched misreading. Spitzer was a dashing polemicist who, although he did not always win, never lost. Among his many adversaries are numbered Américo Castro, Bloomfield, Bremond, Dámaso Alonso, Frank, Gilman, Gamillscheg, Green, Hall, Heidegger, Klemperer, Lovejoy, Pei, Poulet, Sayce, Schmidt, Sturtevant, Wasserman, and Wechssler. As a polemicist, scholars have described him as acerbic, belligerent, contentious, and feisty, a man of ardour, élan, and impetuosity.[5] That, from his friends. His enemy, Yakov Malkiel, preferred the terms intemperate, partisan, peevish, sarcastic, and vitriolic.[6] The Harvard Hispanist Stephen Gilman, wounded by a Spitzer article, complained: 'Spitzer has chosen to sacrifice the masterpiece in order to confront the commentator ... It is rather like hunting quail with an elephant gun or a private soldier with heavy artillery.'[7] Gilman and the others have a point. Not only were Spitzer's assaults devastating; they could also be inconsistent, subjective, and capricious. Nevertheless, we in the humanities ought to treasure genius even in its more eccentric manifestations and, sometimes, especially in such eccentricities. Furthermore, the historical context of these polemics is important. It was a time of contrasts, when, under the impulse of the refugees, American universities were coming of age. What one would give to have seen the reaction of

Spitzer's colleagues – sherry-sipping gentlemen for whom scandal was even more threatening than ideas!

What was Leo Spitzer? I should like to begin with what he was not. He was not a theorist, not a historian, and actually, not a writer of books.

Spitzer was no more or less a theorist than other humanist critics of his generation. The 'philological circle' is a metaphor or an analogy taken from the 'hermeneutic circle' in Friedrich Schleiermacher and Wilhelm Dilthey. It explains Spitzer's own approach to literature – a unique approach – yet it cannot be compared seriously to theory as it is practised today, or even as it was practised by the New Critics and the myth critics. Geoffrey Green has rightly underscored the personal and even the mystical in Spitzer's method, which Spitzer himself accounted for as a habitual procedure of the mind, not a rigorous program.[8] It is symptomatic that the most important statements Spitzer made are contained in autobiographical essays in which he relates the procedure of the mind to the stages in his career. Not only this. He also confesses:

> Such [Spitzer's] results, if correct, do not seem to me representations of any particular method but a simple reading based on the good sense that every good reader should exercise. I arrive at the conclusion, therefore, that there is no specifically 'Spitzerian' method. Good sense is a critic's only guide. By means of his good sense he discerns the method of reading suggested by the work itself, one whose imperative he must obey without superimposing extraneous categories on the text ... Further, this empiricism, whereby every text is considered a unique and unrepeatable experience, can perhaps excuse what has been pointed out by so many critics: the absence in my work of an aesthetic philosophy capable of organizing my various experiences.[9]

Only Spitzer can be Spitzer. Although, like Curtius, he was attacked by his contemporaries for doing something other than philology and literary history and for taking up contemporary writers, he simply persevered in doing what he did, and he persevered over a lifetime. There was a buoyant, aggressive optimism in Spitzer – a healthy mixture of the choleric and the sanguine, with no room left for phlegm and melancholia – that enabled him to overcome his adversaries by writing more and better than they did and, wherever feasible, by outliving them. Perhaps Spitzer's generation had an advantage over ours in that they could dispense with the obligatory first three theoretical chapters, and for that matter, with the first three theoretical books.

Green proposes that Spitzer and Auerbach were historically oriented whereas Vossler and Curtius partook more of formalism, and indeed that Spitzer and Auerbach became attuned to history as a result of their experience of exile, while Vossler and Curtius, remaining at home, turned to an ideal of literature as the timeless.[10] Green's thesis is to distinguish, in intellectual terms, those who left the Reich from those who stayed and, at least implicitly, Jews from non-Jews. I don't agree. Spitzer's and Auerbach's visions of literature and of criticism form two unities, from their earliest writings to their last. Spitzer did insist that the macrostructure pole of the philological circle evolved over the decades: from the author's psychological make-up to the work's inner form to a cultural archetype or even to the *Geist*. He also wanted an Italian audience to believe that he had shifted from French to Spanish literature and later from Spanish to Italian.[11] However, a perusal of the Spitzer Bibliography will convince the observer that the great man engaged all three literatures throughout his career. More importantly, the philological circle itself, as a habitual procedure of the mind, remained the same. It remained grounded in the close reading of individual texts, and it remained an inherently immanent criticism.

Secondly, as scholars have observed, Spitzer was relatively unscathed by the Second World War and its aftermath, and he adamantly refused to indulge in the bashing of German culture. Significant in this regard is a luminous article published in 1944 that refuted A.O. Lovejoy's contention that certain ideas – *Ganzheit*, *Streben*, and *Eigentümlichkeit* – form a historical continuum from German romanticism to Hitler; Spitzer also insisted that neither German romanticism nor the German cultural tradition be held responsible for Naziism.[12] If anything, it is Vossler and Curtius who changed their critical approach and their field in response to and in protest against the Führer. During the 1930s Vossler shifted his attention from Italian to Spanish, partially in reaction to the policies of Mussolini, and Curtius reverted from the modern to the medieval. As we shall see in chapter 2, Curtius's commitment to the Latin Middle Ages – an endeavour to locate the historical as well as rhetorical origins of modern high culture – was also a gesture of protest against the Nazi repugnance for high culture and a plea for Goethean humanism.

All the great German philologists knew history, having amassed an incomparable historical and linguistic culture. However, some bequeathed to us a vision of the history of literature, and others did not. Of the four discussed here, Vossler was probably the most historical and Spitzer the least. Spitzer argued, in any number of articles, for a structural or immanent reading of texts and for the scholar not to be restricted to the findings of the then dominant logical-positivist literary history (which included the life of the author). In his later years especially, Spitzer denounced literary history and the distortion that a reliance on cultural background and historical relativism can bring to our reading of a text. On more than one occasion he announced that he would remain inside the text in question and, for the purposes of the article, never leave it. In his later years, Spitzer exalted the 'eternal character of the work of art,' 'the eternal meaning of art,' and the 'immanent, organic criticism' that can, in Ezra Pound's words, 'make it cohere.'[13]

Furthermore, Curtius's vision of the rhetorical tradition and topos – which extends from antiquity through the Latin Middle Ages and then nourishes the modern vernaculars for centuries – or Auerbach's vision of the mixed style – Christian in origin, which, after having given rise to a powerful, concrete representation of reality in writers such as Dante, was to fuel a tradition of realism in the modern centuries – have altered forever our conception of the evolution of culture over time. There is nothing comparable in Spitzer. His occasional striving at synthesis, concerning national character inherent in a work of art, can go awry: the famous lecture of 1943 contrasting the Spanish baroque, as an *imago* of *España eterna*, to *l'âme française* ends in school clichés, which Spitzer himself had the good grace to recognize as outmoded, given subsequent discovery of the exciting, dynamic French baroque (which he did not know much about).[14] In order to articulate a vision of history, it helps to write a big book: *Mimesis* or *European Literature and the Latin Middle Ages* or Vossler's *Medieval Culture: An Introduction to Dante and His Times*.[15] That wasn't Spitzer's way. Spitzer wrote articles, hundreds of articles. True, the MLA Spitzer Bibliography identifies forty-nine items as books or monographs. However, following René Wellek, I submit that all forty-nine (fourteen of which are posthumous) are either collections of articles and pamphlets published separately or occasional articles that attain monograph length (because, for example, the author has cited every example he can find of François Rabelais's word formation and because it was his doctoral dissertation).[16] Spitzer's most influential book in English, *Linguistics and Literary History* (1948), is a collection of five articles.[17] His most influential books in German are the two-volume *Stilstudien* (twenty-eight articles) and the two-volume *Romanische Stil- und Literaturstudien* (fifteen articles).[18] Less influential yet of equal intrinsic importance would be the compilation summa of Spitzer's later years, the 1959 *Romanische Literaturstudien* comprising forty-nine articles. I suggest that if one is fascinated by words and the style and texture of particular books and has extraordinary literary sensitivity and imaginative empathy, one will not need to reflect on theory, or to elaborate a vision of history, or, for that matter, to aim at a synthesis and, therefore, to write books. All that would distract from the phenomenological reality: the text and one's reading of it.

So what was Leo Spitzer? And why is he important? He bequeathed to us his life as a *miles philologicus* or *philologicus iratus*, ever in combat against *l'infâme* and for *der Geist*. In a sense, he is our Voltaire. Above all, simply, Spitzer was and is, in range and scope, in production and accomplishment, a superb practical critic, the most notable with whom I am acquainted.

According to my calculations (based on the Spitzer Bibliography with my own additions and subtractions), Spitzer wrote 258 essays on literature. These treat topics in French literature (95), Spanish (65), Italian (36), German (20), Occitan (14), English (13.5), Latin (8.5), Catalan (3), and Greek, Rhaeto-Romance, and Romanian (1 each). Spitzer composed his articles in the following languages: 104 in German, 61 in English, 52 in French, 21 in Italian, and 20 in Spanish. Of the 258 pieces in his repertoire, 106.5 were devoted to the Middle Ages, 97 to the period extending from Columbus to Robespierre, and 54.5 to the nineteenth and twentieth centuries; these latter include some of the longest.

Spitzer's achievement, like that of Auerbach and Curtius, was to work in the Middle Ages and in the modern. He was a pioneer in modern literary studies with path-breaking work on Henri Barbusse, Charles-Louis Philippe, Jules Romains, and Marcel Proust.[19] He was one of the first serious scholars to pay attention to Michel Butor and, in his seventies, envisaged an extended study of *nouveau roman*. Also, again resembling Curtius, prior to the Nazi takeover, he penned essays on xenophobic tendencies in the speech of German xenophobes.[20] Finally, toward the end of his career, he performed an extraordinary – for the times – tour de force, the structural analysis of an advertisement for Sunkist orange juice.[21]

As a medievalist, Spitzer treated old literature as literature, subjecting it to the same scrutiny as the modern and deriving from it similar critical or aesthetic readings. This practice went against the common wisdom of the profession. Spitzer was able to do it, in part, because he never went so far as to deny the importance of cultural surroundings. Indeed, he benefited from a full command of the medieval Christian mindset, including St Augustine. His sense of the Christian mindset dictated pieces such as 'Le style "circulaire,"' 'Note on the Poetic and Empirical "I" in Medieval Authors,' and the posthumous *Classical and Christian Ideas of World Harmony*.[22] The Christian mindset justified Spitzer's proclamation of a literature of tradition and convention, without imposing on it the romantic desire for originality and what C.S. Lewis called the 'Personal Heresy.'[23] Christian readings of the medieval can be rigid; they can lead to distortion. For example, D.W. Robertson and his disciples in English studies – practitioners of the typological or exegetical approach – interpreted all medieval works of art from an Augustinian vantage point. According to them, all 'serious' books in the Middle Ages had to exalt *caritas* and denounce *cupiditas* or *concupiscentia*. Any book that appears not to do so must, then, be read ironically.[24]

Spitzer avoided such extreme positions. He read Christian texts from a Christian perspective, and secular texts from a secular perspective. Given the extraordinary richness of the courtly secular, especially in France, he would have been the last to deny the existence of *fin' amor* (courtly love). Thus he remained always an open, creative, enlightened reader of texts, the practitioner of 'La critique des beautés.'

Spitzer's essays hold up today. Whether forty or eighty years old, they retain acuity and insight to an extent that can be said of no other critic living or dead. The larger portion of his studies remain the best or among the best that have been written on the particular text in question, from any perspective and in any language. I offer a few medieval examples.

In an extended essay from 1944 Spitzer discusses *amor de lonh* in the chansons of Jaufre Rudel.[25] First he demolishes Grace Frank's botched misreading of the lady from afar as an allegory for the Holy Land, in the process demonstrating how she consistently mistranslates the Occitan text. Spitzer himself relates the spring topos or *Natureingang* of the first stanzas to the Augustinian notion of world harmony, and he insists on what he calls 'le *a priori* chrétien.' It is this Christian a priori which helps define the Eros of the troubadours, an Eros frankly erotic and powerfully sexual: desire to possess the lady and desire not to possess her, love which is both real and unreal, authentic and a dream; a forbidden love that is also a good love encouraging the lover's socially productive growth in the community; and, finally, a love that employs the sacred register and yet is not sacred. Spitzer repudiates the narrowly historical and biographical approaches of his predecessors in favour of studying literary genres, myths, and *Geist*, and privileging tradition and convention. He finds in Jaufre Rudel structures and a coherence comparable to those we recognize in Dante. The troubadour, exploiting the same motifs as his colleagues, expounding the same concept of *fin' amor*, will nonetheless grant his own work a unique tone, and the tone will vary from poem to poem. This is what today we call archetypal criticism.

In an article from 1930, Spitzer analyses the functioning of the symbol in Marie de France's *Lais*.[26] He discusses the knot and the girdle in *Guigemar*, images that pledge love and concretize intimacy, that separate the lovers from others yet also, in a sense, juxtapose their naked flesh and unite them, making them one. He considers the restorative potion in *Les deux amants* that, despite the lovers' deaths, will nourish the life of plants, for it is also a love potion, and love is good, natural, and given to creating life. And he shows how the little nightingale in *Laüstic*, which sings of love and sings what the lovers would say to each other if they could, is the love in their hearts that keeps the lady awake. Slain by the husband, its memory will endure. Its death is the *aventure* of the lai; written down by Marie, it becomes a symbol of symbols and the memory of a memory. Spitzer insists upon the power of the symbol to confer meaning and a sense of *tremendum* to the lais. In a poetry of remembrance, of commemorating the pseudomemory of oral pseudosources, Marie's symbols create the memory and imbue the ancient story with contemporary immediacy. Later, in 1943–4 and 1946–7, Spitzer explores the prologue to Marie's lais in terms of medieval scholastic gloss and medieval humanism; and he examines the nature and function of the symbol – the pared hazelnut tree carved with the name 'Tristan' – in *Chevrefoil*.[27] This is what we today call metatextuality.

In a revisionist article from 1948,[28] Spitzer opposes the then standard Hispanist reading of the *Poema del Cid:* Ramón Menéndez Pidal's thesis that the *Cid* is immediately historical and grounded in actuality as well as being 'popular,' and that, because of its historicity and realism, the poem differs from all other epics and is, therefore, quintessentially Spanish. Spitzer, on the contrary, insists that the *Cid* is fictional and a work of art. He argues that the narrative structure – the Cid's greatness, fall from grace, and return to grace – is traditional to epic and romance. García Ordóñez and the infantes de Carrión embody the epic function of the traitors at court, typical of chanson de geste. The Cid himself, at the same time a rebel baron and a good vassal, presents a synthesis of two figures in medieval epic: Girart de Roussillon or Rüdiger von Bechlaren the rebel and Guillaume d'Orange the good vassal. According to Spitzer, the Cid does not grow or evolve in the course of his adventures. Inherently great from the beginning, his greatness in adversity leads to the recognition that he is great and, therefore, to the overcoming of adversity. Virtue is made manifest in external recognition (honour) and in external achievement (riches). In addition, the poem is in no way democratic: as a nobleman, the Cid has to fight, whatever his personal circumstances; whatever they may be, he will remain ever noble; and the final manifestation of his recognition and honour is derived from the fact that his daughters are to become mothers of kings. Finally, it is wrong to compare eternally the *Chanson de Roland* and the *Poema del Cid*, for they belong to different literary kinds, the former being 'epopeya mítica' and the latter 'biografía epopeyizada.' This is what today we call genre theory and the study of *mentalités*.

In a study from 1942, Spitzer comments on Canto XIII, the suicide canto, of the *Inferno*.[29] First he discusses Dante's Christian adaptation of Ovidian metamorphosis: how the plant-man (*uomo-pianta*) – a human soul endowed with a new, subhuman plant body – is to be considered a monstrosity, a disgusting hybrid *contra naturam* which utters speech only in a monstrous, disgusting, subhuman manner – as the hissing of wind combined with the flow of sap (blood) – and only in the process of tearing and wounding. The harsh-sounding, disharmonious speech and the twisted, contorted syntax in this canto reflect then the twisted, tortured disharmony of the subject matter: suicide and its punishment. Finally, Spitzer argues for the unity of the canto, saying that Dante intentionally contrasts the central figure, the magnificent, literary, powerfully individual Pier delle Vigne, with the lowly, vulgar, anonymous suicide at the end, a Florentine who symbolizes all suicides and *tutta Fiorenza*, Dante's homeland, which never ceases to make war on itself. Later, in 1944 and 1955, Spitzer explores farcical elements in *Inferno* XXI–XXIII and also addresses to the reader throughout the *Commedia*.[30] In this latter essay he lists nineteen distinct interventions by the narrator and describes how they function to mold reader response by presenting the narrator as one close to the reader yet also his spiritual guide. This is what we today call narratology.

In an article from 1934, Spitzer argues that the *Libro de buen amor* is not a naive, primitive, realistic poem, nor does it express, in a modern way, the personality and subjectivity of its author, the Archpriest of Hita.[31] Spitzer reads the *Libro* as a Christian work reflecting medieval Christian culture. Typical of this world view are the Narrator's stance that his book is important, that he can make mistakes and be corrected, and that any number of differing glosses can and should be employed. In any case, according to Spitzer, the book has greater significance and a deeper meaning, for inside the shell we find an allegorical kernel, the conflict between *buen amor* and *loco amor*. Furthermore, the I-narrative is not literally autobiographical. The shift from wit and humour to the most serious of discourses is eminently medieval and preclassical; it would mirror the life of fallen mankind, the Old Adam. Female beauty and the very unbeautiful Trotaconventos are both conventional, 'types' of *loco amor*. The Archpriest's book can be envisaged as lyrics embedded in a humorous (pseudo)autobiography embedded in an ascetic-moral treatise. Spitzer thus anticipated (but with deeper insight and genuine literary taste) the school of exegetical or Robertsonian criticism.

As a superior version of exegetical criticism, we can also cite the analysis of three Middle English lyrics from 1951.[32] Here Spitzer's approach is *explication de texte*, a close reading in the line of New Criticism yet richer and more nuanced. He demonstrates how, in a secular lyric, the motifs of courtly love – the physical external portrait, the psychological inner portrait, love sickness, the debate, and the allegory of love – are included within and reflect a Christian world view and the specifically Christian practice of allegory. This is more apparent, and is as cogently argued, in a Marian song where Spitzer finds the sacred connotations of Mary the Rose, a branch from the Tree of Jesse, and the rosebush itself bursting forth with the Flower of Christ, a bush with its branches piercing down to hell, covering the earth, and rising up to heaven.

Finally, in an article from 1940 on Villon's 'Ballade des dames du temps jadis,' that amplifies an earlier article from 1930,[33] Spitzer offers a reading of the text that includes the following points: the procession of the ladies in space corresponding to the recital of the poem in time; the circularity of the poem's structure cum refrain and of human life, *ex nihilo ad nihil*; the aesthetic power of the refrain, 'où sont les neiges d'antan'; the correspondence between woman and nature; and the poetry of women's names. He also argues for an immanent reading of Villon and of medieval literature generally, aesthetic rather than historical, as literary criticism rather than source hunting. Therefore, the fact that Villon's ballade comes at the end of a thousand-year tradition of 'ubi sunt' texts is useful knowledge but tells us nothing about the beauty of his poem. Furthermore, the fact that 'antan' meant 'last year' in the fifteenth century and has only come to mean 'yesteryear' in our age is useful knowledge but must not be allowed to inhibit our twentieth-century appreciation of its beauty, which includes the poetic overtones in 'yesteryear.' (Here Spitzer, unknowingly of course, sides with the New Critic William Empson and the *nouveau critique* Roland Barthes against their scholarly adversaries.) Finally, if Alcibiade was a man in ancient Greece and a man to twentieth-century scholars, she is a woman in Villon and, as a woman, lives eternally in poetry. Spitzer also composed a number of studies on individual lines in Villon, pointing out (long before Jean Dufournet) the sexual innuendo therein. The sexual innuendo, today taken for granted and even dignified by the term 'psychocriticism,' shocked Villon scholars in the 1930s.

I chose these seven examples. I could have cited equally magisterial studies on the Renaissance, the baroque, or the modern. They all are and remain the best.

The editors of the admirable and superbly conceived *Leo Spitzer: Representative Essays* express a genuine concern. I shall let them speak:

> In the quarter century since Spitzer's death, the various movements that have crossed the critical scene ... may well have made certain of the values that Spitzer proclaims here seem obsolete. Among these values one might cite his faith in the autonomy of the individual work of art, his refusal to pursue a single line of inquiry to the exclusion of all other lines, his belief that great literature is different in kind from other forms of writing, and his insistence ... on the critical act as a display of love for a particular poem and for the language in which it was written ... Spitzer's humanistic faith ... will doubtless seem archaic and idealistic to readers of the late 1980's.[34]

In the foreword John Freccero also alludes to 'outmoded aesthetic values' and 'out of date ... ideology' (xv, xx). Other critiques can be heard, from time to time. Benjamin Bennett makes a leftist critique of Emil Staiger, Martin Heidegger, and Spitzer because each one claims authority for his own reading of Eduard Mörike's poem 'Auf eine Lampe,' and because all three fail to address the political dimension in their controversy.[35] The powerfully intelligent theorist and critic Emily Apter, while otherwise quite positive in her response to Spitzer, does fault him for what we can call his insufficient political correctness.[36] She seems to feel that when he cites a joke about railroad porters, he should have raised the issue of Jim Crow; when he alludes to *Mein Kampf*, he should have discussed Hitler; and when he praises a passage in Louis-Ferdinand Céline, he should have made something of the anti-Semitism.

In my opinion, the observations, as observations, are largely accurate. Spitzer was intensely authoritarian: he did not fancy multiple readings of a text, nor did it enter his psyche that someone else's interpretation could be as valid as his own. He was unabashedly eclectic. In his own words:

I exposed myself to the oft-repeated charge of eclecticism. In response to this I contend that the only important issue is whether the category used by the critic really suits the phenomenon in question, and not whether it is original ... In the field of literary criticism there are in fact too few rather than too many categories that might help us describe the phenomena that we examine.[37]

Spitzer indeed practised a *critique des beautés*; he believed passionately in the greatness of the great books and in their inherent superiority over other cultural artifacts (though he could also pen the extraordinary analysis of American advertising). It is significant that, for the most part, he addressed the masterworks in the canon, seldom rediscovering a neglected work that ought not to be neglected. Finally, Spitzer's approach was *Stilforschung*. Literary structures and literary language were more important to him than ideology.

The observations are correct. Whether or not Spitzer ought to be condemned because of them is another matter. I shall address that question in chapter 9. Here I can say only that, yes, the profession has evolved since Spitzer's time and that, today, we do many things in a different way. Yes, it is true, one element in the profession, oriented toward theory, especially in the domains of cultural studies, feminism, and the new historicism, could respond negatively to Spitzer, just as it has responded negatively to the New Criticism and to Northrop Frye. On the other hand, no such element or current is ever univocal. So many currents flourish today, including those within cultural studies and feminism, as to preclude universal condemnation. As it turns out, a number of scholars, both contemporary-oriented and traditional, theoretically grounded and from differing perspectives, praise Spitzer and launch their readings of texts or their theoretical constructs by taking off from a Spitzer article. These include, among others, Donald H. Hook, Roger Pensom, Orrin N.C. Wang, Amy Wygant, Jules Brody, Richard Klein, and Emily Apter.[38] In addition, I am not certain that the theorists stand alone as readers in the late 1980s or the 1990s, not to speak of today. The profession contains a powerful conservative strain: all who are opposed to deconstruction, feminism, and what they deem to be MLA Po-Mo chic. Finally, there is an element (my element ...) fascinated by the new scholarship and its insights and incorporating large portions of it (in my case, narratology, intertextuality, postcolonialism, and gender theory) while maintaining the humanist vision of our fathers, which includes belief in the great books and in the great chain of civilization extending from Homer to Proust, or, to be more universal, from *Gilgamesh* to Julien Gracq and Claude Simon. I believe that a good number, perhaps the majority of us in literary studies, throughout North America, and the majority of scholars working in the older centuries, share Spitzer's faith in the enduring grandeur of language and of texts, and in the faith that moves us and him to revere them. That is why, throughout the world, since his death, people have collected, translated, and published Spitzer's essays in book form fourteen times.

Finally, I think Spitzer exhibits a very special sort of dignity, the dignity of a master 'philologian,' and is, in his domain, a *grand seigneur*, by his ability to cite Céline's most notorious anti-Semitic book, *Bagatelles pour un massacre*, and to praise its Rabelaisian gusto in language without deigning to denounce the anti-Semitism, scarcely alluding to it at all.[39] That Leo Spitzer, an Austrian Jew driven out of Europe by anti-Semitic fanatics and yet alive and a great professor in America, gave the lecture and published the article was and is plain to all. The magnificent irony in the situation enhances Spitzer, not Céline. It is one of Spitzer's great humanist moments, a moment of victory – the victory of tolerance over prejudice, reason over the emotions, health over psychosis, and Enlightenment over fanaticism.

A personal story (*non è vera, mica vera, ma è ben trovata*). When students come to my office bursting with enthusiasm – they have just discovered the Archpriest of Hita or Pierre de Ronsard or Novalis or Giovanni Verga – they beseech me, what can they read to deepen their understanding? When this occurs, I tell them (rather, should this ever occur, I would tell them): 'Go look at the MLA Bibliography on Leo Spitzer. If Spitzer has written on your discovery, read him, meditate on him, and assimilate all he has to say on your author and on the nature of literature and criticism. Joy in Spitzer. If he hasn't written on your topic, come back, and I'll give you Brand X.'

2 The Continuity of Western Literature: Ernst Robert Curtius

In 1983 Earl Jeffrey Richards published *Modernism, Medievalism, and Humanism: A Research Bibliography on the Reception of the Works of Ernst Robert Curtius.*[1] Over the next ten years a number of major conferences were devoted to Curtius: at Heidelberg in 1986, at Bonn in 1986, and at Mulhouse and Thann in 1992. The proceedings of all three colloquia were then published.[2] Haijo J. Westra, of the University of Calgary, reviewed the Heidelberg collection in the 1992 *Canadian Review of Comparative Literature.* This review, an insightful, well-written essay, gives the impression of being, among other things, a jeremiad against Curtius. In addition to questioning Curtius's character and politics, Westra alludes to 'the subjective-ideological aspect of Curtius's conservative-restorative scholarship ... [his] more dubious views and positions.' *European Literature and the Latin Middle Ages* is said to be 'still a convenient standby, in particular for scholars in other fields.' However, Westra also lists the 'well-known' objections to Curtius: 'formalism, functionalism, a- or supra-historicity, undervaluation of originality and poetic individuality ... and orality ... exclusion of non-Latin elements ... and disregard of the manuscript matrix and its implications, or the concept of audience and reception.' He also states: 'The "tradition" inevitably involves imitation, mediocrity, and a closed canon. [Curtius's] answer to this problem is traditional as well: the cult of genius (Virgil, Dante, Goethe), a supra-historical concept of Beauty, and personal preference ... Theory was not Curtius's *forte* ... ' According to Westra, 'a revival is not desirable. The need for figures such as Curtius today is questionable ... It is the merit of this collection of essays to have demonstrated one more time to what extent Curtius is a dated phenomenon.'[3]

If I cite Westra at such length, it is not to launch a polemic. Admittedly, I shall take Curtius's defence. In the 1950s, as a student, I was attracted to the great German school of humanist critics: Spitzer, Auerbach, Curtius, Vossler, and Hatzfeld. This happened to quite a few of us in the United States, Argentina, Italy, the Netherlands, and so forth. In taking Curtius's defence, however, it is only fair to let the other side speak, to recognize that, perhaps unlike Spitzer and Auerbach, Curtius was, from the beginning, a figure of controversy: in the 1920s and 1930s, again after the Second World War, and also today. I quote Westra because he is a respected North American scholar who writes in English. He does not stand alone. A number of comparable assaults from the Left have appeared both in French and in German. Their passion and brio offer irrefutable evidence, I should say, as to the vital, living presence of Curtius today as a scholarly figure and an intellectual force.[4]

Now, if Curtius is such a figure and embodies such force, it is of course as a medievalist, yet also because he is other than a medievalist. All five names I cited above – Spitzer, Auerbach, Curtius, Vossler, and Hatzfeld – were Romance philologists in the total sense of the term; they wrote with mastery on at least three Romance literatures in all periods. This granted them a particular strength. They saw the Middle Ages as a continuum, as an integral, organic part of the whole of Western culture. Because of this they avoided, in my opinion, the error of some more recent figures, such as D.W. Robertson and Paul Zumthor, who set off their own abstract model of the Middle Ages against a no less abstract model of the modern.[5] The binomial opposition is conceptually pretty and intellectually seductive, yet it inevitably, I believe, distorts the reality of the Middle Ages and of the modern – to say nothing of the pedagogical crisis unleashed when one declares modern reality to be the central Self and one's field of research and life commitment a marginal Other.

Curtius avoided this error by his own total engagement with the modern as well as the medieval. After publishing his dissertation – a critical edition of the beautiful early Anglo-Norman translation of the Book of Kings[6] – he devoted the next twenty years of his life to exploring contemporary French literature and mediating between it and the advanced German literary public. From these years come monographs on Ferdinand Brunetière, the leading French academic critic at the turn of the century, the novelist and publicist Maurice Barrès, and Honoré de Balzac.[7] In addition, *Die literarischen Wegbereiter des neuen*

Frankreich contains seminal essays on André Gide, Romain Rolland, Paul Claudel, André Suarès, and Charles Péguy;[8] *Französischer Geist im neuen Europa* treats Marcel Proust, Paul Valéry, Valery Larbaud, and Henri Bergson.[9] Although Spitzer also penned studies on contemporary French authors (Henri Barbusse, Charles-Louis Philippe, Jules Romains, and Proust),[10] Curtius was unique as a philologist and a university professor in his scholarly commitment to the modern and contemporary, in his insistence that there should be no conflict between philology and criticism, and in his humanist commitment to building a bridge of culture between the two warring nations.

On the one hand, these books are very good criticism indeed. The Balzac volume and the Proust essay (one hundred and fifty pages later severed from *Französischer Geist* and published as a monograph) hold up today among the best that have ever been written on Balzac and Proust.[11] Curtius, in his magnificent 543-page study, is the first modern academic to break away from the standard French view of Balzac as the founder of realism in the novel and the first in a line of French novelists of realism. Curtius envisages Balzac differently. His Balzac is a writer obsessed: with secrecy, the secrets of the universe, and secrecy and deception in society, and with magic, occultism, augury, second sight, magnetism, and alchemy, ever seeking a vision of the all, the quest for the absolute. The novels of *La comédie humaine* tell of men's passions, a quasi-cosmic energy made manifest in desire or will to power, with the result that Vautrin, a synthesis of Prometheus and Lucifer, a creator and rebel, becomes the greatest Balzacian hero. No less important would be Balzac's Rabelaisian gusto for life, French society, and French politics, his fascination with all aspects of the contemporary, in a word, his modernity. Finally, Curtius underscores the central place of religion in Balzac's universe, his juxtaposition of traditional Catholic Christianity and the various strands of occult and esoteric syncretist faith from the eighteenth century. As the German critic sees it, syncretism gives the impulse to Balzac's quest for a total work of art that will encompass the totality of existence, therefore novels opening out to poetry and drama and forming a metaphysical epic that will conquer and reveal the mysteries.

The Proust study, published in 1925, is noteworthy for the fact that Curtius isolated the major Proustian themes and motifs without having read the last two volumes of *À la recherche du temps perdu* – *Albertine disparue* and *Le temps retrouvé* – which had yet to appear in print. Curtius sees art and the life of the artist dominating the thematic of the *Recherche*.

However, art is knowledge, to be taken very seriously, and not just aesthetic pleasure. Memory gives rise to artistic creation because art is the reality of life, and life is made meaningful through present and past art. Among the major Proustian patterns of imagery are found music as structure and metaphor (here Curtius anticipates our current understanding of *mise en abyme*) and space – land and soil, centred around Combray, not Paris, with the functioning of floral and vegetation images. Finally, Curtius recognizes in Proust the failure of love, therefore the tragedy of passion, jealousy, and solitude, where the last remaining hope is a Platonic yearning for the eternal, for the spirit, which can be attained only in the novel itself, which recounts the tragedy and the yearning.

These two studies, and the others, are modern criticism of a calibre beyond anything published in French or English during the 1920s. They anticipate by a decade or two the best work of the Geneva school (phenomenology) and of the pioneers in American studies (myth criticism). Curtius's taste and his recognition of what was truly important in contemporary French literature are uncanny. Between 1918 and 1925 no one else in France or abroad recognized that Gide, Claudel, Péguy, Proust, and Valéry were the names that would endure. No one in the German-speaking world recognized, as he did, the importance of T.S. Eliot and James Joyce.[12] Of the critics discussed in this book, and for that matter in the entire annals of modern criticism, Curtius is unique in the quantity and quality of ties to major contemporary creative writers and in his stance vis-à-vis them – an equal speaking to equals.[13]

Secondly, I should like to underscore the humanist and heroic aspect of Curtius's early writings. In an age when so many conservative German intellectuals indulged in Gallophobia, including Thomas Mann in the *Betrachtungen*, Curtius appealed to his countrymen to notice and profit from the best of the 'enemy's' literature (with the implied lesson that it was better than their own). Moreover, he specifically chose for study Barrès, the epitome of French nationalism; Claudel, a Catholic patriot; Gide, notorious for sundry sorts of scandal; and Rolland, the socialist pacifist who had, it was rumoured, contributed to sapping the will to resist on both sides. It is also true, that as a German intellectual born and raised in Alsace who, compared to others, knew France from the inside, Curtius did not hesitate to critique his authors; he disapproved of Barrès's extreme nationalism, Claudel's intolerant Catholicism, and Brunetière's unscholarly theory of the organic growth and decay of literary genres, a theory that privileged French classicism and failed to appreciate the great literature in Old French. In general, Curtius singled out for praise the 'unclassical' France, works and writers more 'irrational' and spiritual in nature. However, his main thrust was to denounce the current German stereotypes on the French (French *esprit* and French decadence), to hold up French writers as a model for the intellectual rebirth of Germany, and to help find a place for Germany in the new Europe.[14] For this, Curtius was attacked by a number of fellow Romance philologists, including Victor Klemperer, Eugen Lerch, and Oskar Schultz-Gora: for writing on the contemporary, for taking these contemporary figures too seriously, for being too close to the Frenchies, for an absence of scholarship, for appealing to the general literary public, and for his unseemly elegant prose.[15] It is fascinating to note that Curtius was appointed to the chair in Romance philology at Bonn over the objections of the philologists, including the incumbent, Wilhelm Meyer-Lübcke. It is not an accident that the Gide-Curtius correspondence bears witness to this cosmopolitan, transnational humanism in a decade we normally associate with surrealism and expressionism.[16]

In 1930 Curtius published *The Civilization of France: An Introduction*, a curious, fascinating book which has not received the attention it deserves.[17] To begin with, the title of the English version is unfortunate. Curtius is reacting against the then current distinction in German intellectual circles between 'French civilization' – deemed to be a superficial manifestation of parliamentary democracy and modern improvements, its literature political and social – and 'German culture,' a deeper, more profound, and more spiritual private embracing of tradition and the metaphysical. By entitling his book *Die französische Kultur,* he was questioning this particular German nationalist myth.

Curtius goes beyond the simplistic portrait of the neighbour to the west then current, whether in Germany or in France; he will not be limited to a republican, Jacobin, freethinking France, or to its counterrevolutionary, monarchic, Catholic antithesis. He devotes insightful chapters to space (the provinces, with their own traditions and history, in a healthy antithesis vis-à-vis Paris), history (the importance of the old feudal, monarchical tradition in helping to shape and, in a sense, fusing with the modern, centralized republic), and religion (the supremely rich cultural and intellectual history of the French church and the no less rich tradition of Gallicanism and anticlerical skepticism). He is good on Paris at the centre and on France as the child and inheritor of Rome. He notes the central importance of literature as the expression of national consciousness, more so than for any other country, and the unbroken continuity of French literary culture from the early Middle Ages to the present, a vital and unique wholeness that explains French respect for the book and is one aspect of French 'universality.'

Curiously, Curtius's weakest chapter is the one on 'Literature and Intellectual Life' (98–128). There he proclaims German superiority in philosophy, music, and lyric poetry; he simply ignores French music from the Gregorian chant to Jean-Philippe Rameau and François Couperin, and French poetry from the chansons de geste to Jean de La Fontaine and Jean Racine, and for that matter to Alphonse de Lamartine and Alfred de Vigny. And, in the last chapter, he makes unfortunate generalizations about France as a nation of permanence and maturity, of style and craftsmanship ('un peuple de finisseurs,' 233), of taste, and of prose.

This nonsense can be partially explained away or even, to some extent, justified by the fact that Curtius states in the beginning and reiterates throughout that he is not presenting his personal vision of France but the French vision, how the French think of and explain themselves, thus 'an explanation of its [France's] values and systems of ideology ... an "introduction" to the *understanding* of French civilization' (8). By so doing, he anticipates our current fascination with national myths and the 'institution' of culture – in a word with cultural studies. It is also possible that, under the influence of Gide and his other French friends, and with the need to distinguish France from Germany, Curtius came to believe the cultural stereotypes. In any case, whatever the blemishes and even though some of his German critics were right to condemn an amateurish venture into the alleged psychology or spirit of peoples (*Völkerpsychologie, Volksgeist*), the distinguished man of letters Charles Du Bos was not inaccurate when he wrote: '*Die französische Kultur* est l'écrit le plus magistral qu'un étranger nous ait consacré.'[18]

In the early 1930s Curtius reverted from the modern to the medieval; he re-became a medievalist. There were personal reasons for his *Kehre* and, I should say, above all, political reasons. Curtius could no more speak admiringly of contemporary French writers, including Jews and homosexuals, under Hitler than Victor Zhirmunsky could continue to praise contemporary formalism under Stalin. So Zhirmunsky turned to oral epic in Central Asia, and Curtius turned to the Latin Middle Ages. Furthermore, as early as 1932, when Curtius published *Deutscher Geist in Gefahr*, a 132-page essay denouncing Nazi barbarism and the Nazi repugnance for high culture (their *Kulturhass*), he made a plea for Goethean humanism, stating however that the new humanism should be grounded in medievalism, not the Renaissance, and not classical antiquity.[19]

Deutscher Geist in Gefahr is a fascinating, highly controversial book that has been both praised and attacked by scholars.[20] Curtius writes as a

Christian conservative. Some of his options – opposition to the Weimar Republic's parliamentary democracy, opposition to mass education and entrance to the university for vast numbers of students – today appear anachronistic and wrong-headed. It can be argued that in 1932 more important issues were at hand than the defence of *Geist*. On the other hand, Curtius also attacks the Conservative Revolution intellectuals associated with the journal *Die Tat*, and he upholds the values of the Enlightenment and of nineteenth-century German liberalism.

As Curtius sees it, the West in general, and Germany in particular, are in a process of decline and are threatened with collapse. The danger comes from mass movements and the demagogy of the masses – on the Left and on the Right, from communism and from National Socialism – movements which call for revolution. In Germany, in 1932, the danger meant above all Hitler and the Nazis. They especially fetishized the present and denigrated the past; they especially were the fanatics of extreme German nationalism, xenophobia, and hatred for *Bildung* and *Kultur*. Hence, the two chapters entitled: 'Bildungsabbau und Kulturhass' (11–32) and 'Nation oder Revolution?' (33–50). In his polemic against what he calls 'Soziologismus' and its attendant spirit of relativism and materialism, Curtius anticipates our polemics today over postmodernism; in his defence of the university and academic freedom from state control and political demagogy, and for that matter from intellectual levelling and the overemphasis on preprofessional training, he anticipates our debates over the function of the university, the decline of the liberal arts, and the pressures for political correctness.

In sum, as Curtius sees it, cultural nihilism, political extremism, nationalist supremacy, and the cult of the present are united: they lead from one to the other. In response, this German patriot calls for a new Christian humanism, reaching out in space to include all of western Europe, with its centre in Rome, the Rome of Virgil and Dante, and reaching back in time to include all of Western civilization, because it is grounded in Virgil's Rome. This means high culture, tradition, continuity, and internationalism. By exalting Rome and by leaving Greece aside, Curtius undercuts the myth of German cultural supremacy based on the alleged German closeness to the Hellenic world. On the contrary, he distinguishes two Germanies: the one, Goethe's Germany, situated in the Rhenish domain, classical, humanist, and cosmopolitan, looking toward France and Italy; the other situated in Berlin, irrational, mystical, open to extremism from the East. Goethe vs Hitler and Stalin. The Nazis understood. *Deutscher Geist in Gefahr* was denounced and its author designated *persona non grata* during the years of the Reich.[21]

When *European Literature and the Latin Middle Ages* was finally published in 1948, it had an impact comparable to that of Auerbach's *Mimesis* of 1946, a world impact not limited to German-speaking academe.[22]

One immediate discovery of Curtius was the topos. For the first time, in a rigorous and totalizing discourse, he made a case that, for ancient, medieval, and postmedieval literature – say, from Statius to Denis Diderot – the determining structural element and the means of transmission were the topos or rhetorical commonplace. Because of the topoi, scholars now saw literature in a new way: they now could envisage a new, more powerful thematics of medieval literature and a new criticism that would begin by weighing and nuancing these themes and motifs. I cite at random: affected modesty, something never said before, the world upside down, *florebat olim, puer senex, aut puer aut puella, mundus theatrum*, ought a man to marry? *fortitudo et sapientia, locus amoenus*, and the book as symbol. Thus Curtius anticipated one current of structuralism with what has been called a phenomenology or morphology or archaeology of literary types. I remember how, in graduate school, a few of us dreamed of adding to the list, of making our fame by discovering new topoi. I believe we came up with *scholasticus asinus*.

Others took the topoi more seriously, with more adult fervour, than we. For a time a school, or at least a current of criticism, developed in Germany devoted to *Toposforschung*.[23] German-language scholars did discover or invent new topoi, defined the topos in its relation to theme and motif, explored the evolution and transformation of topoi in the various literary domains, and scrutinized their functioning. For a time Curtius was associated with that school and approach.

From the perspective of medievalism, it is significant that an approach originally applied to or derived from the Middle Ages and related to studies in medieval iconography by Aby Warburg and Erwin Panofsky could be especially illuminating for the study of postmedieval literature.[24] Although Curtius himself preferred the terms mannerist and mannerism, it is the baroque period that benefited the most from his insights. Books were written on judicial, political, and panegyrical oratory and on biblical and theological poetics of the baroque. Still more important, a number of his topoi – world upside down, world as theatre, devotional formulae, and 'all must die' – were used, in one form or another, to define the baroque as a literary period style to the extent that, today, students may well conceive of them as uniquely seventeenth-century phenomena.

Also significant for our comprehension of the Middle Ages are the implications of the Curtius method, implications often neglected by both the master's disciples and his detractors. The aesthetic of the topos flourished in a culture of rhetoric – judicial, deliberative, and panegyrical – and of school education grounded in study of the *auctores*, who were often known through collections of *sententiae* and *exempla*. This was a powerfully literary culture, more literary than any we have known since. By emphasizing the literariness and rhetoricity of medieval literature, Curtius helped to refute the generally held romantic belief (à la Gaston Paris and W.P. Ker) going back to German romanticism, in a naive, popular, oral Middle Ages. Curtius, along with Spitzer and Auerbach, made the Middle Ages a period of serious literature worthy of serious literary study. This vision can serve as a model for us today – we who believe in the literariness of literature and the textuality of texts – and also as an antidote to those belated romantics or purveyors of paradox – say, those who distort the ideas of Bernard Cerquiglini and, by so doing, propagate a Middle Ages without literary high culture.[25]

'Imitation, mediocrity and a closed canon' (dixit Westra)? I think not. By insisting upon an aesthetic of *imitatio*, Curtius refutes the romantico-symbolist valorization of sincerity and originality. On the contrary, he indicates how the greatest beauty derives from and is created in the study of earlier literature, in rhetorical and typological cultivation of the *exempla maiorum*. This is a genuine anticipation of our current notion of intertextuality: that all texts are created and read in the confluence, in the present, of other texts and of the tradition of textuality. As it turns out, as much as any medievalist, Curtius opened the canon as part of his vision of history, which extended from antiquity to the Enlightenment and, therefore, had to include writing in Latin, the corpus from Prudentius to Petrarch, excluded from the modern school curriculum first of all by professional Latinists. Putting it bluntly, to know the European tradition, and for that matter to know the Middle Ages, one has to immerse oneself in medieval Latin literature because of its inherent value and because it transmitted ancient culture to the modern vernaculars. Curtius also opened the canon to heretofore neglected elements in the Renaissance and baroque extension of the process. By these I mean especially the masterpieces of the *siglo de oro* in Spain. By insisting upon the book as symbol in Pedro Calderón de la Barca and Baltasar Gracián, the *artes liberales* in Calderón, and the *puer senex* in Luís de Góngora, and by commenting at length on *ingenio, concepto,* and *agudeza* in Spanish poetics, Curtius expanded the domain of the European Renaissance such that subsequent scholars could ignore it only at their peril.

It is, I think, not entirely a coincidence that *European Literature and the Latin Middle Ages* was published one year after *Fearful Symmetry* and less than a decade before *Anatomy of Criticism.*[26] On the one hand, Curtius and Frye, each in his own way, sought to valorize literary studies by insisting upon criticism or scholarship as restricted to literature, as no longer dependent on and a secondary manifestation of history, biography, or manuscript editing. On the other hand, they both called for criticism-scholarship that would reach beyond the single text to encompass more inclusive structures of literature taken as a whole, a phenomenology of literature. As it turns out, the Middle Ages was not one of Frye's strong points. His sense of postbiblical culture really begins with Edmund Spenser and can be seen to centre on John Milton and William Blake. For Curtius, on the other hand, the Middle Ages is the centre, without which the great tradition in its totality is inconceivable.

Here one can observe that the archetypes and the topoi appear to embody divergent visions of literary creation. It is true. Yet I personally find them complementary, not in irreconcilable antithesis. In teaching and in writing on, say, the *locus amoenus* or the girl-rose metaphor in Guillaume de Lorris and in Ronsard, surely one has the right to propose that these literary structures are topoi *and* archetypes. The divergence is, in any case, superficial. Frye's archetypes are transmitted textually. And scholars have noted Curtius's positive citing of Carl Gustav Jung; according to Wellek, the topoi are to be explained as rhetorical figures from antiquity or the creation of great writers or Jungian archetypes. Reading Curtius can help us to grasp the functioning and the beauty of the text.

I say beauty intentionally. Critics have accused Curtius and Frye (again Westra is not alone) of neglecting individual writers and texts. Here I have to state that such criticism is grounded in an insufficiently broad acquaintance with the men in question. *European Literature* and *Anatomy of Criticism*, given their function as anatomies, could not include close readings of texts, although we sense Curtius's love of the great books on every page, and the Dante chapter speaks for itself. It is in other works that the genuine practical criticism is made manifest. Frye authored four brief books on Shakespeare, one on Milton, one on English romanticism, and one on Eliot: these are delightful essays in practical criticism.[27] In addition to his books of the 1920s and 1930s, over the decades Curtius wrote a number of papers on the great figures of the Western canon: Virgil, Calderón, Goethe, Balzac, Miguel de Unamuno, José Ortega y Gasset, Stefan George, Hugo von Hofmannsthal, Hermann Hesse, Eliot, and Joyce, collected in *Essays on European Literature*;[28] and, from the 1920s we have almost one hundred dense pages on Henri Bremond, published in the 1952 *Französischer Geist im zwanzigsten Jahrhundert.*[29]

No less important, from 1944 to 1952, Curtius published some two hundred pages entitled 'Über die altfranzösische Epik,' a continuing sequence of articles in *Zeitschrift für Romanische Philologie* and *Romanische Forschungen* which were then collected in the *Gesammelte Aufsätze* of 1960.[30] As to be expected, Curtius insists upon the learned, cultured, rhetorical, topical structure of chanson de geste, a welcome counterweight to Jean Rychner's championing of orality.[31] No closed canon either. Curtius was the first to insist that the golden age of the medieval French epic is the reign of Philip Augustus at the end of the twelfth century, not the time of the *Song of Roland.* And he was one of the first to state that the problem of the origins is a non-problem and that he would deal uniquely with literary questions. Curtius dealt openly with the problems of genre and reception. For him, so much of chanson de geste was *Unterhaltungsliteratur,* like Alexandre Dumas or Victorien Sardou, but then, superficially identical to the pulp, exploiting the same themes and motifs, the masterpieces stand out in contrast, each with its own unique literary reality: *Girart de Roussillon, Renaut de Montauban, Garin le Lorrain,* and *Aspremont,* among others. These masterpieces, including the original *Chanson de Roland,* are works of literature of the highest quality. They incorporate elements from the Bible, from classical Latin, and from medieval Latin. They are products of a Christian culture and the first major example of modern Christian epic seeking to rival Virgil with the rhetoric of the True Faith.

These two hundred pages are important in that they demonstrate how the generalities of *European Literature and the Latin Middle Ages* can engender literary criticism of specific texts and in the vernacular. They also bear witness against those who claim that, from 1930 on, Curtius felt revulsion toward France and ceased to write on anything French.

Finally, a word about history. Curtius and Frye both have endured attacks that they were (are) excessively formalist and that they ignore history. One response to this accusation would be that they create a new kind of history, the history of topics and archetypes, a history of literary structures. After all, the accusation usually comes from those who recognize only social and economic history. Nowadays, we also include the history of *mentalités,* no less important than the other. In addition (here I think Curtius has the advantage over Frye), because of his reliance on the facts of medieval education, medieval rhetoric, and medieval poetics, Curtius adheres to what we know of composition and reception a millennium ago. For what it is worth, Bernard of Chartres and Jean de Meun would have understood and approved of Curtius's ideas, which is not the case for those of a number of other people including my own.

Curtius the medievalist was also extraordinarily modern in a number of respects, and I believe these constitute his legacy to us.

1 What matters is the critical reading of old texts, not scholarly disputes over the manuscripts and the origins.
2 Medieval literature is profoundly literary, like the literatures of antiquity and of the Renaissance and baroque. All literature is conventional and, as we would say, intertextual. Romantic exaltation has no role in criticism.
3 The reality of Western civilization, at least from Virgil to Diderot, is a continuity of high culture and of aesthetic high civilization. The similarities are more cogent than the disparities.
4 Divergences, over *longue durée*, are stylistic: the shift back and forth between classicism and mannerism, between striving for classical perfection and striving, beyond the classical, for mannerist play, tension, and excess.
5 This said, the history of our civilization does give rise to periods of striving and periods of decline. After every period of decline, renewal is possible. In our time, we can struggle for such renewal.

I have reserved the sixth point for last, a theme (or topos, if you will) that I first elaborated in discussing the modernist writings of the 1920s: Curtius's commitment to humanism. In the forward to the English version of *European Literature and the Latin Middle Ages* the author reveals how the book came into being, what it means for him, and ought to mean to us.

Virgil and Dante have long had a place in the innermost circle of my admiration. What were the roads that led from the one to the other? This question increasingly preoccupied me. The answer could not but be found in the Latin continuity of the Middle Ages. And that in turn was a portion of the European tradition, which has Homer at its beginning and at its end, as we see today, Goethe.

This tradition of thought and art was severely shaken by the war of 1914–18 and its aftermath, especially in Germany. In 1932 I published my polemical pamphlet *Deutscher Geist in Gefahr.* It attacked the barbarization of education and the nationalistic frenzy which were the forerunners of the Nazi regime. In it I pleaded for a new Humanism, which should integrate the Middle Ages, from Augustine to Dante ...

When the German catastrophe came, I decided to serve the idea of a medievalistic Humanism by studying the Latin literature of the Middle Ages. These studies occupied me for fifteen years. The result of them is the present book ...

What I have said will have made it clear that my book is not the product of purely scholarly interests, that it grew out of a concern for the preservation of Western culture. It seeks to serve an understanding of the Western cultural tradition in so far as it is manifested in literature. It attempts to illuminate the unity of that tradition in space and time by the application of new methods. In the intellectual chaos of the present it has become necessary, and happily not impossible, to demonstrate that unity. (vi–viii)[32]

This utterance, in its discreet pathos and its hope, is equalled only by the comparable 'confession' at the end of *Mimesis,* and by André Malraux's credo in *Les Noyers de l'Altenburg.* Other statements from Curtius's masterwork come also to mind:

For literature, all the past is present, or can become so ... I can take up Homer or Plato at any hour, I 'have' him then, and have him wholly ... With the literature of all times and peoples I can have a direct, intimate, and engrossing vital relationship (14).

The 'timeless present' which is an essential characteristic of literature means that the literature of the past can always be active in that of the present (15).

A community of the great authors throughout the centuries must be maintained if a kingdom of the mind is to exist at all. But it can only be the community of creative minds. This is a new kind of selection – a canon if you like, but bound only by the idea of beauty, concerning which we know that its forms change and are renewed. That is why the House Beautiful is never finished and closed. It continues to be built, it remains open (397).

If this is 'conservative-restorative,' so be it.[33] However, it is my conviction that Curtius's humanism is derived from the French and German Enlightenment in addition to the conservative-restorative. Goethe and Schiller, Victor Hugo and Anatole France, Jean Jaurès and Léon Blum would have understood; Gide and Hofmannsthal did. Humanism in our age is also embattled. We also endure a mindset grounded in indifference to or hatred of culture, humanism, and the great books, and inevitably accompanied by contempt for the past. With Curtius in mind, we can see him as he saw Goethe, the last classic – as one with the consciousness of forming a link in the chain of culture over the millennia, a vital creative mind in the present whose *pietas* allied him with the Fathers of old, all this a legitimation and corroboration of his mission and a sign of our succession. With Curtius in mind, we also can pass on the torch of culture and help preserve and renew the *exempla maiorum*.[34]

3 The Evolution of Western Literature: Erich Auerbach

Conferences at Stanford, Marburg, and Groningen commemorated the fiftieth anniversary of Erich Auerbach's *Mimesis*.[1] 'Tis sixty years since – more than sixty – when appeared the first German edition of a scholarly volume that was recognized immediately to be one of the great books of criticism in our century.[2] Charles Muscatine reviewed the English translation as 'one of those rare books that speak to everyone in the literate world.'[3] René Wellek, who had reservations about *Mimesis*, nonetheless characterized it as follows:

> a book of such scope and breadth, ranging as it does from Homer to Proust, combining so many methods so skillfully, raising so many questions of theory, history, and criticism, displaying so much erudition, insight and wisdom, that it was hailed as the most important and brilliant book in the field of aesthetics and literary history that had been published in the last fifty years.[4]

Sixty years later, at the beginning of a new century, Auerbach's masterwork has lost little of its luster or even its immediacy. Whatever the criteria – translations of books into English, books in print, paperback editions readily available, sales, symposia or conference sessions devoted to him, books and articles written about him – it would appear that, in America, as a foreign-language critic Auerbach stands with Mikhail M. Bakhtin, Roland Barthes, and Walter Benjamin in terms of continuing presence. Whatever the evolution of our profession in methodology or in the acquisition of knowledge, students, their mentors, and public intellectuals turn to Auerbach with much the same enthusiasm and sense of discovery or of recovery as in the past. Among a host of examples, two must suffice: in a powerful essay from a powerful mind, Marc Escola rereads Molière, Jean de La Bruyère, and Auerbach, centring on Auerbach's interpretation of Molière and La Bruyère, and treating all three as 'classical texts'; the reputed contemporary novelist Margaret Drabble grounds her discussion of modes of realism in the British novel since 1945 in a respectful and sympathetic reading of Auerbach.[5] Many of us would say that *Mimesis* remains the most important single work of criticism in the modern age and, therefore, that Auerbach deserves a place among the handful of supreme literary scholars and critics.[6]

As I have stated previously, Auerbach, together with Leo Spitzer, Ernst Robert Curtius, Karl Vossler, and Helmut Hatzfeld, form a circle or current of German-language academic criticism – humanist critics – the finest in their day. These German and Austrian scholars combined vast scholarship and historical knowledge with a rare literary sensitivity and imagination; they specialized in all three major romance literatures, from the Middle Ages to the twentieth century; and they authored a rich, extensive corpus of original critical scholarship. Yet whatever their similarities – and there were many – they were scholars grounded in the tradition of classical German-university philology and literary history: each arrived at his own way of writing philology and literary history, that is, at his own approach.

The method, in *Mimesis* as in *Literary Language and Its Public*,[7] is to submit a number of brief excerpts from longer texts to close reading – stylistic analysis concerning features of grammar, syntax, and diction – which then leads to the consideration of broader questions of culture and society in their historical dimension, which then leads to or includes one of Auerbach's central concerns – the literary public and its social response to texts. Somewhat like Spitzer, Auerbach proceeds, back and forth, from the individual passage in a work of art to the style typical of the age, from the particular text on the page to universal principles. W. Wolfgang Holdheim and Michael Holquist have analysed with especial pertinence Auerbach's approach: Holdheim elucidates the Auerbachian *Ansatz*, the text in question or a question about the text, which then launches a process leading to understanding, not unrelated to the Heidegger process; Holquist situates Auerbach in the tradition of classical German philosophy, and more specifically, in a neo-Kantian meditation on representation and history.[8] It is not surprising that Auerbach's version of 'the philological circle' transcends *Stilforschung* or, rather, juxtaposes and fuses *Stilforschung* with what Wellek calls 'historical sociology' – hence

Spitzer's complaint, citing Aurelio Roncaglia, that his colleague was not a stylistician.[9] Because of his work in the historical sociology of literature, in what Holdheim calls historical understanding, Auerbach, unlike Spitzer, is himself aware and makes his readers aware of historical process and change.

Auerbach's mastery of stylistic analysis on the page as well as of the broader social and historical context enabled him to appeal to philologists, historians of literature, formalists, and Marxists, pretty much at the same time. The close reading and the exaltation of a tradition of great books explain why the impact of *Mimesis* in the United States did not wane over the decades of New Criticism, structuralism, and deconstruction; whereas the history of literary publics explains why, in 1977 when the book was finally translated into French, it was hailed in Paris as Marxist *sociocritique*.

Auerbach has always been a favourite of medievalists. This is true for a number of reasons. First of all, as stated earlier, like Spitzer, Curtius, Vossler, and Hatzfeld, he was, throughout his career, both a medievalist and a modernist. Secondly, influenced by Giambattista Vico and the founders of German historicism, Auerbach committed himself totally to what he calls historical perspectivism. Historical perspectivism states that each historical epoch and civilization has its own capacities for aesthetic creation. The universally human is to be perceived in the finest works of each epoch, manifest in a form or style unique to it. This is the formulation Auerbach gave to his legacy from Vico: 'the conviction that every civilization and every period has its own possibilities of aesthetic perfection; that the works of art of different peoples and periods, as well as their general forms of life, must be understood as products of variable individual conditions, and have to be judged each by its own development, not by absolute rules of beauty and ugliness.'[10] It is his credo, as a child of historicism, to appreciate the culture of all periods as part of a universal human condition. Thus he stands at the farthest possible distance from what Lee Patterson designates as Whig literary history, whose adepts, for example, praised Dante and Chaucer for being non-medieval, that is, for allegedly anticipating our modern psychological portrayal of character and our modern social democracy.[11]

Assuming we are allowed to count Gregory of Tours as medieval, seven of the original nineteen chapters of *Mimesis* (it later became seven of twenty; the Cervantes chapter was written for and first published in the Spanish edition) are devoted to the Middle Ages. The medieval centuries, with their differing styles, publics, and mental attitudes perceived

as variety and multiplicity, not a single, simple medievalness, are offered
maximum scrutiny in a book that treats Western culture as a whole, one
in which the Middle Ages occupies a place of honour. Like Curtius,
Auerbach has a vision of Europe: centred on the Mediterranean, and
more particularly on France and Italy, Europe manifesting a unique
consciousness of reality, of history, and of intellectual inquiry, in antiquity, the Middle Ages, and the modern. In addition, like Spitzer,
Auerbach was committed to a single methodology – his own – which he
applied to the medieval and the modern equally, and which produced
similar results across the centuries.

Perhaps still more significant is the fact that, instead of the usual
approach, that is, applying modern insights to medieval texts (what
most of us, who think of ourselves as theoretically progressive, do all the
time), Auerbach does the opposite. He defines man's conscious and
unconscious apprehension of reality, his attitude toward the world, and
his artistic expression of that attitude as shaped by two cultural phenomena that date from the Middle Ages and from classical antiquity.
Auerbach concentrates on *figura* and on the hierarchy of styles – these
are examples of his *Ansatzphänomen*. The classical triad of high, middle,
and low styles in antiquity, when it breaks down due to the impact of
Christianity, gives rise to a mixed style; and the figural Christian vision of
history (today, under the influence of D.W. Robertson, we call it allegorical or typological),[12] allows for random events in the present or the past
to prefigure or postfigure momentous events in history. Thus emerged
the possibility of writing in the vernacular where the low can be treated
with high seriousness.

In Dante human existence is fulfilled in its ultimate destiny; the individual in his earthly existence and the individual in eternity both are
concretely real. In Dante we find a mixture of styles in which *sermo humilis* (vernacular Italian) is, on the one hand, the vehicle for a *commedia* in
the low style, with low, vulgar characters, the contemporary grotesque
and obscene, and, of course, a happy ending. On the other hand, it is
transformed into a new sublime style embracing historical existence and
the cosmos, just what the authors of the New Testament did with and for
demotic Greek. Dante makes the claim that his comedy is also an epic
under the aegis of Virgil and Apollo, and a *poema sacro* under the aegis
of Christ. It contains all of history in time and all of the cosmos in space,
while at the same time, it dignifies the individual, his body, his memory,
and his earthly existence – reality for its own sake and as participation in
God's plan.

This powerful, concrete representation of reality in Dante was then, because of *figura* and because of a second collapse of the hierarchy of styles that had been re-established by French classicism, to fuel a tradition of realism in the modern centuries culminating in Balzac, Stendhal, Gustave Flaubert, and Émile Zola. As Holquist has observed, for Auerbach reality is comprised of the entwining of the individual experience and those external socio-economic forces that shape the individual and also history. Modern realism allows for the lower classes and their social concerns to be depicted as and in historical reality, in the dynamic concreteness of history, their unique historical peculiarity; it also allows that they be granted value and thus be treated not as comedy but with depth and the problematic seriousness of tragedy, the tragic seriousness heretofore reserved for Virgil's Aeneas and Racine's Nero. The French novelists' achievement in endowing the humble and the quotidian, the random everyday occurrence, with the dynamic concreteness of history – that is, with historical significance and with high tragic seriousness – occurs as a modern secular replication of Dante and as a cultural phenomenon that could occur only in the West because of Christian *figura* and because of the (now broken) hierarchy of styles. Thus, the medieval is not depicted simply as a precursor of or introduction to the modern. Instead, with two summits – Dante and the nineteenth-century French novel – the two periods exist in a structure of dynamic tension wherein the modern is shaped by the medieval and is a direct outgrowth of it. Hayden White has even proposed that this structure is figural, a secular, aesthetic figural pattern of the history of literature according to which the medieval foreshadows the modern which then fulfils the medieval.[13]

Auerbach made major contributions to the criticism of early literature and of the modern. His starting points – the three styles and *figura* – became genuine methodologies in their own right (rhetorical criticism, typological criticism), exploited now by two generations of scholars. His readings of individual books made their mark and continue to have an impact. They are still regularly footnoted.

To this day, a significant number of scholars uphold Auerbach's vision of the *Song of Roland*: a poem written in a new sublime style in the vernacular, a paratactic style that corresponds to and reflects a narrow, rigid, and predetermined Christian world view in which the major questions are settled in advance – where we are offered a clear, obvious choice between the light and the dark, between good and evil, and where life is never problematic and tragedy is impossible. Similarly, for at least a generation, scholars saw Chrétien de Troyes with Auerbach's eyes. Here, in contrast to chanson de geste, we find the representation of a courtly romance world, one in which a place is made for external realism – charming vignettes of established custom, courtly ritual, manners, a life of graceful amenity. However, this external realism serves only to enhance the individual knight's career – a life of adventure, with the quest and its adventures the only reason for his existence and for the romance as a literary genre. The world view is class determined, in that the life of adventure is extrahistorical, above earthly contingency, and reserved to the courtly, chivalric, aristocratic society, a community of the elect.[14]

The same is true for Auerbach's studies of the Old and New Testaments. The same is true for the essay on *Don Quixote*, which launched a revisionist current in Cervantes studies, emphasizing the comic in reaction to the then dominant quasi-existential high seriousness of the Unamuno school; and for the essay on Zola, which was one of the first examples of *sociocritique* to counter the orthodox Marxist belittlement of Zola compared to Balzac. The chapter on l'Abbé Prévost's *Manon Lescaut* and on Voltaire was one of the first critical texts to take the eighteenth-century novel seriously and to treat it as more than something that happened to precede Balzac and Stendhal; it was one of the first critical texts to point the way to understanding and defining a literary rococo. Thus, Auerbach underscored the importance and the uniqueness of the eighteenth-century period style, whether it be Prévost's erotic and sentimental intimacy, plus the juxtaposition of the realistic and of bourgeois sentimentality, of the crassest material concerns and of high-flown moral rhetoric; or whether it be the graceful, elegant, and charming demystification of high-flown sentiment in Voltaire's prose and verse, a pleasing middle style intentionally devoid of the tragic and of high seriousness.

In terms of influence, to cite but one example (my own), I profited from the idea of typology as a way into Renaissance and baroque French epic and into Catholic writers of the twentieth century.[15] And the Schiller chapter, with its insights into a sentimental ideology of rural or burgher virtue, exalting domestic intimacy and the warmth of the peasant or middle-class home where the concerns of little people are granted dignity and treated with seriousness, helped me to explore the phenomenon of Biedermeier in a European context, in writers as disparate as Lamartine, Henry Wadsworth Longfellow, Théodore Aubanel, and Stephen Phillips.[16]

Finally, it is important to remember that Erich Auerbach is not just the author of *Mimesis*, although this work represents the crowning point of his career. From the 1920s and 1930s, in addition to a number of important articles, he penned a dissertation on the fifteenth-century novella in France and Italy, a translation of Vico, and what turned out to be one of the most significant and innovative contributions to Dante studies in our century.[17] *Dante, Poet of the Secular World* makes a unique synthesis of the secular, human Dante and the deeply Christian Dante – the two poles of *dantista* scholarship over the centuries. The 'Christian revolution' offered Dante both an inspiration and a model for the valorization of his Italian vernacular – the ennobling of *sermo humilis* – and the valorization of secular courtly love, with desire now allied to the metaphysical quest for the ideal. The new Christian epic will treat, following upon Aeneas and Saint Paul, the turning point in a man's life and in history, a voyage to and a vision of the other world, grounded in the Thomistic conception of man's individuality and free will. In this other world, even in the depths of hell, human beings retain their individual traits, their reality, and their dignity, for the earthly is now eternalized. With these people, time is frozen, nothing new can transpire, their essence is fixed. The Narrator, Dante the Pilgrim, alone offers personal testimony as a witness while struggling for his own salvation; he alone evolves.

From the 1940s on Auerbach continued to produce. Medievalists are familiar with his *Introduction aux études de philologie romane*, and with the essays contained in *Literary Language and Its Public*, which make a statement on Latin prose during the so-called Dark Ages and on the language and audiences of early French romance and Dante.[18] As in *Mimesis*, he is concerned with the rise of literary vernaculars – in twelfth-century France and fourteenth-century Italy – how under a particular form, in particular levels of style, they came into being and became meaningful for a particular social class and literary public.

Of equal importance, especially for North American readers, are the essays published in the 1959 collection, *Scenes from the Drama of European Literature*.[19] In 'La cour et la ville' (131–79) Auerbach conducts a meticulous sociological and lexical analysis of how the meaning of the term *public/publique* evolved during the age of Louis XIV from the body politic to the new literary public, the first public that was conscious of its identity and that used the term. This new public was made up of the monarch, his entourage, and an emancipated high bourgeoisie including writers, the *honnêtes gens* who are cultivated and who appreciate the arts. 'The Aesthetic Dignity of the *Fleurs du mal*' (199–226) sketches Charles Baudelaire's achievement in depicting modern horror and despair in a sublime style, granting dignity and a vital sense of reality to his personal vision of death, vile physicality, the sensuality of artifice, and the absolute denial of transcendence and of any hope for redemption.

The fact that, toward the end of his life, Auerbach made such a commitment to French literature, from the *Eneas* to Baudelaire, gives the lie to that assertion, heard now and then, that the master's primary concern was always for things Italian. On the contrary, Auerbach was a genuine Romance philologist; his field was *Romanistik*. Although he lacked some of the range of Curtius and Spitzer, he nonetheless paid major, continuing attention to centuries of French, Italian, and Latin literature. Despite the cavil from susceptible teachers of English, such as Robert Gorham Davis and, for that matter, Wellek, *Mimesis* is a legitimate and fair reading of the central tradition in the literature of our civilization.[20]

Were one to criticize *Mimesis*, half a century later, it would not be for Auerbach's overall vision of literature or his approach(es). They hold up. Nor would it be for his commitment to a tradition of great books and the high culture that they nourish (see below). However, one can express reservations about the reading of individual texts.[21] Brilliant, provocative, and partial as they are and would have to be, Auerbach's readings can be, and over the past five decades actually have been, nuanced and enriched by those who come after. To cite some medieval examples, today most of us would deem the *Song of Roland*, *Yvain*, and the fabliaux as deeper, more complex, and more problematic, according to Auerbach's own criteria for the representation of reality, than he himself recognized them to be in 1946.[22] In addition, we could propose other texts from roughly the same time frame and genre or mode – *Raoul de Cambrai* or *Girart de Roussillon*, Beroul's *Tristan*, Thomas's *Tristan*, or the *Prose Lancelot*, and the *Roman de Renart* – all of which manifest significantly greater historicity, density, and the concreteness of everyday life. More importantly, they also are grounded in immediate political and social issues; all but the beast epic radiate tragic seriousness of one kind or another; and they are composed in a genuine mixture of styles à la Dante and a juxtaposition of voices à la Dostoevsky (as read by Bakhtin). These observations on the early medieval are applicable also to the books of antiquity and the books of postmedieval modernity.

Thus, today we have a more complete and problematic picture of Homer, or Chrétien de Troyes, or the century of Voltaire and Rousseau than Auerbach did. This is due in part to the torrent of criticism devoted to all the major writers since the 1950s. Our discipline is progressive. Literary criticism resembles the sciences in that we build upon the discoveries of our predecessors just as our successors will build upon ours. Given that, in some sense of the term, we see farther than Nicolas Boileau, Charles Augustin Sainte-Beuve, and Matthew Arnold, so also we see farther than F.O. Matthiessen and Erich Auerbach. The medieval cliché is apt in this context: we are dwarfs standing on the shoulders of giants.

A second explanation lies in the nature of what it means to write literary history. Here we should recall Auerbach's commitment to Vichian historical perspectivism and to history as such. As much as any of the great critics of our century, he was sensitive to historical process and evolution. He said: 'My purpose is always to write history' (*Literary Language* 10).

In a book of seminal importance, *Is Literary History Possible?*, David Perkins argues (without alluding to Auerbach, of course) that such literary history must be structured by and according to an implied narrative.[23] The implied narrative proceeds from a beginning to an end, almost always underscoring the complexity of the evolution to the summit (the end) and oversimplifying the origins (the beginning) from which the evolution is derived. The narrative itself determines, more or less arbitrarily, which texts will be chosen and how they will be read. Given that most scholars favour their own field of research while remaining to some extent uninformed about other fields, I should add that most monographs devoted to a century, a movement, or a current will attribute 'good' qualities to the century/movement/current and significantly less good qualities to the preceding century/movement/ current from which it arose. Whig literary history also applies here. Medievalists have a right to bewail the number of studies on the Renaissance which proclaim any number of 'modern'-seeming traits in the sixteenth-century – subjectivity, individual psychology, political and social concerns – set off against the Middle Ages, the latter (Christian, unproblematic, uniform) depicted in terms two generations out of date. Medievalists can take heart, however, from the fact that specialists on classicism or the baroque do to the Renaissance what the *seiziémistes* did to the Middle Ages. The phenomenon continues, unabated, to the

present, where a number of studies on the postmodern attribute uninformed cliché-traits to the masters of modernism: W.B. Yeats, James
Joyce, Ezra Pound, T.S Eliot, and William Faulkner.[24]

Of all men, Erich Auerbach avoids this kind of provincialism. Of all
men, Auerbach avoids Whig literary history. Nonetheless, he is not com-
piling a series of essays or an encyclopedia. He writes literary history.
Therefore, despite the historical perspectivism, despite the particular,
unique beauty of each time and place, given the narrative of figural realism, Dante and the nineteenth-century French novel embody or fulfil
the representation of reality in ways that other authors and genres do
not. Those works that lead up to (precede) Dante or that lead up to
(precede) Balzac will inevitably be faulted, in one sense or another, for
not (yet) being Dante or Balzac. Perhaps for this reason, and this reason
alone, Auerbach's readings of single texts do not hold up as well as
Spitzer's, for Spitzer never published a book of literary history but,
instead, collections of discrete critical and linguistic essays. I think
Perkins would say that to write a book of literary history you have to be
willing to pay the price.[25] The relative distortion of certain books, easily
correctable, is a small price to pay for Auerbach's masterwork and the
master narrative that it structures.

As much as Spitzer and more than any critic writing in French or Italian, and without ever having read the likes of F.R. Leavis and F.O.
Matthiessen, Auerbach made a contribution to American critical modernism.[26] For this reason, *Mimesis* has recently been studied as a historical
phenomenon in its own right. Especially prevalent in the Stanford proceedings is this wish to 'historicize' Auerbach and, as some have said, to
make him timely rather than timeless. However, in today's climate of politically charged scholarship, it should surprise no one that analysing *Mimesis*
as history can lead to the analyser displacing his own ideology onto Auerbach or criticizing Auerbach's ideology in favour of his own. Historicizing
Auerbach also allows distinguished critics whom I admire (Terry Eagleton
and Herbert Lindenberger) to portray him as a dated phenomenon,
obsolete in some sense of the term, and of diminished relevance today.[27]

As I mentioned in chapter 1, Geoffrey Green proposes that Spitzer
and Auerbach were historically oriented, and indeed that they became
attuned to history as a result of their experience of exile and, in more
specific terms, their exile as Jews. According to Green and to Jesse M.
Gellrich, Auerbach's vision of literature and of history – the foreground-
ing of a passionate, depth-oriented style in the Hebraic Old Testament,
the restated crucial importance of the Jewish Bible in the figural chain

of meaning, and the evolution of a tragic, modern realism leading to fragmentation and disruption – is to be related to the fate of Auerbach's Jewish contemporaries under the Third Reich and can be identified as his response to their fate. In other words, Auerbach's work, defined by Hebraic historicity, would be the expression of his sense of responsibility for and kinship with the lost Jews of Europe.[28]

I do not agree. First of all, as in chapter 1, I should argue that Auerbach and Spitzer differed enormously as to their own critical practice and conception of literature vis-à-vis history. Secondly, Auerbach's vision of literature and history forms a unity from his earliest writings to his last. To the extent that personal testimony can contribute to such discussion, I remember Auerbach telling me that, like Goethe, he had the ideas for all of his books in his head at age twenty-five.[29] He never indulged in Germany-bashing. On the contrary, on another occasion he volunteered to me that he never truly felt at home as a professor in America. He would have accepted the offer of Curtius's chair at Bonn and returned to Germany but for the fact that his son Clemens was a scientist established in America, not far from New Haven. Finally, although it is certain that figural typology reasserts the link between the Old and New Testaments and between Judaism and Christianity, and also offers the reminder (alas! that the reminder is needed) that it is impossible, indeed a flat contradiction in terms, for a genuine Christian to be anti-Semitic, *figura* is a complex, problematic notion which also asserts that the Old Testament and the history of the Children of Israel are devoid of interest and of meaning other than as prefiguring the Advent of the Saviour and, therefore, forming stages on the road of *Heilsgeschichte.* Northrop Frye discovered this complexity with the negative reviews of his studies on the Bible and literature that denounced his version of biblical typology as insensitive to or insulting of Judaism.[30]

In my opinion, Martin Elsky is closer to the truth when he observes that Auerbach does not identify as a Jew.[31] In Auerbach's correspondence with Walter Benjamin, the great critic alludes only to their shared 'origin.'[32] And, in the very important 'Epilegomena zu *Mimesis,*' Auerbach proudly affirms his German identity, that he is a German intellectual, and that *Mimesis* is unthinkable other than as a German book grounded in the intellectual tradition of Germany.[33] Elsky compares brilliantly two great German intellectuals of Jewish descent, masters of *Bildung*: Victor Klemperer, a convert to Protestantism who turned to the French eighteenth-century Enlightenment for inspiration, and Auerbach, who sought his inspiration ultimately in French Catholicism. Spitzer also was attracted to the Catholic Church, in his case by way of the Spanish Golden Age.

A variation on the Jewish reading of Auerbach could be called the Muslim/exile reading. We know of Edward Said's interest in Auerbach as a great European intellectual authoring the great book of the European intellectual tradition, doing it as a Jew, exiled from Europe in a Muslim land, Turkey, which had embodied for centuries the greatest threat to Europe.[34] Interestingly enough, we know, again from the correspondence with Benjamin, how, on 3 January 1937, Auerbach denounced the reformist regime of Kemal Atatürk. As he sees it, the New Turkey resembles the New Germany and the New Italy – with the attendant hatred of Western civilization, extreme nationalism, and eagerness to extirpate its own culture of the past. When I asked him whether he had learned Turkish, Auerbach replied that people of his generation were less interested in such things and, also, that the Turks with whom he conversed were fluent in either French or German. The transnational, transcultural, nomadic, and migratory condition, so in vogue today, may have had less of an impact on him than some of today's scholars would have it; or, rather, cosmopolitan, French-oriented German intellectuals had all the stimulus they could handle, whether or not they left the Reich.

Paul A. Bové, a noted spokesman for the academic New Left, finds in Auerbach evidence for and a confession of the cultural exhaustion of bourgeois humanism – that is, Auerbach's tragic consciousness of the defeat of Western bourgeois humanist culture.[35] He finds two or three passages in Auerbach that bring grist to his mill; he analyses them in depth with brio. Bové also sees in Auerbach a representative of the humanist mandarin professoriat in Weimar Germany, the professoriat that recoiled from modernity and from democratic/progressive politics. Employing the common cultural studies argument, Bové continues:

> Another way of saying this is that Auerbach is what Foucault might call 'a relay of power'; taken up by the American professoriat his work completes a circuitry that makes available for American appropriation intellectual discourses, practices, and images that empower the academy's elitism, satisfy its needs and interests in reproduction, and legitimate its existence in its own eyes and, given the eccentric role of humanistic education in the United States, that of the state and other powerful institutions. (128)[36]

Holquist, while he does not share Bové's leftist anti-intellectualism, would agree with him as to the consciousness of end/failure/exhaustion/defeat/death:

The West that is the site of history in Auerbach's sense is less an end, in the sense of a telos, than it is a development that has come to an end, in the sense of its conclusion. *Mimesis* is ultimately an elegy for the difference and otherness that he has named the West ... The West that is the hero of Auerbach's tale, the subject of whose biography tells of a growing courage to see randomness and difference without appeal to the opium of religion – is dead.[37]

Yes, we do find in Auerbach historical urgency and, occasionally, the tone of elegy. However, he was scarcely unique in this domain. Most of the great exiles despaired at one moment or another as they envisaged the New Order in Europe – the Führer and his thugs dominating the continent of high culture and their homelands for what appeared to be the foreseeable future. Similar passages can be found in Georges Bernanos, Thomas Mann, and St-John Perse, to name three of the most eminent. Stefan Zweig committed suicide. Yet the others did not commit suicide. They arose from their own ashes to reclaim the heritage of Western civilization, their own. Auerbach's *Lebensdenken* can be distilled from his work, all his work; this work is not and never was an admission of defeat.

I have more sympathy, therefore, with those – Arthur R. Evans, Jr., Paul Zumthor, René Wellek, and Jan M. Ziolkowski – who assert that Auerbach cannot be limited to ideology, or be seen only as a symptom of the history of his time.[38] Or, at least, grounding him historically in his age has to be done in a more subtle, complex, and problematic manner. In any case, I would argue that Auerbach never repudiated scholarly or creative humanism and that he never spread a pall of gloom about him. He maintained to the end his faith in 'the inner history of the last thousand years [which] is the history of mankind achieving self-expression' and in the capacity of the literary scholar, including the young who emerge, to recover that history and make it live.[39] It is in the mode of resistance and of affirmation that I interpret the oft-cited passage that concludes *Mimesis*:

With this I have said all that I thought the reader would wish me to explain. Nothing now remains but to find him – to find the reader, that is. I hope that my study will reach its readers – both my friends of former years, if they are still alive, as well as all the others for whom it was intended. And may it contribute to bringing together again those whose love for our western history has serenely persevered. (557)

In contrast to the 'high civilization' of Western culture Auerbach did observe and deplore what he called 'levelling,' 'standardization,' and 'imposed uniformity.'[40] He dreaded a sterile, undifferentiated world without standards, where the individual consciousness would no longer find a place. He was alluding to the Soviet Union but also to the United States, the then so vaunted American Way of Life. I see him as having anticipated, with brilliant prescience, among other things, today's phenomenon, the spread of American pop culture over the entire world, though he could not have foreseen the academic adulation of the spread, what Irving Howe called 'glorious infatuation with trash.'

Throughout the history of Western culture, from Homer to Proust and beyond, there have always been Greeks and there have always been barbarians. The tension between them constitutes one of the more exciting chapters in that history. One legacy of Auerbach is that mankind always has a choice, and that three thousand years of culture are the result of the choice – culture which, thanks to the historicism that he so honoured, now not only is but also is known.

4 Albert Béguin and the Origins of Literary Modernism

Albert Béguin was a leading member of the French-language current designated as the critics of consciousness or the Geneva school (l'École de Genève). This phenomenological school of criticism came into prominence as a school in the 1950s and 1960s as the most important element of the French-language *nouvelle critique* in reaction against traditional French literary scholarship – that is, the positivist literary history à la Gustave Lanson associated with the Sorbonne since the latter decades of the nineteenth century. Béguin, his older colleague Marcel Raymond, and their younger colleagues and disciples, Georges Poulet, Jean-Pierre Richard, Jean Rousset, and Jean Starobinski, are the most important representatives of this movement.[1]

Although less famous in the English-speaking world than some of the others, Albert Béguin has enormous standing on the Continent, especially in France, Germany, and Italy.[2] Like Curtius and Auerbach, he is best known as the author of one major book, the published version of his 1937 doctoral dissertation entitled *L'âme romantique et le rêve: Essai sur le romantisme allemand et la poésie française*.[3] René Wellek deems this two-volume, 800-page monument to be 'one of the finest productions, or even the finest, of French literary scholarship in this century.'[4] Taking into consideration the book's impact in both German and French studies and its contribution to the shaping of modern literary history – indeed, to our idea of modernism – I agree with Wellek.

Béguin was among the first to see the modern as a development from certain French writers in the second half of the nineteenth century: Charles Baudelaire, Arthur Rimbaud, Gérard de Nerval, and the late Victor Hugo, whose influence and presence extend on to surrealism. He does not imagine that this bursting forth of the modern came *ex nihilo*; on the contrary, he finds the most likely predecessors (not sources) of the French moderns to be the writers of German romanticism: Jean Paul, Novalis, Ludwig Tieck, Achim von Arnim, Clemens Brentano, and E.T.A Hoffmann.

The focus of analysis – the key to modernism, so to speak – is the dream. Béguin explores the broadest possible semantic field for *le rêve*: dreaming at night, daydreaming, reverie, the mystical trance, the vision, the unconscious, prophecy, and what we can designate as the phenomenology of the psyche. He is fascinated by dreaming as related to collective myths, memories of childhood, reality beyond the empirical, waking world, and the romantics' striving to regain lost unity or the world-soul. The individual capable of rising to this higher level and attaining (or merely wishing to attain) universal consciousness proves to be a magus, seer, and poet, with the result that artistic creativity is implicated in all aspects of the romantic dream experience.

Although in rebellion against Sorbonnard literary history, Béguin retains one important element of the tradition – the intellectual background. From its very conception, his book is as much a work of philosophy as of literary criticism. In fact, the entire first volume, some 300 pages, is devoted to late eighteenth- and early nineteenth-century thinkers, and it is not the least of Béguin's achievements that he grounded his critical readings historically in the writings of these relatively obscure, little-known philosophers.

Even though, from Béguin's perspective, the end of the eighteenth century marks a reaction against the rationalist and the mechanist currents of the Enlightenment, he finds two traditionalist thinkers who are also fascinated by dreams and the dream experience. Georg-Christoph Lichtenberg relates, in a timid manner, dreams to myths and to the representation of being and death. More interesting is the case of Karl-Philipp Moritz, who, in two autobiographical novels, *Anton Reiser* and *Andreas Hartknoph*, resembles Proust in his anguished quest to recover the past in memory and in the symbolism of place.

Far more important are a group of thinkers contemporary with the romantics, the *Naturphilosophen*, a circle of friends, disciples, and contemporaries of F.W.J Schelling. Béguin brought to light these obscure mystical polymaths, the most important being Ignaz-Paul-Vitalis Troxler, Gotthelf Heinrich von Schubert, and Carl Gustav Carus. Troxler was a pre-Bergsonian who denied pure intellect. For him, our dreams in sleep are a superficial residue of the grand Lifedream, which includes sleep and the waking state, the soul and the body. Other avenues to Life and the Lifedream are the child's preconscious, magnetism, and mystical ecstasy. Schubert, the author of *Ansichten von der Nachtseite der Naturwissenschaft* (1808) and *Symbolik des Traumes* (1814), proposed a mythical history of mankind: from unity to the fall to striving to recapture the unity. Dreams play a crucial role in the striving; allied to poetry and to prophecy, they are a language to be deciphered, the seeds of our higher and better next existence. Carus denied the traditional dualities. As he saw it, God is to be found in us, in the external world, and in his realm beyond. We and nature are in a state of transformation – becoming and rising. In sleep the conscious and the unconscious (*Unbewussten*) are joined; their joining, their wedding, gives rise to dreams.

In the second volume of his dissertation Béguin delves deeply into and comments with acuity on six of the principal German romantic writers: Jean Paul, Novalis, Tieck, Arnim, Brentano, and Hoffmann. Reading him is to participate in an extraordinary magical voyage into the life, thought, and spirit of one of the greatest generations of men who made our culture. With a passionate insight, Béguin reclaims, so to speak, their vision of the cosmos and of mankind.

To give a few examples, we see the 'blaue Blume' in Novalis's *Heinrich von Ofterdingen*, a dream flower that the protagonist will seek for all his life, his dream world more real than the waking one, and his dream the consciousness of a higher realm. The poet and the seer can rise to that realm because of the creative imagination; they can attain universal consciousness.

We find an extraordinarily 'modern' situation in Achim von Arnim where two characters who never communicate when awake do so in their common dreams. Truth and insight are derived from each person's dreams and from the unconscious. They are even given, in interior monologues, to automatic writing.

We observe in Clemens Brentano a German Catholic Baudelaire preceding Baudelaire. In Brentano love opens the gate of dreams; love, night, and dreaming, now joined, are morally superior to daytime reality. Since prophetic and allegorical dreams are to be interpreted, their interpretation reveals the mysteries.

The French chapters in Béguin are less extensive and devote less space to individual writers. Nevertheless, the Swiss scholar does trace the evolution of dreams and dreaming from the eighteenth-century *Illuminés* to Proust and beyond. He argues for the central, seminal contribution of Nerval, Hugo, Baudelaire, and Rimbaud. Béguin was perhaps the first critic to separate Victor Hugo from the other early French romantics. It is in Hugo's late, apocalyptic verse, especially *La fin de Satan* and *Dieu*, that we find the dreamer welcoming all that God can communicate to man, and the notion of the dream as transgression, as an act of defiance grasping the forbidden. In Hugo all is myth, all is cosmic totality.

As Béguin sees it, the French romantics prior to Baudelaire, Nerval, and the late Hugo, manifest certain generic traits of the movement, including grand sentiment and the cult of the individual; however, they lack the metaphysical dimension, plus the depths and the authenticity to be found in German romanticism. The German romantics were the first to consciously base an entire work of art on the dream experience and to relate dreaming to artistic creation, to make the dream world the subject and the structure of a poem and to seek inspiration and a literary structure in dreams. They create a modern sensibility which includes nostalgia for a better, more harmonious world, myths of a lost golden age, exaltation of the unconscious and the irrational, and the eternal striving, the quest for the world-soul, a quest which leads also to the creation of works of art.

After defending his grand thesis, Béguin was offered a chair in French literature at the University of Basel. He continued to publish at an enormous rate for the next twenty years, but his post-1937 writings have received less notice than *L'âme romantique et le rêve*, and have been compared, unfavourably, to the masterwork. This is due, in large measure, to the direction taken by Béguin following upon his conversion to Catholicism and his baptism by the great theologian Hans Urs von Balthasar. According to Sarah Lawall, 'after his conversion in 1940 he never again studies an author who does not consider religious themes.'[5] According to Wellek, 'Béguin's leading preoccupation was always religion, and poetry was only a means to it … late in life he allowed [aesthetic values] to be overshadowed by his concern for religion.'[6] Other scholars, including those most sympathetic to Béguin, notice similarly a narrowing of vision.

A number of factors can explain these judgments. The old, traditional French *Thèse d'état* (and its Belgian and Swiss equivalents), ranging from 500 to 1,000 printed pages, was expected to make a definitive statement on a topic; it would normally take one or two decades to complete and would make a scholar's career. Just as few poets compose more than one epic, so also few scholar-critics contribute additional studies of the weight and impact of their thesis. Béguin's life was further complicated by the Second World War and the occupation of France – he participated in the intellectual Resistance – and by his decision, in 1946, to leave Switzerland and the world of academe in order to become a freelance writer, translator, and editor in Paris.[7] As with Edmund Wilson and for the same reasons, Béguin's later books were, to some extent, collections of materials published previously as articles or as introductions to volumes that he himself had edited or translated. It can also be noted that non-Christian academics – the majority of academics – have a tendency to assume that a scholar who writes on Christian authors or who comments on Christianity suffers ipso facto from a narrower vision if not major myopia. Especially in French studies, where the spirit of laïcité is embraced by so many in the profession, the Christian tradition, central to our civilization, is often treated as if it were merely one among a number of secondary currents, examples being le roman catholique or la poésie des Guerres de religion.[8]

This said, I should like to argue for the originality and brilliance of the later criticism, for its quality and its importance.

Béguin wrote two books on Balzac.[9] Following Curtius, Béguin was the first scholar in the French world to oppose the then-dominant view: Balzac as a realist, a scientific observer of society who launched the French tradition of realism in the novel. Instead, alongside the realism, contributing to and surpassing it, Béguin offers his Balzac, a visionary and creator of myths. As Béguin sees it, Balzac's greatest characters are creatures of excess, devoured by passion, ambition, and greed, themselves searchers for the absolute. With them, Balzac creates myths: the androgyne, the courtisane, the usurer, the travelling salesman, and the demiurge. Perhaps the greatest is that of society itself portrayed as a living organism. With these myths, Balzac creates his own universe, one powerfully allegorical and with special ties to the supernatural.

Béguin wrote two books on Nerval.[10] Responding to the then general view of Nerval as a minor figure in French romanticism, a lightweight eccentric (or madman) important only as a precursor of Rimbaud, Béguin insists upon what can be termed the existential element in Nerval. He underscores the theme of the quest, life as a titanic struggle and a heroic voyage through darkness, allied to rebellion, the Nervalian speaker refusing to accept that he is insane or that his insanity is bad. Logic and 'real life' are deemed inferior to the imagination, to layers of symbolism, and to the quest within. The details of autobiography and of reality are willingly suppressed in favour of literary structures that emphasize the dream and the symbol, that will help the speaker to achieve atonement in his inner life and in the act of writing, writing itself conceived as transfiguration and mystery.

Béguin wrote two books on Léon Bloy.[11] More than anyone, he brought to the attention of the French literary public this weird, eccentric Catholic of the late nineteenth and early twentieth centuries who denounced optimism, progress, and modernity while foreseeing, indeed predicting, the horrors of our age, including Naziism. Bloy's vision of history is grounded in what, today, we would call Christian typology. In place of the current progressive conception of differing centuries and periods, grounded in one form or another of meliorism, Bloy envisages all of history derived from and responding to the Incarnation. Throughout history, because of the communion of saints, all of us re-enact the passion; we either wipe the filth from Christ's body or spit in his face. Since the end of the Middle Ages society as a whole has chosen to separate itself from Christ, in a mad dash to the Apocalypse. In response, Bloy denounces the rich who, in their greed, construct an idol out of their gold and silver and thus re-enact Christ's betrayal by Judas. He associates himself with the poor, the *pauperi* close to Christ, who, in their suffering, bleed Christ's blood and are Christ. He denounces anti-Semitism. And he wills pain upon himself, seeking the grace of suffering in order to share in Christ's agony. Because of Bloy's passion – agony in his person due to Christ's absence and to his desire to imitate Christ, agony due to the recognition of his personal lack of holiness – the writer is metamorphosed into a prophet, one who foretells the future and denounces the iniquities of the present, including his own.

Béguin wrote three books on Charles Péguy.[12] Péguy resembles Bloy in his vision of history, with the Incarnation as the dominant event that speaks to everyone. Christ is always present, because of the sacraments and because of the chain of the faithful, so that we all partake of his crucifixion and resurrection. However, Péguy differs from Bloy in temperament. He sees hope in prayer, in the community/communion of the people (Christ's body), and in his own quest to regain lost purity, the purity and innocence of the child, the old French village, the parish, and even the act of breaking bread.

Toward the end of his life, Béguin published two volumes in the 'Écrivains de toujours' series published at Le Seuil. Normally these are mere editions of selections from a well-known author. However, the one hundred or so pages of introduction gave Béguin the opportunity to make an original and compelling statement that most of the other editors ignored. In *Pascal par lui-même* Béguin recognizes the tragic anguish which makes Blaise Pascal appear to be so strikingly modern.[13] He also underscores the power of Pascal's mind, his achievements as a scientist and philosopher; he proclaims Pascal to be a style-conscious writer and master of rhetoric; and, finally, demystifying the fetishization of Jansenism on the part of the freethinking French academics, he notes Pascal's presence in the Church as one among so many seeking redemption.

A number of literary events mark Béguin's life – for example reading Péguy as an adolescent, and the first encounter with Jean Paul in a Paris bookstore. Perhaps the greatest was his discovery of Bernanos. A passionate admirer of the great Catholic novelist, Béguin edited a number of his books, helped publish others, encouraged the project of the *Œuvres complètes*, and himself began to edit Bernanos's papers and correspondence. In addition to a host of articles, he also did a *Bernanos par lui-même*.[14] Béguin finds in Bernanos a world of night and an obsession with death, and also the hope of escaping the dark by a return to childhood or, instead, by regaining the childlike quality of goodness which is inherent in the saints but which the rest of us have lost. His heroes are priests, forced to serve in a post-Christian age. Their three graces are lucidity, suffering, and love; because of the love, they have supreme insight, above that of mere psychologists, as has their author, Bernanos himself.

Admittedly, of these six writers, four are consciously, wilfully Christian. Bloy, Péguy, and Bernanos, with some others, constitute a Catholic movement, school, or renaissance in the twentieth century. However, Balzac and Nerval, whatever their personal leanings, are not Catholic writers in any meaningful sense. With all six, Béguin moves out from the heritage of German romanticism to a more general, synthetic understanding of the modern in literature, and especially the twentieth century. Not only that; as the Pascal volume demonstrates, Béguin's engagement with Christianity also inspired him to go back in time, to explore French literature prior to 1800. Therefore, I propose that the Swiss scholar's conversion and his wartime and postwar activities led to a broadening, not a narrowing, of his vision. We can see this in three posthumous collections of his essays: *Poésie de la présence*, a project which was on Béguin's agenda, and two collections chosen and edited by Pierre Grotzer, *Création et destinée: Essais de critique littéraire* and *Création et destinée II: La réalité du rêve*.[15]

In *Poésie de la présence,* Béguin reaches out to the distant past, with five essays – seminal essays – on writers and books from the twelfth to the seventeenth century. As he sees it, Chrétien de Troyes is a writer of great maturity whose works, language, and world view are more urbane – not more primitive – than ours. His is a world of symbols and of the meaning behind them, a lay aristocratic world of love, heroism, chivalry, and honour of great spiritual depth. *La Queste del saint Graal* is shown to be congruent with Cistercian missionary zeal, a book of complex and interacting structures: linguistic, psychological, spiritual, and allegorical, a book of high civilization. Maurice Scève appears as a Renaissance poet comparable to Stéphane Mallarmé and also superior to him in a number of respects. Although Scève is a difficult poet, his symbolism is always grounded in concrete physical reality. Few poets have ever delved deeper than Scève into the complex problematic of jealousy and desire, with desire transfigured by and in adoration, contemplation, and, ultimately, redemption. Béguin devotes two briefer pieces to freedom, exaltation, and glory in Pierre Corneille, and to light vs dark and speech vs silence in Jean Racine.

In addition, *Poésie de la présence* and *Création et destinée II* contain studies on a range of twentieth-century poets, some in the Catholic school and some fiercely opposed to the Church: hypermoderns, surrealists, and poets of the Resistance. In alphabetical order, these are Louis Aragon, André Breton, Paul Claudel, Paul Éluard, Pierre Emmanuel, Max Jacob, Pierre Jean Jouve, Charles Péguy, St-John Perse, Pierre Reverdy, Jules Supervielle, and Paul Valéry. And, as additional evidence for Béguin's increased attention to prose fiction during his later years, in *Création et destinée II* we find some 150 dense pages on the novel, with particular attention paid to *Madame Bovary,* Balzac, Bernanos, C.F. Ramuz, Julien Green, and Jean Cayrol. Cayrol can be thought of as a Béguin discovery.[16]

Given the importance of the *nouvelle critique* and given Béguin's contribution to it, a number of major figures, including the other Geneva scholars, have written on Béguin and, more especially, have defined his approach as a reader and critic. These include, in addition to Lawall and Wellek, J. Hillis Miller, Gaëtan Picon, Georges Poulet, Marcel Raymond, Jean Rousset, and Jean Starobinski.[17]

What is Béguin's method? his approach? He opposes psychoanalytic criticism and other 'external' approaches (history, biography) that would concentrate on the author, his life, or his medical history, and thus separate him from the work. Similarly, he will not be subject to the tyranny of scholarship, and especially to the listing of sources or to artificially imposed scholarly grids such as Corneille vs Racine or Balzac vs Stendhal, or, for that matter, the medieval vs the classical and the classical vs the modern. Béguin's method is one of sympathy or affinity for a writer's work that leads to something like identification. He seeks to penetrate and to explore the consciousness manifest in the work, its mental structures and life experience, his consciousness of their consciousness. His is what Raymond has called a morphology of the spirit. Béguin unveils the myths that make up a writer's universe, and the intense life of that universe on the edge – the boundaries between the real and the imaginary and between the material and the spiritual. The great poets offer a Heideggerian sense of Being or Presence, an absolute tension, anguish, and *tremendum* that surpass the historically quotidian and respond to man's *Ur-Angst.* As such, Béguin finds in himself, and offers to us, the astonishment that people at an earlier stage in history felt in the presence of the *numen,* a consciousness of that greater reality or transcendence, forbidden to us but which we seek throughout our lives, an aesthetic incarnation whereby the spiritual is made present to us. Thus the critic undergoes his own quest for the Grail, one sought also by the poets.

Béguin reveals his personal reasons for writing *L'âme romantique et le rêve.* He was attracted to the topic, drawn by the surrealist poetry he discovered in his youth and the romantic tales he read as a child (I: xiv–xix). He precedes the study of the six great German romantics by his own encounter with each one, drawing a sketch of their homes, their regions, and themselves as men (II: 11–16). In one essay he echoes Roland Barthes's famous distinction between a readerly and a writerly literature by positing his own opposition between the *lecteur* and the *liseur.* The *lecteur* reads, as a professional or an amateur. He has a vocation or an avocation. The *liseur,* who reads with passion, gives his life to reading; his life is transformed by what he reads. His is a calling.[18] Reviewing a recent edition of Pascal's *Pensées,* although he praises the editor's scholarship, erudition, and the analytic skills deployed in reconstituting the text, Béguin insists that what is most important is to offer to readers today a version of Pascal that will be readable, a text both coherent and meaningful:

La reproduction fidèle des manuscrits, en leur état de désordre provisoire ou d'ordre momentané, ne saurait suffire à ces fins de l'oeuvre pascalienne. Il importe que les *Pensées* demeurent, ou redeviennent, parole vivante, parole d'homme à homme, eau vive capable de désaltérer nos soifs. C'est là qu'est leur vérité, c'est cette vérité-là qu'il faut permettre à n'importe quel lecteur d'apercevoir, sans qu'il ait à refaire pour son compte un travail de déchiffrement et de synthèse qui incombe à l'éditeur.[19]

Therefore, we are not surprised when, as early as 1936, he states openly that the critic should always seek a work's meaning and power for us today rather than indulge in a futile effort to relocate himself in some foreign century contemporary with the author:

> Mais nous sommes qui nous sommes; et toutes les précisions d'une exacte analyse ne nous rendront pas semblables au poète du XVIIᵉ siècle ou à ses premiers lecteurs. La poésie ne demeure vivante qu'en se faussant au gré de l'évolution spirituelle. À la limite, on imaginerait une oeuvre dont aucun élément ne serait plus compris dans son sens originel, et qui pourtant resterait efficace.[20]

Significantly, as early as the 1950s Béguin praised the French *nouveaux critiques*, especially Barthes but also Poulet, Richard, Gaston Bachelard, and Lucien Goldmann.[21] His one caveat directed at Goldmann's *Le Dieu caché* concerns the Marxist assumption that Pascal and Racine can be explained, first and foremost, by their social class. As to be expected, Béguin portrays the writer as a lone individual, imprisoned in his unique solitude and exalted by his unique freedom to create, for himself and for the community.

Such readings of literature will inevitably be subject to critique. In particular, a later school of Germanists has pointed out weaknesses in *L'âme romantique et le rêve*. These include the following: Béguin chooses a few isolated dream experiences in a writer's corpus, to the exclusion of other quite divergent themes and motifs, including the protagonist's active life in society. He does not analyse an individual writer's style nor does he distinguish sufficiently between the various German-language romantics. Perhaps most of all, he views them through the prism of Nerval, Baudelaire, and the surrealists, failing again to make crucial distinctions. Guilty of anachronism, simplifying to an excess, and oblivious to the historical contextualization, Béguin can himself be envisaged as a romantic poet writing on the romantic poets. Thus said Walter Benjamin.[22]

To some extent the critiques are justified. Yet it must be remembered that Béguin, like Curtius, or for that matter, like Frye, does not write literary history or even literary criticism in the traditional manner. As Joanna Zurowska observes, he practises something more akin to *Stoffge-schichte* or *Problemgeschichte*, others would say he explores the phenomenology of literature.[23] Furthermore, like Spitzer, in the wake of his phenomenology of literature Béguin has produced some superb critical readings of texts, practical criticism at its best. I have noticed, among others, essays on Novalis's *Heinrich von Ofterdingen* and *Hymnen an die Nacht*, individual poems by Arnim and Brentano, especially the latter's *Romanzen vom Rosenkranz*, Hoffmann's *Die Elixiere des Teufels*, Balzac's *La fille aux yeux d'or*, Nerval's *Aurélia*, Péguy's *Ève*, Bernanos's *M. Ouine*, Scève's *Délie*, and *La Queste del Saint Graal*. Again, like Spitzer, Béguin has been cited for the quality of his criticism, for having authored the most 'penetrating' book on Pascal, dense and brilliant; for rich, dense, and masterful work on Péguy; for the best book ever on Ramuz, etc.

Finally, and I think this is especially significant, for a man who paid no attention to literary history as it was practiced in the French-speaking world, Béguin's greatest contribution was, paradoxically, in the domain of canon formation, with his reconsideration of which books are and have been important in our culture and why, and, therefore, which literary currents have defined our culture (and why). In this and in other respects he resembles Curtius. As much as anyone, and as early as the 1930s, Béguin defined the tradition of modern literature – what today we call modernism – as a line of poetry extending from Nerval, Baudelaire, and the late Hugo up to and including French surrealism. The great predecessors of the French modernists were not the French romantics but the German romantics. Theirs is a literature not only of formal innovation but, in addition, one of epistemological and metaphysical striving, of a quest for a deeper reality, beyond reason, to be had through the dream-experience, mysticism, and the imagination. He was one of the first, and the very first in the French-speaking world, to make a claim for the German romantics, not only vis-à-vis German classicism but also as a major presence in and major contributors to world literature. Due in large measure to Béguin, French writers since the Second World War have been influenced the most by their confrères beyond the Alps and the Rhine. In passing, Béguin was one of the first to call for the recognition of the irrational, unconscious, mystical, and visionary strain in literature and to grant it a place of honour.

Later in his career, Béguin isolated a second major current in poetry, which includes Paul Verlaine, Guillaume Apollinaire, Péguy, Supervielle, and Éluard, a poetry of simplicity yet which resonates with *tremendum*.

Unlike most pundits in Paris or elsewhere he could appreciate and encourage all schools in twentieth-century verse, specifically both the heirs of arcane modernism and the poets of the Resistance. Béguin upheld *l'honneur des poètes* in all camps and on all fronts. ·

And, of course, he was the first academic to insist upon the importance of a Catholic school or current in the twentieth century, in prose and in verse. Béguin's vision has stood the test of time. We see modernism and the Catholic renascence in part as he saw them, because of him. With regard to this, and always working from individual writers, Béguin altered our perception of Pascal and Balzac, he rehabilitated Nerval, Hugo, Bloy, and Péguy, and he first called attention to one of the greatest, Georges Bernanos.

Reading the accounts of those who knew him makes us realize the extent to which Béguin was a vital, human presence in French intellectual life, a public intellectual. In this he resembles some figures in the Anglo-Saxon world (Lewis, Leavis, Frye, Wilson, Kazin, and Howe) and differs from the more private and very scholarly German philologists. Béguin was, of course, a man of books, the eternal reader, and, because of this, a man of passion, his passions unleashed and his life transformed by books. For him, as for Alfred Kazin, 'writing was everything.'[24] With writing and books, Béguin's was always a relationship of engagement and passion, even identification. His was a quest for their struggle and their truth, and for his own. He sought their 'présence' and he found it. The power of his vision was felt by all around him.

The vision was, from early in Béguin's career, oriented toward the world. He observed that we today no longer enjoy what Sainte-Beuve could take for granted: wealth, leisure, an amateur standing, and disengagement. We are condemned to read books in relation to our current situation and our destiny; and this way is better: 'Non, Sainte-Beuve n'était pas enviable, avec sa paix, sa solitude, ses échelles de jugement. Il n'était qu'un critique littéraire, si peu indispensable. Le critique actuel revendique d'autres responsabilités, et connaît d'autres joies: les joies d'un homme mêlé à tous les risques de la vie des hommes'.[25] In January 1934 Béguin gave up his post as Lektor in a German university and returned home. Prior to this, in 1933, he withdrew his membership in the Jean-Paul-Gesellschaft because it had withdrawn the editorship of Jean Paul's complete works from Eduard Berend, who was of Jewish descent. In 1939 Béguin made a major effort to help Berend flee the Reich.[26]

As a Professor at the University of Basel, Béguin considered it his mission to uphold faith in France and in French civilization among the prudent, lukewarm Swiss with their bourgeois passivity and apathetic philistinism. His conversion to Catholicism was, according to Grotzer, first of all a conversion to the Christian tradition of France.[27] Therefore, intransigent, unlike Marcel Raymond (and, above all, unlike Paul de Man), he could find no good whatsoever in the 'German revolution' and its New Europe.

This commitment then found a practical outlet in the editorship of *Cahiers du Rhône*, which gave a voice to the Resistance poets, a voice silenced inside France, and later in the editorship of *Esprit* from 1950 to his death in 1957. Béguin became a voice for Christian humanism during Hitler's war and, after it, a voice for the new France in what was becoming a totalitarian world:

> Devant cette complicité monstrueuse des petits bourgeois rationalistes avec les tyrans en démence, devant cette alliance des idéologies abstraites avec les peurs et avec l'énorme crime hitlérien, il fallaît que s'élèvent et que s'unissent toutes les voix qui persistaient à protester au nom de la Liberté, de la Fraternité, de la Justice, au nom de la personne humaine.[28]

> Si la guerre nous a appris quelque chose, c'est que l'homme *tout entier* est engagé dans l'histoire, et qu'aucun des problèmes de l'homme n'est inutile à élucider, si nous voulons chercher à vaincre les monstres.[29]

As a Christian socialist, he defended the worker-priest movement shut down by the Vatican. In the 'Affaire Finaly' he supported the laws of the Republic which forced the Church to return to their relatives two Jewish boys baptized during the war. He attacked the French armed presence in Algiers and the Soviet armed presence in Budapest. Through all these years he spoke out against Catholic reaction, capitalist exploitation, bourgeois opportunism, and the Sartrean and pro-communist extravagance.[30]

Reading the accounts of those who knew Béguin, one comes to understand his *présence*, resembling C.S. Lewis in the impression he made on friends and colleagues as a quasi-prophetic figure and a man, the extent to which he was loved. Such is also the incandescent quality of his prose, again like Lewis's, the prose of a writer. His was the conscience (one conscience ...) in one of the most dynamic intellectual periods of our time.

5 Academic Criticism at Its Best: Jean Rousset

Like Albert Béguin, Jean Rousset is Swiss, a critic and scholar associated with French *nouvelle critique* and the Geneva school. Like Béguin, he spent a number of years teaching in Germany, where he was influenced by German literature, architecture, and intellectual life. In other respects, however, Rousset differs from Béguin and from the concern with consciousness deemed central to the Geneva critics. Born in 1910, he is, except for Frye, the youngest figure whom I examine in this book, and he is also the only one whose work came into being in its entirety after the Second World War. As I see it, the fifteen years or so that separate *L'âme romantique et le rêve* from *La littérature de l'âge baroque en France* are crucial. Unlike Béguin, Rousset spent his entire postdoctoral career as a university professor in Geneva;[1] unlike Béguin and other *nouveaux critiques*, he pays scrupulous attention to the text and to history. In a sense, more than the others, he does – at a significantly higher level – what many in the profession try to do. That is, he examines literary texts with rigour, integrates the insights of literary history, cultural history, and source studies, is aware of and receptive to the approaches of other critics, and, last but not least, as a consequence he documents the work of his predecessors. Perhaps also as a consequence, he resembles many in the profession in being known primarily to specialists. Although Rousset is the least famous of the figures whom I study, he is included in part because of the enormous impact he has had in French studies and because I consider his practical criticism, in scope, quantity, and quality, to be the finest that I know in or on French literature.[2]

A final similarity to Albert Béguin, Jean Rousset had the greatest impact with his first book: *La littérature de l'âge baroque en France: Circé et le paon*, published in 1953.[3] In the French university system and in the

French-speaking 'institution of literature,' pride of place had always been accorded to 'les grands classiques' of the generation of Louis XIV. It had been tacitly assumed, or more often proclaimed outright, that Corneille, Molière, Racine, La Fontaine and their contemporaries were unique in world literature, that they represent the summit of French literary accomplishment, so that the other masterpieces from the other periods lead up to or fall away from these classics. In addition, they were deemed to embody the French spirit in its essence – to be Frenchness – as no other works did, past or present. It was this institution of cultural Frenchness that Rousset helped to decentre by exploring the literature of the first half of the seventeenth century – the age of Louis XIII.[4]

Although he was first inspired by German and, even more, Italian architecture, Rousset prefers an inductive to a deductive approach, leaving the discussion of Roman monuments by Gian Lorenzo Bernini and Francesco Borromini to later in his book (161–80). Instead of imposing on literature categories borrowed from the fine arts, Rousset finds his categories illustrated in the literature itself; in other words, he offers us a phenomenology of the baroque text and of baroque cultural practices. Rousset analyses certain themes or bundles of motifs: the spectacle of death (horror, blood, cruelty, the torturer and victim, the funereal landscape); the world in movement (flame, snow, clouds, the rainbow, soap bubbles); and, within that world, water in movement (streams and fountains). Writers may joy in the movement or recoil from it. In the latter case, especially, it is perceived as ending in the permanence of death.

Still more interesting, perhaps, is his scrutiny of three non-canonical theatrical forms: the court ballet, the dramatic pastoral, and the tragicomedy (13–78). Here, fully aware of seventeenth-century stage practice, Rousset anticipates our current interest in paraliterature and cultural studies. This theatrical world is grounded in movement, metamorphosis, enchantment, inconstancy, illusion, disguise, deception, the mask, doubling, dream vs reality, and the play within a play. The *ballet de cour*, under the influence of Torquato Tasso – in particular, the garden of Armida and Ismen's forest – revels in enchantments. In this domain of Circe and Proteus, reality is unstable, people themselves are subject to metamorphosis, and the world is a stage. The action in the *pastorale dramatique* occurs in a décor of stylized illusion and the fantastic: a dark forest with magical fountains and secret grottos. Lovers seek after and flee from each other; if they themselves remain faithful, the Hylas-figure, a pastoral Don Juan, revels in his own inconstancy. In spite of the happy ending, tragicomedy presents a much darker world, in which the precarious and the capricious are assigned to Dame Fortuna, and the characters doubt themselves and their existence. Disguise and illusion contribute to a mysteriousness that can lead to insanity. In sum, myriad manifestations of metamorphosis allied to spectacle and ostentation; in other words, Circe and the peacock.

Later in the volume Rousset draws conclusions and implications (229–53). He argues for a new French literary history that would recognize a Renaissance classicism (Ronsard, Joachim Du Bellay, Robert Garnier) followed by the baroque (ca. 1580–1665) followed by the traditional classicism of Corneille, Molière, and Racine. Actually, with the term 'long classicism,' Rousset wished to include the eighteenth century, a period that today we are more likely to associate with the rococo. The thrust of the book, as a whole, denies outright the notion that François de Malherbe and Nicolas Boileau imposed order on chaos and, thus, saved France from bad writing. A new sensitivity, a new kind of literature, exists and demands to be recognized.

Rousset also tries to isolate the specifically French aspects of the baroque (196–228). He concludes that the French texts are, for the most part, grounded in spectacle and ostentation but not in mobility and metamorphosis. He also sees in Malherbe and Corneille strong baroque tendencies which then shift toward the classical. The early Corneille writes comedies on the subject of inconstancy in love; with the inconstancy and in response to it, come deception, disguise, metamorphosis, and the will to appear what one is not. L'illusion comique is a total and complete baroque play in all respects. In time, however, Corneille shifts from comedy to tragedy when he creates a new hero constant to himself and immutable in his glory. Nevertheless, this classical character retains one major baroque trait – ostentation. The heroic tragedy of triumph is predicated on the hero's playing a role and establishing the self as a standard for others; this permanence is enunciated by means of an external façade of dissimulation and, when necessary, prevarication. In sum, Rousset finds the French baroque less baroque than the Italian, for instance, and of less literary weight than the classical.

Here I wish to critique Rousset, who could have gone farther. Rather than assign a list of categories and, based on whether or not writers partake of them all, judge the writers for being more or less baroque and revealing a pure or impure baroque, he might have taken the baroque where he found it and, thus, differentiate between the national currents within the baroque age. Today we do not hesitate to designate Nicolas Poussin and the palace at Versailles as French baroque. In addition, had

Rousset chosen Agrippa d'Aubigné, Jean de La Ceppède, Antoine
Gérard de Saint-Amant, and Jean Rotrou as his test cases, he would have
arrived at a French literary baroque that adheres to the international
style in its totality and that is in no way inferior to the comparable writers of classicism.

Scholars have critiqued Rousset on more serious grounds. Some, in
the French literary and educational establishment – the 'institution of
French culture' – were outraged by what they perceived to be an assault
on the French classics and on Frenchness. Others believe that Rousset's
vision of the baroque is excessively formalist, that he fails to take into
account factors of dynamism, movement, history, and historicity, and
that he removes books from their context, isolating traits chosen before-
hand and neglecting the rest.[5]

The first critique is symptomatic: it pays tribute to the importance of
La littérature de l'âge baroque and its impact – that of creating a paradigm
shift – on French literary studies.[6] The second charge is more valid,
although we have to admit that Rousset's purpose here was not to write
literary history or to do practical criticism. He sought to acclimatize the
idea of the baroque in France and to elaborate a phenomenology of the
mental structures of that age. In this, he succeeded admirably.

However, the concern for taking literary works out of context does
apply to Rousset's two-volume *Anthologie de la poésie baroque française*.[7]
This was and is still the most successful, most famous anthology in
France, for any period and any genre. Rousset establishes six categories:
Proteus or inconstancy; bubbles, birds, clouds; water and the mirror;
from metamorphosis to illusion; the spectacle of death; night and light.
These categories are grounded in the phenomenology of *La littérature de
l'âge baroque*. What Rousset does, however, is to select individual poems
and even bits and pieces from longer poems, and to include them in
one of his six sections in order to illustrate the phenomenology of the
section. For example, religious sonnets that form part of a sequence
devoted to the death and resurrection of Christ are ranged under the
category 'le spectacle de la mort' or 'la nuit et la lumière.'

This said, the anthology also has sterling features. The poems and
pieces of poems are teachable; one can ground a class in the scrutiny of
texts, which can include restoring them to their original context. The
notes and bibliography are superb. Most important of all, the anthology presents offerings taken from little-known or under-recognized figures. Among the writers Rousset rehabilitated or discovered in the first
place, are (this is only a partial list): Agrippa d'Aubigné, Jean Bussières,

Jean-Baptiste Chassignet, Martin Drelincourt, Du Bois Hus, André Mage de Fiefmelin, Jean de La Ceppède, Siméon-Guillaume de La Roque, Pierre Le Moyne, Martial de Brives, Honoré d'Urfé, and Théophile de Viau. In my own case, inspired by Rousset, I wrote a monograph on Pierre Le Moyne and three chapters on baroque epic.[8]

The critiques evaporate when one takes into account Jean Rousset's next statement on the baroque, the 1968 *L'intérieur et l'extérieur.*[9] This is one of his finest books. Here he expands his vision of the baroque: in addition to the earlier categories, Rousset writes insightfully on illusion and disillusion/disenchantment, duality and doubling, and the concetto. Above all he establishes a new field for the baroque imaginary – the exterior façade, with its decoration, dispersion, disguise, deceit, and movement, yet which is always in a state of tension with the interior, inner self, the self of religious and mystical devotion and the yearning for unity, stability, and permanence. The devotion and yearning call for a greater presence of the religious elements than was the case in *La littérature de l'âge baroque.* To illuminate the thesis, he offers superb readings of texts, practical criticism at its best. These include, among others, the structure of the sonnet sequence from Du Bellay to La Ceppède, light and darkness in sacred poetry by Claude Hopil and Du Bois Hus, the play within a play and the actor as hero in Rotrou, and the structure of the Don Juan plays. Especially cogent, and especially historical, is his analysis of the introduction of Italian stagecraft (the box stage) and its implications for baroque and classical French drama.

The 1960s mark a decisive turn in Jean Rousset's critical writings, one much less familiar to scholars. This second, and longer, phase in his career manifests a turn toward the modern – he now treats literature from the seventeenth to the twentieth century – and toward more contemporary critical approaches: structuralism and narratology. His genre of predilection becomes the novel. It is perhaps artificial, on my part, to distinguish between structuralism and narratology. The two approaches overlap, in that the various functions of narrative technique determine structure and that, except for the brief lyric, all structures in works of literature relate to the narrativity or narratizing element inherent in them.

Rousset's collection of essays *Forme et signification* created quite a stir, capped off by a respectful yet strongly stated caveat from Jacques Derrida.[10] *Forme et signification* was perceived as structuralism with a human face, structuralism/formalism in the tradition of Roland Barthes, Claude Brémond, A.-J. Greimas, Roman Jakobson, and Tzvetan Todorov, yet written with elegance and highly readable.[11] Rousset insisted upon the notion that form – a given structure – is the essential component in a work of art that determines, so to speak, its meaning and our reading of it. Among his more notable forms or metaphoric structures are the figure-eight pattern in Corneille, the antithesis of protagonist and spectator in Marivaux, the 'plunging' view from a window in Flaubert, the circle in Proust, and the separating screen in Claudel.

In the case of Pierre Carlet de Chamblain de Marivaux (45–64), Rousset distinguishes between the novels and the plays. In *La vie de Marianne* and *Le paysan parvenu*, the older Marianne and Jacob, as narrators, observe and comment on themselves, their actions, and their motivations when they were young, when they performed the activities that make up the plot. They function as spectators to themselves as actors. In the plays the functions are separated. The masters assume the role of unconscious, unlucid romantic leads. It is their servants and confidantes who observe, comment upon, and manipulate the masters. They manage also their own love affairs, paralleling the masters. Although everyone is playing a part, the servants do so consciously and with full lucidity, and thus function also as author figures.

With regard to Proust (135–70), Rousset wrote in 1962 what has come to be the principal thrust in criticism on the *Recherche*. Rousset elaborates on the strands that make up the Proustian circle: time and the intemporal in *Combrai* resolved in the end by the revelation of time and the intemporal in *Le temps retrouvé*, when the protagonist joins with the narrator, becomes the narrator, because, now that he remembers all, including the beginning, he can tell his story and be a writer. The quest for an aesthetic becomes the novel's aesthetic and the subject of the novel. As narrative doubles – models and countermodels – Swann and Charlus embody the conflictual nature of love and art. Love and art, love vs art, are also exemplified in the characters' favourite books. Rousset analyses brilliantly what today we would call the intertextual presence of Balzac, the duc de Saint-Simon, Georges Sand, Mme de Sévigné, and the *One Thousand and One Nights*. Marcel's true vocation as an artist and his quest for the vocation function as the circle. Inside it, contained within it, we and Marcel discover the world of love, that is, the false loves and the false lures that destroy failed artists.

In the same general line we can place Rousset's book, *Le mythe de Don Juan*, which postulates three non-variables or invariants essential to the Don Juan myth: the apparition of the dead man (the statue), Don Juan himself as protagonist, and the women whom he seduces (who, in the plays, range from one to four).[12] In the tradition prior to romanticism, the tradition from Tirso de Molina to Mozart, what matters is not character but the situation, the functioning of forces and relations that make up a structure.

Rousset's furthest reaches and most extensive theorizing in structure are to be found in the 1981 *Leurs yeux se rencontrèrent* and the 1990 *Passages*.[13] In the first book, perhaps inspired by the microanalysis in Barthes's *S/Z*, Rousset examines in depth and with rigour one increment to be found in most novels: the scene of first encounter – that is, the first meeting between the protagonist and his/her love interest. He then elaborates on the structures or aspects of this increment in order to construct a model. The model includes a static *mise en place* – space or décor, time, the characters, their relative positioning, the other's portrait, and the other's name – and a dynamic *mise en scène* – the encounter that gives rise, either in this particular scene or later in the fiction, to three elements: the effect (love at first sight, initial repulsion, etc.), the exchange (the first speech or gesture, the first communication), and the crossing or bridging (*franchissement*, contact or understanding of an erotic nature). The rest of the book explores the permutations offered by narrative texts – primarily French novels from the seventeenth to the twentieth century – in the domain of effect, exchange, and crossing, followed by a long chapter on 'Écarts et transgressions' (149–201), the manifold exceptions to the model. The second book, *Passages*, contains some one hundred additional dense pages on 'l'échange entravée' (125–230), the blocked or prevented exchange.

Among a number of scholars, Philippe Carrard is favourably impressed. He believes that Rousset constructed the model not for its own sake but in order to help us read texts; he also observes the extent to which Rousset treasures the exceptions.[14] John E. Jackson praises the book as 'le plus attachant, peut-être, des ouvrages formalistes de l'auteur.'[15] Roger Francillon alludes to 'la richesse de ce beau livre' and describes it as an 'ouvrage majeur et exemplaire'; he also praises Rousset for the exceptions.[16] No doubt … Still, since it may well be that I don't have the mind for rigorous structuralism, I am not convinced that the 'première rencontre' merits so many hundreds of dense pages. Did not perhaps Rousset indulge in a bit of 'overkill' and, consequently, might not some of his readers benefit from a less exhaustive and more compact presentation?

Whatever reservations I hold as to Jean Rousset's scene of the first encounter, they disappear with regard to his contributions to narratology, two books of capital importance. The first of these, *Narcisse romancier,* treats of novels told in the first person.[17] Rousset's work on narrative technique places him on a level with Wayne C. Booth, Gérard Genette, and Franz Stanzel.[18] In a 'préambule semi-théorique' of only twenty pages (15–36), he comes to grips with any number of elements or increments that relate to first-person fiction. Among these are the position of the narrator: first-person vs third-person, the narrator as protagonist or observer, first-person narrative inserts in a third-person novel, authorial intervention, mock authors and mock readers; mixed and multiple narrators; the epistolary form; and dialogue. No less important is the temporal order, whether it be retrospective, past, and chronological as in pseudo-autobiography or a memoir; or prospective, present, and subjective as in letters, a journal, or an interior monologue; and the permutations made possible by mixed forms, insertions, and the disruption of chronology. Narrative perspectives are organized with regard to focalization and point of view: inside and outside, coherent and intermittent, and, again, first-person and third-person.

After this extraordinarily rich introduction, laid out with clarity and elegance, Rousset proceeds to analyse categories in novels that extend from Paul Scarron's *Le roman comique* to Alain Robbe-Grillet's *La jalousie.* The readings are brilliant, the insights illuminating. Also, although the chapters are not ranged in chronological order, that is, following the composition of the novels or the career of the authors, Rousset devotes two chapters to the origins of the French I–novel in the seventeenth century (37–66). He demonstrates how, although dramatic soliloquy and the autobiographical or confessional form went out of favour during the heyday of Jansenism and of classicism, two genres came into prominence which would not only replace, in a sense, these forms but also feed into the rise of the novel: memoirs or pseudo-memoirs and collections of letters. Rousset concentrates on the eighteenth century, with studies devoted to Robert Chasles, Prévost, Marivaux, and Crébillon fils. By so doing, he contributes, as in his studies on the baroque, to the rehabilitation of neglected writers. He also contributes to the rehabilitation of an entire tradition. The pre-eminence of the French novel, from Balzac to Jean-Paul Sartre and Albert Camus, has lead to a relative denigration or misinterpretation of novels in other periods, such as medieval romance and contemporary *nouveau roman* and surfiction. The same is true for the eighteenth century, treated as a harbinger of the nineteenth, meritorious in some ways but deficient in nineteenth-century realism. Rousset emphasizes that eighteenth-century fiction can and should be studied in its own right, as a major contribution to the history of the novel, comparable to the century of Balzac, Stendhal, and Flaubert. He also underscores the 'modernity' of the great eighteenth-century texts, the extent to which their narrative experimentation and play anticipate similar manifestations in our time, and also that reliance on first-person fiction is endemic to both the eighteenth and the twentieth centuries, in contrast to the third-person structure dominant in the nineteenth.

An example of such fecund revisioning would be the chapters on Marivaux (103–13) and Prévost (127–38). Both novelists adhere to the conjunction of character and point of view; with both, the reader cannot know more than the I-narrator, therefore the reader is obliged to share the narrator's subjective vision. However, whereas Prévost's older narrators do not 'improve' upon their younger selves and, consequently, remain relatively blind as to their own and other people's passions, Marivaux's Marianne, blind concerning the others, has come to know herself. Significantly, the subjective, limiting obsession with the self coincides with Marianne's essence as a character, for, as protagonist, she loves herself, past and present, and is eager to be loved by and reflected in her suitors; and, as narrator, she loves herself, past and present, and is eager to be loved by and reflected in her readers.

A second example would be Rousset's last, chapter 10, a contrastive essay on Prévost's *Histoire d'une Grecque moderne* and Robbe-Grillet's *La jalousie*, both texts viewed as examples of the restricted narrative field, and both of them molding the reader to conclude that the textual voice is in error or lying and that there is a truth behind and beyond what we are told, even if no way exists for us to discover it. In addition, as Francillon observes, the reader will feel more sympathy for Robbe-Grillet's second-person voice – cold, mute, and invisible, a thinking void – than for Prévost's first-person voice, so un-lucid and non-introspective, so grounded in its own bad faith.[19]

Equally masterful is the volume entitled *Le lecteur intime*.[20] The most important section ('Le destinataire dans le texte,' 19–137) concentrates on the reader in the text. In his habitually brief yet seminal opening chapter (23–35) Rousset observes that much more criticism has been devoted to the narrator than to the reader. Then, building on the work of Gerald Prince, Gérard Genette, and others, he discusses the external or extradiegetic reader (the public), alluded to either overtly ('Dear Reader, you may be asking ...') or obliquely by seemingly trivial signifiers in the narrator's discourse.[21] The narrator performs a selective process on his inscribed narratees: they are chosen by gender, social class, geography, and taste. The reader can be subject to assimilation or exclusion. The narrator can raise himself up or lower himself down vis-à-vis his public. Rousset then offers a similar classification of the internal or diegetic/intradiegetic narratee: a reader or listener who functions within the narrative, deemed to be singular, plural, or collective; stable or mobile; and subject to an internal narrative that is written or oral or both. Note that for all cases – internal and external – Rousset is discussing inscribed narratees whose existence and whose functioning can be determined by a careful reading of the text, who are inscribed in the text. In this he differs from Wolfgang Iser and his followers who study a more abstract entity – the implied reader with its variants: the competent reader, the ideal reader, the average reader, etc.[22]

Examples of Rousset's style of criticism in *Le lecteur intime* include his analysis of the 'staging' of a reading process in La Fontaine's *Psyché* (73–82): within the narrative frame, Poliphile delivers orally – by reading his own prose text – a reworking of the story of Psyche and Eros. Interactions abound between the myth and the narrator who recounts it, between the myth, Poliphile's text, Poliphile, and his three listeners, and between all of them and the architecture, sculpture, and gardens at Versailles.

On the oft-studied *Les liaisons dangereuses* Rousset also makes an original contribution (83–94) by observing that, in this epistolary novel, certain readers of letters read more than their share; they become 'pirates,' reading the letters meant for others. Because Valmont and Merteuil become multiple narratees for a number of discrete narrators and, consequently, break the epistolary contract, they obtain knowledge of the others and from that knowledge power over them. The irony and double meanings are for them alone, not for the others, to be savoured and then used to empower. Valmont and Merteuil share the extradiegetic readers' knowledge (we readers know *all* the letters) while remaining within the narrative and, therefore, having the power to shape it at will as we cannot.

Despite the subtitle 'From Balzac to the Journal,' Rousset ranges over several centuries of French literature, as he did in *Forme et signification* and *Leurs yeux se rencontrèrent*. He writes on Corneille, La Fontaine, Jean-Jacques Rousseau, Choderlos de Laclos, Balzac, Jules Barbey d'Aurevilly, and Guy de Maupassant. In addition these essays are not limited to the novel and the novella; chapters are devoted to the theatre, to the philosophical essay, and to travel guides.

Le lecteur intime concludes with a long section on another genre whose very existence is determined by the tension between writer and reader: the *journal intime* (139–218). Rousset separates the elements that constitute the diary or journal (present or very recent past time, chronological order, fragmentation) from those of autobiography and first-person fiction (past time, authorially-determined order, unity). He also distinguishes the narratees of a genre purportedly meant to be a secret text, without readers. These include the (implied) author himself, external inscribed readers (one's beloved, one's descendants), and the literary public, whether posthumous and unauthorized (Henri-Frédéric Amiel) or, in some sense, presumed (Gide, Julien Green). Rousset's practical criticism is, as always, insightful and illuminating. Particularly impressive is the essay on Gide's *Voyage au Congo* (195–206), in which the voyage itself grants the journal narrativity and a structure. It might have been desirable for Rousset to scrutinize the seeming contradiction in a 'journal intime' by Gide or Green, in which the implied author explores among other things his own desperate striving for authenticity, dialoguing with his own conscience in the most authentic of genres, yet which he knows (inauthentically) is destined by himself for high-level mass publication in the not-too-distant future. Perhaps he avoided such questions because they would take him away from the structures and the forms.

What is Rousset's method? Does he have a theory? The most scholarly and most recent critic included in this book, Rousset offers a methodology, usually (like so many of us) in his introductory and concluding chapters. Working within the French-speaking university system, with its institution of literary study – then one of the more conservative in Europe – Rousset first of all upholds criticism as a discipline. He observes that his criticism treats the work itself, not the author's project or his intentions, in other words the text not its author. Similarly, the I–narrator in eighteenth- or twentieth-century novels is understood to be a character inside the text, functioning inside the text, and not the author; this means that the narrator's discourse is not to be read as the author's autobiography or as evidence for it. For his studies on the baroque, Rousset defends the legitimacy of applying to French literature insights and entire categories taken from foreign literatures and from the fine arts, and to apply to the old books twentieth-century readings that the author and/or his public might not have understood:

À vrai dire, la transposition était double: à la translation d'un art à un autre, d'un langage à un autre langage s'ajoutait l'extension à la France de critères

fondés sur des réussites étrangères. Belle occasion d'arracher le passé français
à un isolement excessif ... L'idée de Baroque se trouvait alors disponible, elle
s'offrait dans sa relative fraîcheur comme un instrument approprié à ce travail de rénovation ... L'instrument était trop moderne, trop étranger aux
préoccupations du XVIIe siècle, qui n'avait jamais songé à en faire une
catégorie critique? raison de plus pour avoir recours à lui; c'est parce qu'elle
est une création de notre temps, liée aux aspirations de notre art et de notre
poésie que la notion de Baroque était apte à jeter une passerelle du XXe au
XVIIe siècle, à ramener vers nous cet archipel qui s'éloignait.[23]

In the essay entitled 'Pour une lecture des formes'[24], Rousset compares himself to Leo Spitzer, noting how close he stands to the great
Austrian scholar. Rousset describes how the critic (himself) enters into a
book, takes it, and is taken by it. He discovers a motif or a stylistic feature that can reveal the total structure of the work. The text itself determines the form and deep structure; it is the critic's job to allow the text
to do this in his mind, and not impose his own predetermined form on
it. Thus you can grasp the totality of the book, for instance its space and
its time, from beginning to end. The style will always be individual and
deeply a part of the book, never external artifice. To do this, Rousset
favours a process, resembling Spitzer's, of coming and going, into the
text and outside it, from the particular to the general, in Rousset's own
version of the philological circle.

Given the passionate, powerfully emotional stance of Spitzer vis-à-vis the
texts on which he wrote, here is perhaps the place to take note of Francillon's thesis that Rousset embodies 'la passion de la lecture,'[25] that his critical stance is that of a lover driven by passion and desire; Francillon goes so
far as to suggest that the lover's 'première rencontre' with his beloved can
be read as a *mise en abyme* for Jean Rousset's critical method throughout
his career (21–3). The very distinguished French *seiziémiste* Gisèle
Mathieu-Castellani also designates Jean Rousset as a 'critique amoureux,'[26] Perhaps the Swiss manifest passion in other ways than the rest of
mortals. Perhaps Rousset's passion is dampened by a number of protective
rhetorical devices. However, I find him to be the least passionate and most
mentally precise of the critics studied in this book. The apparent lack of
emotion can explain why figures as disparate as Jeanneret and Derrida
agree that Rousset's structural readings fail to account for the force, the
tension, and the dynamic vitality of a work of art.[27]

Although Rousset insists that his concern is always with the individual
book and not with the author's total corpus or his mind, he states also

that the forms reveal mental structures and that he seeks to grasp a form which is also the author's imagination: 'Est-il possible d'embrasser à la fois l'imagination et la morphologie, de les sentir et de les saisir dans un acte simultané? C'est ce que je voudrais essayer.'[28] Here Rousset was probably seeking to align himself with his colleagues in the Geneva school. Miller observes that Rousset demonstrates how the author's mind becomes itself and reveals itself and that he proceeds from form to its dynamic source, the spirit at the origin, the organizing power that gave it shape, a presumed intentional consciousness.[29] According to Poulet, Rousset begins with forms in movement only to end with consciousness, thus proceeding from the objective to the subjective.[30] Unfortunately, Poulet does not clarify whether the subjectivity belongs to the critic or to the writer whom the critic is investigating. However, Carrard notes correctly that in his subsequent books Rousset drops all allusions to mental universes and intentional consciousnesses or imaginations. The scholars agree that Rousset stands as an exception in the Geneva school, that he is closer to the American New Critics and Russian Formalists than to Poulet and Starobinski, or for that matter to Barthes and Richard.

Also in contrast to some of the *nouveaux critiques*, Rousset adopts a problematic and by no means hostile stance toward history. On the one hand, in doing battle with the Lansonian school of literary history then dominant in the French system – just as the New Critics had done a generation earlier in Great Britain and the United States – he stakes a claim for criticism as opposed to history. He observes that literary history is important but must always remain ancillary to the central endeavour – criticism:

> Qu'on ne voie pas ici une déclaration de guerre ou de dédain à l'histoire littéraire; je la tiens pour indispensable dès qu'on s'attaque aux oeuvres du passé, mais comme prolégomène et garde-fou; elle n'est qu'un moyen au service de la critique et de l'interprétation ... l'histoire, l'érudition, la biographie des oeuvres (non des auteurs) doivent être pratiquées et utilisées, mais à leur place et à leur rang de sciences auxiliaires.[31]

In *L'intérieur et l'extérieur* he justifies applying to the past an intellectual grid or approach from the twentieth century. We study the baroque through our eyes, not the presumed or purported vision of the seventeenth-century public. There is nothing wrong with this, he says; all periods have done it, scholars do it all the time, and, besides, it works.

At the same time, as a scholar, Rousset invokes history and refers positively to its findings. He is concerned to place the baroque in its time;

he reacts negatively to those German scholars who speculated on the possibility of a recurring baroque, a universal style that might alternate with classicism in a series of cycles. Therefore, in *L'intérieur et l'extérieur* he underscores the divergences between seventeenth-century baroque and nineteenth-century romanticism, distinguishing water as mirror in the baroque, a pretext for meditating on illusion, paradox, the *verkehrte Welt*, and the play of external movement, from water as mirror in romanticism, where it is an avenue to a deeper truth, a loved one, the universe, or God (199–224). Similarly, he devotes one-half of the Don Juan book to the evolution of the myth after Mozart, that is, from romanticism to the present, arguing how diachrony alters the original Don Juan structure. As sexual promiscuity and unbelief are judged less pejoratively than they were in Tirso's and Molière's centuries, and as rebellion against social and religious norms becomes an acceptable, sometimes admirable stance, Don Juan the problematic villain evolves into Don Juan the problematic hero. Consequently, one of the three original functions – the apparition of the dead man/stone guest – ceases to operate. And because of the modern perspective on social class and gender, Anna assumes a central, perhaps *the* central, function in the plot, while the servant Sganarelle, Molière's brilliant synthesis of *dolosus servus* and *agroikos*, has long since disappeared. This structural and ideological evolution coincides with generic evolution, as the original stage play and opera give way to narrative fiction with its specific narratological implications.

Does not the evolution of Don Juan also serve as a metaphor for the evolution of Jean Rousset, literary critic? Rather like Béguin, Rousset's career can be divided into two phases. The Swiss scholar's interests originally focused on the phenomenology of a given period in the history of culture: the baroque. He then shifted to questions of structure and narrative technique in works from 1650 to well after 1950. Over the years he turned from poetry and the theatre to the novel, and from general essays to the study of individual books. Finally, we note an evolution in Rousset's criticism away from history. His studies on the baroque, especially the first one, can be designated as cultural history or even as cultural studies. A number of subsequent volumes are concerned, in part, with the evolution of literary forms such as the first-person novel and, therefore, treat works of literature in roughly chronological order. In other, still more recent books, however, Rousset structures his argument topically and all but totally avoids the historical referent.

Finally, it is a fact that, in his later years, Rousset's interests expanded instead of contracting. In the second half of *Passages* and in his last book, *Dernier regard sur le baroque,* we find essays on non-verbal communication, the relations of text and image, the music of Mozart, and the reading of *nouveaux romans.*[32] Francillon observes that the theoretical essay in *Narcisse romancier* takes so many of its examples from the French New Novel: Michel Butor, Robert Pinget, Nathalie Sarraute, and Claude Simon among others.[33] In his last two books, Rousset publishes four essays on Simon and one on the contemporary Swiss novelist Alice Rivaz. Arguably Rousset was more vitally engaged with the manifestations of contemporary creativity in his eighties than he had been half a century earlier.

Over a publishing career of some four decades Jean Rousset made a number of contributions to the profession: as a historian of *mentalités,* a theorist of narrative technique, a practical critic, and a reviser of the canon. Not at all a theorist, he nevertheless helped shape our critical approaches to literature by demonstrating what one can do with the phenomenology of imagery, narrative stance and voice, and the narratee; and with what rigour and insight one can examine a single recurring increment or episode in a novel. Rousset helped to undermine traditional French judgments on French literature by rehabilitating poetry and theatre in the baroque and the eighteenth-century novel. This helped us rediscover some twenty poets and a dozen writers of fiction. Finally, by the regular (but not overpowering) citation of other scholars, by the use of footnotes and bibliography, Rousset demonstrates, as if it were needed, that one can be a solid scholar and an innovative critic, and that there exists no inherent conflict between the two. And, because he wrote on into the 1990s, as did Northrop Frye, we can take heart in the fact that the tradition of academic humanist criticism is not dead, nor is it an outdated, archaic, passé phenomenon of only historical interest. Frye, Rousset, and the others speak to us today.

6 C.S. Lewis and the Discarded Image of the Middle Ages and Renaissance

Unlike the other scholar-critics discussed in this book, Clive Staples Lewis is much better known as a Christian apologist and writer of fantasy literature than for his contribution to English literary studies. The Oxford don and (toward the end of his career) professor at Cambridge achieved world fame and something approaching cult status for, among other works, *The Screwtape Letters, Mere Christianity,* and *The Chronicles of Narnia.* As a result, Lewis has benefited from the kind of attention accorded to major creative writers: more than 150 books and hundreds of articles devoted to him, in whole or in part, including four serious, full-length biographies plus a 'biography' of the Inklings, the literary group to which he belonged and which he more or less created;[1] three biographies written for young people;[2] a biography of his wife, Joy Davidman, an account of their marriage, and the reminiscences of his stepson, Douglas H. Gresham.[3] The story of the marriage gave rise to a successful stage play and a still more successful motion picture.[4] To this we can add three scholarly journals devoted entirely to the Inklings' current in modern literature plus four semi-scholarly journals published by the most important of the C.S. Lewis societies that came into existence after the writer's death and have grown in strength and in numbers ever since.[5]

Some of this activity is admittedly amateurish. The earlier writings were, on occasion, hagiographic or mere paraphrase, and they often paid scant attention to Lewis the scholar. This said, over the decades he has received more serious scrutiny from scholars, intellectuals, and theologians, including first-class criticism of the fiction and first-class accounts of the critical corpus.[6]

Why do I devote a chapter to Lewis? In part because he had on me, in graduate school, the same electrifying effect, the same impact, as

Auerbach, Curtius, and Frye. I came first to *The Allegory of Love* and only discovered, years later, *Mere Christianity* and *The Abolition of Man*. I should argue that, as a critic and scholar, Lewis attained the greatest heights, and that his achievements in this domain are more rounded, more complete, than in some of the others. I am convinced that his work is the finest, in the English language, that has been devoted to the earlier literatures and that, as a critic overall, he stands with Northop Frye and only a handful of others.

Nevill Coghill quotes his friend C.S. Lewis as having exclaimed one day, 'I believe ... I have proved that the Renaissance never happened in England. *Alternatively* ... that if it did, *it had no importance!*'[7] This, it would appear, when they were students. A few decades later, George Sayer quotes Lewis as declaring to *his* students: 'I think I have succeeded in demonstrating that the Renaissance, as generally understood, never existed.'[8] Finally, in the polemical 'Introduction' to his massive *English Literature in the Sixteenth Century*, he observes that it is acceptable to employ the term 'Renaissance' for the recovery of Greek and the classicizing of Latin. However, if 'Renaissance' is meant to carry additional baggage, it should not be used, and he defines the Renaissance of those baggage carriers who proliferate in academe, as 'an imaginary entity responsible for everything the speaker likes in the fifteenth and sixteenth centuries.'[9]

The convictions behind these *boutades* can be found in the famous inaugural lecture for the chair in English at Cambridge (*De Descriptione Temporum*), where Lewis proclaims his belief in Old West culture, which includes the Middle Ages and the Renaissance, and for that matter what we call nowadays the baroque, the classical, and the rococo.[10] For Lewis, the great divide in Western culture did not occur between antiquity and the Middle Ages or between the Middle Ages and the Renaissance. Somewhat like Arnold Toynbee he situates it in the nineteenth century with the Industrial Revolution and the birth of our modernity:

> my own belief that the barrier between those two ages [Medieval and Renaissance] has been greatly exaggerated, if indeed it was not largely a fragment of Humanist propaganda ... If we do not put the Great Divide between the Middle Ages and the Renaissance, where should we put it? ... I have come to regard as the greatest of all divisions in the history of the West that which divided the present from, say, the age of Jane Austen and Scott. (3, 4, 11)

Austen and Scott partake of Old Western just as Geoffrey Chaucer and Edmund Spenser do, whereas T.S. Eliot and D.H. Lawrence do not.

Lewis prizes that earlier, premodern age which manifests such an extraordinary continuity of culture. By belittling and mocking the term 'Renaissance,' Lewis wishes in no way to denigrate the sixteenth century. On the contrary, the Renaissance, for him, is a period which, at its best, prolongs and embellishes so much of the best that is medieval: feudal loyalty and honour, chivalry, heroism, courtly love and the spirit of the courts, alchemy, astrology, high magic and high daemonology, and, of course, a vital, organic Christian faith. In sum, he exalts the Renaissance by emphasizing its medievalness.

I should like, therefore, to offer a paradox: that Lewis's denigration of clichés concerning the Renaissance and his vision of continuity make a greater contribution to Renaissance studies than to the medieval. It is surely not a coincidence that his most solid and most learned book, in my opinion his masterpiece, proves to be *English Literature in the Sixteenth Century*. A splendid piece of critical and historical revaluation is entitled *A Preface to 'Paradise Lost.'*[11] *The Allegory of Love*, for all its major and still valid contributions to medieval studies, could have been entitled *A Preface to 'The Faerie Queene.'*[12] The goal of this book is to trace the origins and evolution of the tradition of allegory and courtly Eros which shape Spenser's poem and without which it cannot be read or understood. (It should not be forgotten that Lewis wrote more, by far, on Spenser and Milton than on any other single author, medieval or modern.)[13] Finally, *The Discarded Image*, Lewis's most popular scholarly book among non-scholars, which most people deem to be very medieval, is subtitled *An Introduction to Medieval and Renaissance Literature*.[14] In consequence, Lewis makes two contributions to medievalism: an influential twentieth-century vision of the Middle Ages, and recognition of a continuing medieval presence in the subsequent centuries of the early modern period, what French comparatists would call 'la fortune du Moyen Age à l'époque de la Renaissance.'

How does he do this? *The Allegory of Love* insisted, for the first time in English studies, on the central, predominant role of allegory and of courtly love (what today we call *fin' amor(s)*) in the development of early Western literature. Never again could scholars characterize these two 'forms of the spirit' as shallow convention or stylistic artifice. Lewis traced the royal road of allegory from writers in Silver Latin, late antiquity, and the twelfth-century Renaissance to the vernacular explosion in Old French and, later, Middle English, insisting upon the two structures that allegory came to assume at its best: the *bellum intestinum* and the voyage or quest. Lewis was especially innovative in that, more than a decade prior to Curtius, he recognized the importance of the Latin Middle Ages, not merely as background or for the sources, but as an indispensable constituent in our most vital literary tradition. In addition his was a human and humane medieval Latinity, social and urbane, not narrowly monastic. Lewis treated allegory in a sophisticated manner, as a genre or mode comparable to revenge tragedy with the Elizabethans and satire with the Augustans or the novel today; and he explored what role the dominant form plays in a culture, including the eventuality that the form itself becomes a stereotype and attracts bad writers as well as the good ones.

He recognized *fin' amor* to have brought about one of the three or four greatest mutations in the history of civilization and defined its constituent traits – this a decade before Denis de Rougemont. Lewis is especially perceptive in contextualizing *fin' amor,* in relating the literary phenomenon to the culture of its time, and underscoring its contribution, along with allegory, to the evolution of modern psychology and what today we call subjectivity. Then, with deftness and taste, he scrutinized the dynamic, ever-changing interplay of *fin' amor* and allegory in Chrétien de Troyes, *Le roman de la Rose,* and English poetry from Chaucer to Spenser, insisting that the best in both Chaucer and Spenser is their medievalness, rather than a superficial and historically false anticipation of modernity. In an oft-cited Lewis formulation, Chaucer would have 'medievalized Boccaccio';[15] it can also be said that, according to Lewis, Spenser medievalized his immediate sources, Matteo Maria Boiardo, Lodovico Ariosto, and Torquato Tasso.

A Preface to 'Paradise Lost' does for Milton what *The Allegory of Love* did for Spenser, and Lewis does for epic what he had previously done for allegory and *fin' amor.* He categorizes epic as one kind of court poetry: public, aristocratic, festal, and ceremonial. Epic is couched in stock phrases and conventional diction. Neither colloquial vernacular nor the poet's personal speech is valorized, but instead the 'grand style' is grounded in rhetoric and decorum. Virgil is the master of literary epic. Therefore, since Milton does not seek to express his soul but, instead, to choose and cultivate a genre, once it is chosen he cultivates Virgil. No less important, Lewis is one of the first to insist upon the importance of seventeenth-century theological speculation to understanding *Paradise Lost.* His is a Christian reading of Milton, valid, he would say, not because Lewis is Christian but because Milton is (62–72, 82–93). Lewis states that, from Milton's perspective and what ought to be the perspective of the informed modern reader, Satan cannot be the hero. He is a contempt-ible villain, riddled by a complex of self-contradictions and self-denials. In addition, the action of the poem centres not on Satan but on Adam and Eve, the latter guilty of pride and the former guilty of uxorious remissness. Lewis not only rehabilitates Adam and Eve – they are shown to be both noble and courtly, both important and interesting; he also rehabilitates *Paradise Lost* as a total work of art, and not two superb first books which then fall off into orthodoxy and boredom. In sum, Lewis defends his author's language from the strictures of Eliot and Leavis;[16] he defends his world view and its artistic embodiment from the prejudice of 1930s agnostic university faculty in English.

Lewis's most controversial book, *English Literature in the Sixteenth Century*, redefines the focus and the parameters of early English literature. His was perhaps the first major voice in English studies to denounce the old Burckhardtian orthodoxy – clichés about a Catholic and folkloric, pious and primitive Middle Ages happily giving way to our freethinking, Hellenic, and modern Renaissance, superior to the Middle Ages to the extent that enlightenment is superior to superstition and learning to ignorance. Lewis demystifies and undermines the humanist scholars, Burckhardt's heroes, whom he accuses of pedantry, ignorance, and lack of imagination. Because of them, English literature remained in the dol-drums, as 'drab' or worse than drab, up to the 1570s. In contrast, Lewis rehabilitates the Puritans, whom he sees not as prigs or ascetes but as young chic intellectuals, famous for their innovative ideas and intellec-tual rigour. As in the *Allegory of Love*, and more so, he is luminous con-cerning the social and intellectual background, what today we call the contextualization, of the sixteenth-century writers.

Concerning them, Lewis develops a thesis. According to him, the only genuinely good literature from the early period was composed in Scot-land by the Scottish Chaucerians (today we call them the Makars) (66–119); their success is to have adhered to a medieval tradition that is learned, not popular, and to have composed in, among other registers, a high courtly aureate style treating high moral issues. For example, Gavin Douglas is closer to Virgil and a better poet than Henry Howard or John Dryden could ever be. Lewis then goes on to praise the 'golden' style and golden achievements of Sir Philip Sidney, Spenser, Shakespeare, and others, who illustrate finally, as do the Makars, the syncretic wholeness of the century (318–535). For Lewis, the golden style stands as the hallmark of the Elizabethan age at its best, a poetics and a poetry of imagination and invention, young, rich, and bursting with life, in contrast to the 'drab,' plain style that characterizes the first seven decades of the century. Similarly, the sonnet sequences of Sidney, Shakespeare, Samuel Daniel, Thomas Lodge, and Michael Drayton express not personal emotion but, instead, the emotions that all readers can feel and share; these are poetic exaltations and meditations, celebratory, in the same mode as liturgy and prayer.

In *The Discarded Image* Lewis presents the mental structures or, as we say today, the mindset of the Old Western culture. Included are cosmology, astrology, daemonology, man as microcosm, his epistemology, physiology, history, and education. In contrast to the general perception that the Middle Ages was a simple and primitive era, he insists on the bookishness of those times: their emphasis on authority grounded in literacy and their sense of order, codification, and system. Along the way, once again he rehabilitates the Latin tradition: late neo-Platonic paganism, as practised by philosophers who were cultured, ascetic, and deeply spiritual. Recognizing the aura of Arthurian romance as an element apart from 'the Model,' Lewis also demonstrates how the fairies of the Celtic Otherworld were assimilated to the *Longaevi*, one of a number of rational species, including daimons, links between humans and angels. In the Epilogue (216–23) Lewis confesses his liking for and joy in the medieval-Renaissance model. It receded before other models just as our twentieth-century model will recede before others. No one model is more real or true than another; it proves only to be more coherent and to account for phenomena in a more satisfactory manner than its predecessor(s).

Although Lewis is not always given the credit, in addition to his panoramas of the history of literature and his contributions to scholarship, he was a superb practical critic. Virgil, Statius, Andreas Capellanus, Guillaume de Lorris, Guillaume de Digulleville, Chaucer, Lord Berners, Gavin Douglas, Thomas More and William Tyndale, Renaissance pamphleteers and theological polemicists, the *Book of Common Prayer*, Guillaume de Salluste du Bartas, Sidney, Spenser, Christopher Marlowe, George Chapman, Drayton, and Milton – this roll of honour names the writers on whom Lewis wrote superbly crafted literary appreciations.

Here are a few examples. Virgil is shown to be in no way inferior to Homer. A master of 'secondary epic,' he opens up the Homeric world to time and space, he grants it a past and a future, that is, history, so that the trials of Aeneas represent a major turning point in history. As an adult (in contrast to Achilles, who is still a child), Aeneas is torn between vocation, desire, and duty. The founder of Rome who contains within him all that Rome will become, he also evolves, becomes other, as he voyages from East to West, from the Old to the New Troy.[17]

Guillaume de Lorris is seen as a successor to Chrétien de Troyes, who takes Chrétien's characters, allegorizes them, and eliminates the adventures to concentrate on the love, so that the play of allegories becomes the adventure. From the Lover's perspective, the Rose's aspects or moods can be represented by different 'characters,' as can his own aspects or moods and the social forces that favour or hinder his love. The scene is, first and foremost, the woman's heart, her inner self where she struggles against herself. Guillaume creates images of great poetic power, such as the garden, the mirror, the castle, and the rose. With these images, and with the play of allegories, he attains, he recreates, the reality of falling in love and pursuing one's love.[18]

Sidney's *Arcadia* is shown to be a pastoral romance exalting the pastoral ideal yet also a good story well-told with richness of narrative. Noble sentiment is proclaimed by noble characters, who are engaged in war and statecraft in addition to love. Sidney emphasizes this with his forensic conclusion, a full-fledged trial. The whole is embellished in an aristocratic, 'high' register, a sublime prose style for a book which is, in the last analysis, an epic in prose.[19]

Overall Lewis was, above all else, a sensitive, passionate, committed reader of books. We, his readers, sense the passion and the sensitivity on almost every page. More than most great critics of our century, Lewis makes his readers *love* the books that he discusses. It is not surprising, then, that so many of his appreciations have also served to rehabilitate neglected writers and currents. What is true for *Le roman de la Rose* and the Scots Makars is also true for a number of nonmodernist modern authors on whom Lewis also wrote: Scott, Shelley, William Morris, George MacDonald, Rudyard Kipling, and Charles Williams, among others.[20] With MacDonald and Williams, Lewis was the first to call attention to their importance and to make something of them in the world of English literature.

What is certain in Lewis's achievement, and relatively unique in the annals of modern scholarship and criticism, is the extent to which he reshaped the thought and redefined the parameters of the discipline for at least one generation, and not only in his vision of allegory, epic, late antiquity, the Middle Ages, and the Renaissance, but also, and no less so, in his readings of individual poets. Lewis reshaped and redefined how Anglicists think about Chaucer, Spenser, and Milton. Furthermore, today, like Auerbach and Spitzer, he is still quoted and footnoted; indeed, like Spitzer, a number of his readings remain among the best ever written on the subject. Perhaps for this very reason, his readings have ignited controversy. Whereas Spitzer launched almost all of his intellectual wars, for the most part it is others who chose to polemicize against Lewis. It is fascinating to observe the number of essays that seek to refute one or another stance of Lewis and cite him by name in the title.[21] Lewis's adversaries may have leaped into the fray in part out of distaste for his Christian apologetics but also as a response (and, unconsciously, a tribute) to the striking, revolutionary, innovative character of his insights.

Can Lewis be considered in any meaningful sense a literary theorist? What can we say about the theoretical foundations of his work? Lewis himself would have scorned the term 'theory' as it is now used, just as, in the 1950s, he scorned the term 'criticism.' Olaf Tollefsen offers a good philosophical defence of Lewis's practice of aligning or combining relatively objective standards with the individual reader's subjective response, this without a general theory of aesthetic value.[22] Nevertheless, I am convinced that he did publish two books that can be designated as theory. The first treats the writer in relation to the work of literature; the second treats the work of literature in relation to the reader.

In *The Personal Heresy: A Controversy* (in which Lewis debates with the Cambridge don E.M.W. Tillyard), he adopts a strikingly modernist stance, one in congruity with New Criticism and with our more recent theories of narratology and rhetoric.[23] Lewis insists that poetry is never the expression of a poet's personality nor does it reveal his state of mind. It can express *a* personality – what today we call the speaker or the implied author – or an old myth or what today we call an archetype. The poet is not a seer or vates; he is simply 'a man who makes poems,' and 'poetry is an art or a skill – a trained habit of using certain instruments to certain ends' (103). Therefore, the poet rarely seeks to bare his soul or propose a philosophy of life, but rather works within the tradition, cultivating conventional models and genres. And he writes a conventional language, high style or plain style and not his purportedly natural, colloquial speech, for all poetic language is a form of artifice. Here Lewis is combating the romantic and specifically Wordsworthian myth that poets have more enthusiasm, sensibility, and tenderness than the rest of mortals. On the contrary, he writes, ordinary mortals may possess these virtues, and so many poets not at all. Paradoxically seconding Eliot, Lewis is convinced that the value of poetry and its reality lie not in the individual or personal, which he labels 'the idiosyncratic,' but rather in the public and universal, given that poets at their best make us partake of a universal human experience which transcends themselves and us.

In *An Experiment in Criticism* Lewis makes a case for replacing the traditional question in criticism, 'Is this a good or bad book?' with the question, 'What kind of reading does this book encourage?'[24] 'Let us make our distinction between readers or types of reading the basis, and our distinction between books the corollary. Let us try to discover how far it might be plausible to define a good book as a book which is read in one way, and a bad book as a book which is read in another.' (1) He insists that the various categories of reader and reading cross social and professional boundaries, and that the professor of literature is as capable of reading badly, of reading for external reasons, as is the housewife or the retired labourer. He also stands opposed to the notion of rigid boundaries between 'the classics' and 'popular books,' given that some works in the high art category may be there due to fashion and taste whereas some works in the low art category may contain elements of myth – the numinous – and, therefore, give rise to good reading. In essence, good literature permits good reading and bad reading, depending on the reader, whereas bad literature can allow only bad reading. Lewis is especially cogent on bad reading, whether by the unliterary – people concerned only with an exciting story, suspense, and some sort of vicarious happiness, what he calls 'castle-building': 'Let us be quite clear that the unliterary are unliterary not because they enjoy stories in these ways, but because they enjoy them in no other. Not what they have but what they lack cuts them off from the fullness of literary experience.' (38) – or by the literary – those who seek a mirror of 'real life' and/or a deep philosophy for living (27–39, 74–87): 'Dramatists and novelists are praised as if they were doing, essentially, what used to be expected of theologians and philosophers, and the qualities which belong to their works as inventions and as designs are neglected. They are reverenced as teachers and insufficiently appreciated as artists' (74).

Here and throughout *An Experiment in Criticism* Lewis anticipates the more recent schools of reader response (Wolfgang Iser), sociology of literature (Robert Escarpit, Raymond Williams), and aesthetics of reception (Hans Robert Jauss).[25] And, by the meticulous distinction between good and bad books and between good and bad readers, he provides arguments against those individuals who would open the canon to all books regardless of merit or who would deny that value and merit can be applied to literary texts. He would also, no doubt, label simply as bad readers those individuals who come to books, ancient and modern, with a preconceived agenda and who praise or blame the books uniquely with regard to the agenda. In my opinion, however, *An Experiment in Criticism* holds up less well than *The Personal Heresy* because certain issues treated at length in the *Experiment* – debunking realism, for instance – are no longer of interest today, and because the sociology of literature has made enormous strides in the quantifiable, empirical study of publics and their relationship to authors and to the publishing industry. In addition, today most of the bad readers no longer read; they watch television or play videos, and a cultural studies industry is now devoted to fathoming their cultural practices.

It ought to be apparent from my discussion that Lewis was so much more than a traditional academic scholar in English and that his writings on literature anticipate or coincide with some of the major developments in theory since the 1930s. As I have said, *The Personal Heresy* adopts a strikingly modern critical and New Criticism stance in its insistence that the object of literary study has to be the book and not its author, and the way the book adheres to and works upon tradition and convention and not its purported originality. Throughout his career and especially in *An Experiment in Criticism*, Lewis precedes Northrop Frye and parallels Albert Béguin and Jean Rousset by proclaiming that literature is an independent entity, and that the critic must never presume that an approach or a discipline external to literature – say, anthropology or psychoanalysis – can tell us something authoritative about a work of literature. The same is true for the sources. Like Frye, Lewis declared his hostility to evaluation. As we have seen, *An Experiment in Criticism* anticipates more recent developments in reader response and sociology of literature. Finally, Lewis coincides with the *Annales* school of historians in his lifelong passion for the *mentalités* (mindset, mental structures) of the past, structures which shape the literature and which modern scholars must know in order not to misread. One example among many: in *English Literature* (32) he states that the business of the historian of literature 'is with the past not as it "really" was (whatever "really" may mean in such a context) but with the past as it seemed to be to those who lived in it.' I mention all this not because such anticipations necessarily enhance Lewis's value as a critic. The modern approaches come and go. Theorists strive, viciously on occasion, to get on top; after a few years they discover the workings of Dame Fortune's Wheel and what it means to be down and out. Far too often we see a colleague five years out of date denounced as a dinosaur or a fool by one only two years out of date.[26]

What is C.S. Lewis's legacy? Inevitably, after a period of decades, some of Lewis's pronouncements can and ought to be corrected. It is revealing, however, that so much of his work holds up and that the correctors and revisers prove to be more in error than Lewis himself. This is as true in the domain of literary history as in the other facets of his life. Here I note liberal Anglicans outraged because Lewis actually believes in the Incarnation and Resurrection and gives succour to poor benighted Evangelicals who might otherwise see the light;[27] feminists outraged over the fact that the portrayal of Jane Studdock in *That Hideous Strength* does not conform to the current gender studies consensus on American campuses;[28] and, most curious of all, delicate, refined, prissy outrage from the English academic Establishment because Lewis didn't play their game by their rules, because, as an Ulsterman from the middle class, he behaved, according to Dame Helen Gardner, with 'exaggeration and extravagance.'[29]

More interesting are the attacks on Lewis the literary critic from a religious perspective. Some, who accused him of imposing his Christian beliefs onto the criticism of Milton, or for that matter Tyndale, obviously forget how important it is for the critic to sympathize with an author's world view and, historically grounded, to see what the outsider sees not. Spitzer and Auerbach, agnostics of Jewish descent, offered, throughout their careers, superb Christian readings of Christian texts. Resembling them, and in this he was superior to D.W. Robertson and the Robertsonian school of exegetical criticism,[30] Lewis gave a Christian interpretation to obviously Christian books, *Paradise Lost* being the most notable. On all other texts he wisely abstained. It is this restraint, paradoxically, which angers Peter Milward, who blames Lewis the critic for not being Christian enough. Milward wrote an entire book to challenge Lewis's scholarship and criticism.[31] According to Milward, Lewis fails to recognize the all-pervasive Christian spirituality that dominates the Middle Ages – this in contrast to a purportedly more secular Renaissance. Leaving aside Milward's curious hypothesis that Lewis's not being Christian enough comes from his Ulster Protestant background (only an English Jesuit could declare that, because Lewis was a Protestant, he downplayed the importance of the Reformation), Milward's disagreement with Lewis lies for the most part in the fact that Milward accepts Burckhardtian clichés as truth and, in consequence, accuses Lewis of violating the truth because he refutes the clichés.

Preceding Curtius by about fifteen years, Lewis defended Western civ-ilization, considered to be a vast and, in some respects, incomplete project, in which as a central, perhaps the central increment, stands the Middle Ages. Lewis's Middle Ages is vital to the overall evolution of the West and to our understanding of ourselves; like Curtius's Middle Ages, Lewis's is forthrightly secular as well as Christian. It is richly eclectic, urbane, courtly, and aristocratic; it culminates in the best of what fol-lows: Douglas in Scotland and Spenser in England.

At one time, when Robertsonian exegesis (which declared that there is no such thing as courtly love) was predominant in English circles, apolo-gists for Lewis conceded they would have to scrap much of *The Allegory of Love*.[32] Today, it is the extreme Robertsonian formulations that have been scrapped, whereas Lewis's book remains. Today, most of us would say that *fin' amor* did exist then and was as important as Lewis said it was. The age of *fin' amor* and of chivalry – the twelfth and thirteenth centuries in France – was the occasion for one of the greatest transformations of the human spirit and the driving force behind the first great vernacular movement in literature. However, given the number of courtly French romances which end in marriage and the intense scrutiny of love and marriage in Chrétien de Troyes, we do have to modify one of Lewis's four constituent traits defining the concept.[33] Obstacle, not adultery, lies at the core of *fin' amor*. The romance of married love thus occurs in France and Germany long before *The Kingis Quair* and *The Faerie Queene*, and the romance of adultery lives on, magnificently, on the Continent, which may explain why young English gentlemen fancied the grand tour.[34]

Greater knowledge of French and Italian humanism would also have caused Lewis to nuance *English Literature in the Sixteenth Century*. The Humanists did help inspire great humanist poets – Du Bellay and Ronsard, Pietro Bembo and Tasso – to cite the most eminent. These poets, and the French and Italian tradition in general, had an enormous and largely beneficial impact on the Elizabethans. Similarly, most schol-ars today would prefer the designation 'high style' and 'plain style' to Lewis's overly judgmental 'golden' and 'drab.' They might also be annoyed by his rigid and somewhat arbitrary categorization of individ-ual Elizabethan writers and their styles under these designations (plus the third one: metaphysical). And they would supplement his superb study of cosmology in *The Discarded Image* with chapters on medieval-Renaissance Christian typology, political theory, and rhetoric.[35]

The preceding paragraphs demonstrate that, for my part, differing from his adversaries, I wish only to supplement and to nuance some of

Lewis's formulations, which, magnificent as they are, are grounded in a finite command of the non-English materials and which, because they are so magnificent, far-reaching, and innovative, would have to be supplemented and nuanced a generation later in any case. Similarly, and for the same reasons, we can revise – improve upon – some of Lewis's relatively negative judgments on individual writers. I cite, at random, Prudentius, Alan of Lille, Geoffrey of Monmouth, Jean de Meun, William Langland, John Knox, and the Spenser of *The Shepherd's Calendar*.[36]

This raises a fascinating question. The only aspect of Lewis's criticism that bothers me and that I find genuinely dated is his penchant for value judgments, for constantly informing the reader which books are masterpieces, which are mediocre, and which are awful. We don't do that sort of thing anymore. And the C.S. Lewis who does it is the same C.S. Lewis who devotes a section of *An Experiment in Criticism* to denouncing critical evaluation and all those – he calls them 'Vigilants' – who make distinctions within the domain of good literature.[37] This would not be the only example of le maître contradicting himself.[38] The explanation for this contradiction can be found in the 'contextualization' of Lewis's work after he left Oxford for Cambridge. In *An Experiment in Criticism* Lewis was combating the influence of F.R. Leavis and the then dominant Leavisite current in British universities. Leavis's home base was Cambridge. According to Humphrey Carpenter, he had been told that one of the reasons for offering him a chair in English was to counteract Leavis.[39] In fact, going back to the 1930s, Lewis's *Rehabilitations* (1939), with its laudatory readings of Shelley and others, was most likely a conscious rebuttal to Leavis's *Revaluation* published three years previously. Lewis would say that the Leavisite Vigilants condemned major English authors – Milton, for example – and entire periods – romanticism, and in fact all English poetry from Shelley to the Georgians – and, thereby close doors to readers and students, whereas he, Lewis, holds the doors wide open:

> Thus one result of my system would be to silence the type of critic for whom all the great names in English literature – except for the half dozen protected by the momentary critical 'establishment' – are as so many lampposts for a dog.

> Can I say with certainty that any evaluative criticism has ever actually helped me to understand and appreciate any great work of literature or any part of one?

The use of the guillotine becomes an addiction. Thus under Vigilant criticism a new head falls nearly every month. The list of approved authors grows absurdly small. No one is safe.[40]

In more general terms he denies the validity of granting value to some books and refusing it to others on the basis of criteria or a set of privileged conditions such as realism or the New-Critical paradox, tension, and ambiguity. Similarly, when he tells students 'Don't read criticism,' although Lewis appears to will his own books onto remainder piles outside Blackwell's, he alludes again to Leavis and his disciples, who fetishized the term 'critic.' Lewis would have called himself a scholar or a historian.

Brian Barbour has examined in detail Lewis's relationship with and reaction to the Cambridge English faculty over the years.[41] He sees a long-standing, essential, and permanent cleavage between Oxford – literary history, the medieval, and Lewis – and Cambridge – literary criticism, the modern, and Leavis, I.A. Richards, and Eliot. He calls attention to Lewis's 1938 article on Donne, which, by claiming that John Donne is overrated, a writer of specialized but limited excellence and of a superficial and temporary intensity, he challenged the Cambridge version of New Criticism and its revisionist view of the evolution of English poetry.

This said, I also believe that Barbour has oversimplified the complex and multivalent realities of both Oxford and Cambridge. To give just one example, Tillyard, Lewis's friendly adversary in *The Personal Heresy* debate, helped create Cambridge English. He, as much as Leavis, was responsible for it, and he disliked Leavis intensely. In his book of memoirs on the English faculty, Leavis is mentioned only three times, and then, merely as someone who attended meetings.[42]

When I first read C.S. Lewis, I was – like so many others – entranced, enchanted, carried to another level. I was also deeply moved by his claim to be the last Old Western man, the last dinosaur in the old culture of the West.[43] Except that I whispered: 'No, you're not. I am!' After having, over the years, cited this anecdote in class, from time to time a student will whisper: 'No, you're not. I am!' From this I am happy to report that we dinosaurs are reproducing ourselves – carefully, slowly and painfully – but we are.

It has to be said, however, that Lewis's joy in the medieval and his denial of the modern do not make of him a Medieval Man; they demonstrate how much he partakes of medievalism, and therefore, how much he is truly modern, for there is no trait more characteristic of modernism than distaste for modernity and the adoption of a culture from the distant past to counter modernity.[44] It is specifically in our century, and at the end of the nineteenth, that one might declare: 'The more "up to date" a book is, the sooner it will be dated,' and 'It is a good rule, after reading a new book, never to allow yourself another new one till you have read an old one in between.'[45] According to this formulation, Lewis is superbly, authentically Edwardian, and of the school of Chesterton, not the School of Chartres.[46] In this line, we find some witty characterizations of Lewis the last defender of the Old Western civilization: 'He was fighting a perpetual rearguard action in defense of an army that had long since marched away,' or 'He is just a paleontologist pretending to be a fossil.'[47] One strength of the school of Auerbach, Curtius, and Spitzer lies, I have argued above, in the fact that they prized the medieval and the modern and worked splendidly, with enthusiasm, in both areas, actually publishing on the Romance literatures – French, Italian, and Spanish, plus Latin – from the early Middle Ages to the present. In comparison, Lewis appears a trifle thin. We can regret his distaste for Eliot and his incomprehension of the most vital artistic life of our century – from Picasso and Proust to today. We can also note, with a smile, that the English Honour Course syllabus that he and J.R.R. Tolkien introduced at Oxford ended with the year 1830. I often tell my students: If you cannot engage positively with your own contemporary literature and culture when you are twenty, what will you be like when you are sixty?

In the words of the great Scots poet Hugh MacDiarmid, these objections are 'penny wheep' (short ale)[48] and a ridiculously low price to pay for Lewis's accomplishments, for what makes him indeed the greatest English-language critic and scholar of the early literature and, as a critic and writer on literature, at the university and in the public sphere, second only to Northrop Frye overall.

Lewis's criticism does for us what he believes good literature to do for good readers – to take us out of ourselves and enlarge our being, to make us experience what is common to mankind as a whole and not just to ourselves, to grant us a sense of the numinous and the universal. Beholding his best work, as when we behold Auerbach's *Mimesis* or Matthiessen's *American Renaissance*, we can feel wonder and awe, the wonder that mathematicians sense for a supremely great (and beautiful) theorem. Also, because of his medievalism and because he locates the Middle Ages and a medievalized Renaissance at the heart of the Western experience, he helps us reclaim our history and our culture, a sweep of books and centuries that surpass infinitely the peripheral and the ephemeral, 2,500 or 3,000 years of aesthetic creation that are among the best things we have done on this planet.[49]

Ernst Robert Curtius called upon us, the descendants of the medieval clerks, to do our part in passing the torch of culture, to maintain, for ourselves and our descendants, the tradition of great books that extend from Homer and Virgil to the present. Curtius, alluding to Virgil, called this tradition the *exempla maiorum,* which we can translate as the deeds of the ancestors, or the stories of the great ones, or the models from the masters.[50] If we are clerks, even more so is C.S. Lewis the 'grete clerk' of our English-speaking world. By defending and illustrating the old culture, he was indeed worthy to renew with the old warriors and clerks, with the heroes and lovers of geste and the poets who gave them life.

7 The Search for an American Usable Past: F.O. Matthiessen

The vast majority of critics whom I discuss wrote, in addition to other studies of importance, a single, massive book which launched or consolidated their fame and which is their primary contribution to the profession. Francis Otto Matthiessen, however, is perhaps unique in that his 1941 *American Renaissance* helped launch and define an entire professional field of inquiry.[1] The scholars who have written on Matthiessen all emphasize the man's importance and the unique contribution made by his masterwork.[2]

At a time when literary studies in the United States were divided between a newly emergent New Criticism still in its formative stages and a narrow literary scholarship or a no less narrow Marxist or nativist critique of books according to their ideology of protest or their ideology of Americanism, Matthiessen succeeded in combining sensitive readings of texts with the most meticulous scholarly research. As Wellek argues, this book is the 'star example of reconciliation of literary history and criticism in American literary scholarship.'[3] Secondly, at a time when American literature was only in the process of claiming a place in the pantheon, when, for many, it remained an appendage of the English, Matthiessen was the first to accord to American a dignity of purpose and of standing, to legitimize it, and to locate American writers in a world tradition and worthy to be in it.

Matthiessen launched the idea that his five writers – Ralph Waldo Emerson, Henry David Thoreau, Nathaniel Hawthorne, Herman Melville, and Walt Whitman – are worthy of the most rigorous intellectual scrutiny. He invented the term and the idea of an American Renaissance that had occurred in Massachusetts and, tangentially, in New York during a period of concentrated achievement between 1850 and 1855.

More than any other person, Matthiessen gave impetus to what would become a major academic field – American studies – and to the thousands of courses taught every year on 'The American Renaissance.' And thus, also with books on T.S. Eliot and Henry James, he determined the canon of American literature as it would be taught from the Second World War largely up until today. For all these reasons, *American Renaissance* remains the most discussed and the most influential book of criticism published by an American.

Matthiessen's aim was to write a study on Emerson, Thoreau, Hawthorne, Melville, and Whitman, treating their writings as works of art but also incorporating what we would call today their poetics or their theory – that is, their conception of the nature and functioning of literature and how it is borne out in their writing. According to Matthiessen, what gives unity to the age and to his five writers is an aesthetic he calls the 'organic principle,' which Emerson promulgated, and which was shared by Thoreau and Whitman, and influenced Hawthorne and Melville even when they reacted against it. The organic principle is derived partly from the transcendental religion of nineteenth-century New England, and more importantly from romantic philosophy, specifically the ideas of Samuel Taylor Coleridge. For Emerson, the individual soul and its consciousness are central to being. Art is to be considered not as external ornament or embellishment but as an inner form determined by the individual idea or inspiration, or by nature. Art must then imitate or, rather, reproduce nature and experience. For Thoreau even more than for Emerson, nature is placed above art and content above form; life is made equal to nature and also above art. Whitman then carries the doctrine to an extreme where he, the writer, gives himself to the soul or the inner light, ingesting a vision of life and the cosmos as mystery and responding to them with enthusiasm. He concentrates entirely on content and personality, not form. In his hands the extreme organic form breaks down the distinction between verse and prose; indeed, the book, itself an organic whole, should include both verse and prose and anything in between.

Matthiessen traces the organic form to its literary and philosophical origins. He insists upon the extent to which the writers of the American Renaissance read English literature from the seventeenth century. He tells of the appeal of Donne, Sir Thomas Browne, George Herbert, and Milton to Emerson and the others, and notes how the American writers were inspired by the juxtaposition of thought and image, and of the intellectual and the physical, as well as their sense of analogy and allegory, and the mystic strain. Speech patterns close to the spoken vernacular served as a model. The Puritan current that emphasizes the imperfectability of man, stated most explicitly by Milton, was crucial to Hawthorne, just as Shakespeare, with his heightened language, high tragedy, and dramatic effects, was crucial to Melville. Matthiessen even denigrates Hawthorne, compared to Melville, for his correct, slightly archaic prose style in the eighteenth-century manner, the period which Hawthorne so loved. The seventeenth-century analogy is not, for Matthiessen, a question of erudition alone. He is convinced that, because Eliot and the New Critics also treasure Donne and the Metaphysicals, because Eliot is so committed to a similar unified sensibility and heightened yet demotic style, that the writers of the 1850s can appeal to Americans in the twentieth century and can be genuinely understood by them for, perhaps, the first time.

The second factor that the five writers allegedly share and that Matthiessen himself proclaims as a unifying factor is the ideal of democracy:

> The one common denominator of my five writers, uniting even Hawthorne and Whitman, was their devotion to the possibilities of democracy ... Emerson, Hawthorne, Thoreau, Whitman, and Melville all wrote literature for democracy in a double sense. They felt that it was incumbent upon their generation to give fulfillment to the potentialities freed by the Revolution, to provide a culture commensurate with America's political opportunity ... what emerges from the total pattern of their achievement – if we will make the effort to repossess it – is literature for our democracy. (ix, xv)

Similarly, to cite one among a number of statements, in a review that dates from 1942, Matthiessen singles out 'what I would hold to be the chief strength in our American tradition ... "the cult of the common man."'[4] He insists upon the closeness of his writers to the agricultural society of their day, their awareness of the concrete existence of the people, and their inherent sympathy for the common man. In a democratic society form follows function and is not separated from its source in the community; in a democratic society Hester Prynne and Billy Budd can become tragic heroes, eliciting the pity and forgiveness of both author and reader. And Matthiessen posits as a central theme the tragedy of the wilful, magnificent individual, cut off from the community because of his pride and doomed to solitude.

Wellek felt this 'devotion to the possibilities of democracy' to be 'a trivial conclusion obsessively repeated.'[5] The devotion also tells us about the Zeitgeist in the United States just prior to the Second World War and about Matthiessen's own Christian socialism, an idealism and an engagement that he shares with Albert Béguin. It also led Matthiessen to left-oriented readings and even value judgments. He deplores Emerson's justification for class distinction and the accumulation of money. He interprets Thoreau as a left-wing individualist who reacts against the materialism and mercantilism of his day; concerned over the alienation of the craftsman deprived of his craft, Thoreau purportedly recognizes the need for community and for common action in the cultural sphere. Hawthorne is then shown to be conscious of the evil effects of wealth and power extending over generations (*The House of the Seven Gables*) and to favour a collectivist solution to socio-economic problems.

As much as any European criticism of the time, *American Renaissance* is a book of solid scholarship, grounded in the most massive and precise command of the materials available to the author. One instance among so many, Matthiessen cites marginal notes from the books in Melville's library, using Melville's comments to enrich his own reading of Hawthorne and of Melville. He is conscious of the books that his five authors read and was the first scholar to argue the dominant seventeenth-century English impact on nineteenth-century New England. He also traces the impact of the 1850s achievement on subsequent writers – specifically James and Eliot. Finally – I believe that in this feature he surpasses the other humanist critics – Matthiessen brings into focus cultural features of the time that illuminate the Renaissance, both the background and the texts themselves. Splendid brief essays are devoted to the American tradition of oratory and eloquence, our native 'genre' (14–24); the Greek revival and neoclassical style in architecture and sculpture (ibid.); the writings on art by Horatio Greenough, a nineteenth-century sculptor (140–52); the early American stage comedy (Royall Tyler) and fiction (Charles Brockden Brown) (200–2); nineteenth-century opera (558–63); and nineteenth-century landscape painting (596–613). These seeming asides bring a density and richness to Matthiessen's book, and weight to his theses, making the latter more convincing and raising the former to another level, the level of Auerbach and Lewis.

Meanwhile, so to speak, in the midst of such superb scholarly writing, Matthiessen, loyal to his New Critical principles, also makes superb close readings of individual texts, much like Albert Béguin. To list just a few: Emerson's poems 'Days' (59–64) and 'The Snow-Storm' (138–40), Hawthorne's stories 'The Gentle Boy' (215–18) and 'The Birthmark' (254–6) and also *The House of the Seven Gables* (322–37), Melville's *Pierre* (467–87) and passages from *Moby-Dick* (409–66 passim), and Whitman's

'When lilacs last in the dooryard bloomed' (618–24). These readings are neither dutiful nor mechanical (a critique occasionally leveled at the New Critics). On the contrary, very much in the manner of Béguin, they reveal insight, sensitivity, and sympathy; there is a sense that, at this moment, Matthiessen is Hawthorne, he is Whitman, and he makes us identify with and partake of them as well.

Finally, once again in the Béguin manner, Matthiessen arrives at something akin to a phenomenological reading of his authors, and thus, following in the wake of New Criticism, anticipates *nouvelle critique.* That is how I take his insights into Emerson: the image of the seashell, the entire universe in a detail, alive on the shore and dead in one's study; or the structure of the essay, a sequence of paragraphs in no necessary order, and each paragraph a sequence of sentences in no necessary order. Similarly, in Thoreau he finds a universe of bodily functions, concrete, sensual, and alive, evoked in everyday imagery, such as the wooden slate, flowing water, and scything. Matthiessen examines *Walden,* underscoring its organic structure, which is neither absolutely chronological nor absolutely thematic but a combination of both, for the actual twenty-six months that comprise Thoreau's sojourn have been rearranged to form an archetypal year, from summer to summer – the cycle of the seasons and the cycle from arrival to departure. One of Matthiessen's achievements is his revaluation of Thoreau the writer, to be granted his place as a writer of the first rank, in place of Thoreau the naturalist and Thoreau the self-reliant New Englander.

It is also to Matthiessen's credit that he not only perceived faults or weaknesses in his writers but was willing to make a place for them in the book. Emerson, for example, did not accept the discipline of art; he was committed to the sincere outpourings of the heart: matter over form, genius over talent, and poetry as ecstasy. The only person he ever knew was himself. Matthiessen then recognizes that Emerson was faithful to his creed with the to-be-expected results. He had perhaps deep ideas yet no mastery of form, no execution, and what form his works embody can be seen as artificial. In addition, Emerson is faulted for favouring the ideal over the actual, and his mind's optimism over concrete experience. His simple, naïve, unproblematic optimism, grounded in the denial of evil, is perhaps the most negative trait in Emerson, particularly because it is so very American.

Hawthorne had a sense of evil, and Matthiessen, following Melville, sees in him depths of suffering, pain, and sympathy that opened the gates for serious writing in America. Hawthorne had a sense of tragedy, not just situated in the past but related directly to the contemporary world of experience. Yet he often would not carry it through, not maintain something like tragic consistency. The pat happy ending to *The House of the Seven Gables* and the genteel cliché figures that turn up in his fiction indicate a failure of nerve, a limit to his vision of evil in the world, that the world itself is evil, or that even the hero and heroine can be corrupted by power and money.

In the case of Whitman, Matthiessen remains enough of a New Critic to deplore the poet's deep emotions unaccompanied by rigour of mind, and an egocentrism so extreme that it leads to the 'messianic illusion' that Whitman himself is some sort of god. His language – Matthiessen was fascinated by the 'language experiment' – is seen to be the curious juxtaposition of concrete, organic speech, the speech of the masses, including slang, with book terms vaguely remembered, foreign items (mostly French) often misconstrued, and dreadful coinages all his own – in other words the mangled diction of a half-educated man.

Matthiessen's critiques are of interest because of what he says and because of why he says it. In contrast to Lewis and Frye, his touchstone for excellence in literature is high tragedy, the recognition of evil in the world, our contemporary world of experience, and of man's struggle with the world of experience and the evil in it. A second touchstone is the language of analogy, with symbolism and allegory placed above other styles of writing, and symbolism above allegory, ideas that he found in Coleridge and the New Critics. Therefore, he rates Melville and Hawthorne over the others, and Melville over Hawthorne. *Moby-Dick* and, to a lesser extent, *Billy Budd* are upheld as American masterpieces, works of high tragedy and rich, problematic symbolism. It is Matthiessen who launched the idea – some would say the myth – that *Moby-Dick* is the great American novel (or epic) and one of the most important works in world literature. Melville and the others provide a tradition that writes the past to the present and lives for us today.

Matthiessen's critical output was not limited to *American Renaissance*. Some of his books rate little more than a mention. These include a sentimental, self-indulgent, intellectually lax biography of Sarah Orne Jewett, a nineteenth-century regionalist author of tales and sketches; his revised doctoral dissertation on Elizabethan prose translation; and a curious volume, *Out of the Heart of Europe*, part travelogue, part personal reminiscence, part the political musings of a would-be public intellectual.[6] Of much greater importance, indeed work of the first class showing Matthiessen in a different light, are the volumes he devoted to Eliot, James, and Theodore Dreiser.

The Achievement of T.S. Eliot, which dates from 1935 and thus precedes the work on the American Renaissance, helped launch Eliot in academic circles, bringing to English departments the idea that the poet belongs to the very front rank of twentieth-century writers.[7] Matthiessen's volume, a very important study in its day, holds up well more than seventy years later. Whereas most full-length works on Eliot follow his production chronologically and even provide a running commentary on his verse, Matthiessen adopts a topical approach.[8] As he sees it, Eliot's importance to English literature is that he created a revolution – what today we would call the modernist revolution – in both criticism and poetry. He offered a new poetry and a new criticism for the age. Therefore, the poetry explains the criticism and the criticism explains the poetry; bringing them together is necessary for deep understanding. Matthiessen then organizes his reading of Eliot around themes taken directly from the criticism: tradition, the spirit of the age, the objective correlative, the auditory imagination, the integrity of the work of art, and the sense of an age.

Although he avoids the running commentary approach, Matthiessen, a partial disciple of the New Criticism, does splendid close readings of individual passages in the Eliot corpus, such as the intertextual presence of Dante, John Webster, and Baudelaire in a small section of *The Waste Land,* and the past and the present in two passages from *Ash Wednesday.* In a particularly brilliant tour de force he takes a pattern of images found in *Purgatorio* xxvi – gulls, rocks, the sea and the sailor, the city, girls with flowers and blowing hair, desert and rock, fire and water – and locates their recurring presence in the Eliot corpus. Consequently, he explains what we can call Eliot's phenomenology: fragmentation, the waste land, fertility, desert and garden, and death and rebirth. And, in an especially perceptive section, Matthiessen accounts for Eliot's reading, Eliot's own footnotes in *The Waste Land,* and how twentieth-century people can and should read him.

Scholars faulted Matthiessen for having adopted Eliot's own critical dicta for the parameters of his study. According to them, Matthiessen fails to employ a language of his own vis-à-vis Eliot; in other words, there is no critical distance between the poet and the scholar, therefore Matthiessen is not sufficiently independent from Eliot.[9] In my opinion, such caveats are wrongheaded. Matthiessen on Eliot is no better and no worse than, say, Erich Auerbach and John Freccero on Dante, who take Dante's own writings on Christian allegory and typology in the *Letter to Cangrande della Scala* as the key to understanding the *Commedia.*[10] To what extent can any of us, in writing on Rabelais,

Shakespeare, Cervantes, Goethe, Dostoevsky, and Proust, be detached
from our subject, escape his shadow, and maintain a competitive dialogue with him? To what extent would any of this be desirable? The
problem lies perhaps with Matthiessen's critics, who resent the notion
that T.S. Eliot might be one of the very great writers of the twentieth
century and that Matthiessen treats him as such.

Those who critique Matthiessen appear to be men of the Left who
regret that the author of *American Renaissance* does not attack Eliot's
views on politics and religion. Matthiessen was certainly aware of the
problem. He deplores the fact that Marxists hold a prejudice against
religious belief and the poetry of faith. He observes that the reader is
never obliged to share an author's beliefs. At the centre of the work of
art stands the work, not the author or his ideas. In addition, however,
Matthiessen offers a reading of Eliot not dissimilar to that of György
Lukács and Pierre Barbéris on Balzac.[11] Although a man of the Right, it
is in the period from 1920 on that Eliot manifests concern with social
and political issues. He reacts against the power of money that dominates the masses, and against the masses' own obsession with money and
a money-oriented success. He discovers a salvation according to which
one sacrifices the self for others. Thus he arrives at a link between tradition, orthodoxy, and a humane, community-oriented Christianity. As
Matthiessen sees it, Eliot's greatness lies in his version of Christian tragedy – that is, the emptiness of life without belief, the anguished quest
of the individual for belief, and the anguish of the believer confronted
by our fallen world.

With *Henry James: The Major Phase*, published in 1944, just three years
after *American Renaissance*, Matthiessen contributed to launching the
Henry James vogue, the notion that James – not Melville, not Ernest
Hemingway – was the great American novelist.[12] Reacting against Van
Wyck Brooks and Vernon L. Parrington, and for that matter against
Granville Hicks, Matthiessen denied that James was a failed writer
because he left America and did not promulgate the American Dream,
or that he failed because he was a patrician and an aesthete.[13] According to Matthiessen, James has a magnificent tragic vision and is a powerfully moral writer of lived experience; he is a writer of intelligence; and
the intelligence, the lived experience, the moral imagination, and the
tragic vision are seen, at their best, in the James of the great later novels,
the ones most criticized by the Marxists and the nativists.

Matthiessen is superb on narrative structure: the twelve 'books' of
The Ambassadors, each with its own mini-climax; or the fairy-tale analogy in *The Wings of the Dove*, with Milly Theale as an orphan, fabulously

rich and under a curse, to be rescued by the most problematic anti-prince, a fairy tale with a very modernist open ending. He discusses point of view: in *The Ambassadors*, Strether is indeed the centre of consciousness, and the novel is what he sees and comes to know; whereas Milly Theale is seen and known through others and thus retains, for the reader, the very Jamesian sense of vulnerable, delicate beauty and mystery. Matthiessen is at his best elucidating James as the creator of images that are also symbols. These include the city of Paris in *The Ambassadors*; water and animal imagery in *The Wings of the Dove*, with Milly the victim, the dove with great wings pursued by lion, panther, and eagle; and, of course, the flawed objet d'art, the collector's piece in *The Golden Bowl.*

Finally, as Matthiessen insists, James is aware of late nineteenth-century capitalism. He underscores the importance of money, and money as corruption, throughout and for all the principals in *The Wings of the Dove.* In *The Golden Bowl* such questions are dominant. Central to the novel is Adam Verver's immense fortune, new money from California (railroads? mining? land speculation?). Verver and his daughter Maggie are collectors, hence the golden bowl with a crack beneath the surface, a symbol for, among other things, the flawed Italian prince whom Maggie collected. Matthiessen offers an insightful critique of James. As James presents it, Verver and Maggie embody American innocence, which triumphs over European corruption. Yet how innocent can a California robber baron be? How can such a man be a figure of naive love and sensitivity? In addition, after manipulating everyone as she has done, after seeing everything as it is, how can Maggie remain a figure of purity and innocence?

All in all, Matthiessen underscores three major elements in the Henry James universe. One is, of course, the Master's passionate yet so very lucid commitment to art. Like Eliot, he is an American writer as aware of the theory as he is of the practice, and as aesthetically grounded as any European. Hence the powerful central image of the flawed golden bowl, what today we call a *mise en abyme.* Secondly, James treats in a most comprehensive manner Strether's evolution – his learning the need to live; and Milly Theale's tragedy is defined by her desperate will to live, and her failure. Lastly, Matthiessen sees in James the triumph of consciousness and what has been called the moral imagination. James's characters live the drama of ethical choices, and they do so with high conscious awareness. The 'good characters' are conscious of themselves and of others; the villains are blind. Thus James follows Hawthorne and anticipates not only Eliot but also Proust.

James became Matthiessen's central focus in the 1940s. In addition to the book of criticism, he co-edited *The Notebooks of Henry James* and in 1947 published, in two volumes, *The James Family*.[14] This latter work was meant to be the biography of a family, or rather a biography of their minds, and, given the importance of the Jameses, an intellectual history of the United States from Emerson to the First World War. Once again, Matthiessen innovates in a domain, the family multibiography, which will achieve importance decades later. Once again, he brings to the fore previously neglected figures, Henry James, Sr., and Alice James. Unfortunately, the work, rather than simply including selections from the James family writing, is an *anthologie commentée* with immense amounts of text by the Jameses and relatively little by Matthiessen.

The tomes on Eliot and James indicate how close Matthiessen was to the New Critics and how, in spite of his democratic ideology, he could treasure America's greatest patrician authors. Then, at the end of his life, he offended the very same aesthetic humanists with an intellectual biography of Theodore Dreiser.[15] Dreiser was completely out of fashion in the late 1940s. More than one of Matthiessen's admirers believes that, in this volume, the master had lost his critical edge and that only politics can explain why he wanted to work on a novelist so intellectually and aesthetically lacking.[16] William E. Cain, on the other hand, considers that the Dreiser book was a breakthrough for Matthiessen and that it gave him new breadth as a critic and as an American.[17] Cain observes that this is the first study to treat Dreiser's entire opus and to grant him his rightful place in the history of the American novel. I agree.

Matthiessen has empathy for Dreiser, the first important writer with a non-British name, a writer from so humble a background, who had to struggle so hard to become a novelist in the face of grinding poverty and the genteel society that three times censored his books. As Matthiessen sees it, Dreiser is at his best when he writes from lived experience and with sympathy and passion. The thickness or density of experience comes, in part, from Balzac; also from Balzac is a sense of history, of the new replacing the old – specifically in Chicago and New York. What James lacked, Dreiser had in abundance: the concrete sense of wealth, what it offers, how it corrupts, and how it is bound like iron to social differences, to the new class distinctions created by it. Dreiser's most vital, living characters – Hurstwood in *Sister Carrie* and Clyde Griffiths in *An American Tragedy* – are outsiders desperately eager to rise in this new world, who rise and then fall and who are, from beginning to end, creatures of solitude doomed to face victory and endure defeat alone.

In *Sister Carrie* the dominant imagery is of people adrift on water, and also of clothing. Rich, lavish clothes are central to Hurstwood's vision of himself and of where he wishes to go; his fall is evoked most powerfully by seedy suits and, at the end, rags. The equivalent to Hurstwood's wardrobe, in *An American Tragedy*, is a hotel in Kansas City. This hotel, an establishment blatant in its conspicuous consumption and, at the same time, powerfully, irremediably vulgar, is the objective correlative of Clyde's dreams and wish-fulfilment phantasms. Matthiessen is at his best, and insightful as only he can be, in exploring the ways in which *An American Tragedy* is American and a tragedy. The Americanness concerns a society of various levels and distinctions, all of them grounded in money and with money always dominant, for no culture other than the material is to be found, even among the very rich. From a background of poverty and what today we would call alienation, Clyde enters this world; he is as much an outsider to the hotel and the factory as he is to his own family. The tragedy relates to Clyde's efforts to rise to the top and his inevitable failure in the endeavour. He is crushed by nature, by society, and by his own urges. On the one hand, the young man is sensitive and deserving of a better life; on the other hand, he is shown to be superficial and criminally selfish. In the end, in this American tragedy, justice or a parody of justice is enacted, and the murderer – now subjected passively to his destiny – is executed.

Matthiessen never seeks to gloss over Dreiser's inadequacies as a novelist. One such inadequacy would be – in this he resembles his master Balzac – that Dreiser has never experienced high society and that his portrayal of the very rich is made up of superficial clichés. Although *The Financier* is a first-rate novel, the other 'business novels' fail, largely because Frank Cowperwood is too masterful, he adapts to change too easily, he can never be defeated, and, consequently, his career is lacking in conflict and tragedy.

Secondly, similar clichés permeate the passages on sexuality, especially with regard to women. Sister Carrie herself is perceived always from the outside and in the formulas of the time, emphasizing her beauty and even innocence. We are never allowed to sense her as a woman who loves, feels, thrills, and desires. The inability to conceptualize desire, to imagine it novelistically, accounts for the failure of *The 'Genius,'* a book which recounts the interminable affairs of a great painter. All is there, all in the style of Zola; unlike *La curée* or *Nana*, it simply never comes to life. Matthiessen's critiques do not, however, undermine the American Zola who, perhaps for the first time, was accorded the full critical attention that a great critic will accord only to writers of very high calibre.

Dreiser was the only post-Jamesian novelist to attract Matthiessen in a serious way. It is notable, however, that throughout his life the Harvard critic paid a sustained interest in American poetry, especially the poetry of his century and his lifetime. We see this evidenced in his *Oxford Book of American Verse* with its judicious introduction, the chapter on poetry from 1915 to 1940 in the Spiller *Literary History of the United States*, and the essays and reviews collected in *The Responsibility of the Critic*.[18] Matthiessen is extraordinarily prescient concerning the great moderns, whom he admires and whom he helped establish in the canon. Among the poets reviewed we find, in alphabetical order, Conrad Aiken, Hart Crane, E.E. Cummings, Louis MacNeice, John Crowe Ransom, Edwin Arlington Robinson, Delmore Schwartz, Karl Shapiro, Wallace Stevens, Allen Tate, Robert Penn Warren, William Carlos Williams, Yvor Winters, and W.B. Yeats. The *Literary History* article begins and ends with Eliot; it also testifies to the then accepted values in American poetry with, in a constrained format, precious space allotted to the likes of Edna St Vincent Millay, Stephen Vincent Benét, and Archibald MacLeish. The Oxford anthology is especially important. As Alan C. Golding observes, it represents a revision and restatement of the poetic canon. Matthiessen eliminates from the previous *Oxford Book* the popular traditional anthology pieces, and he reduces the selections from the nineteenth-century favourites: Longfellow and his friends. To more than compensate, he introduces material from the colonial period (Anne Bradstreet and Edward Taylor) and the plethora of great moderns, ending in Robert Lowell.

Ideologic criticism directed at literary critics, the practice of attacking an earlier generation of scholars not for their scholarship but for their ideas, has been especially common in the German- and English-speaking lands. Hence, as we saw, the attacks directed from the Left on Curtius. We shall observe the same phenomenon with Northrop Frye. It is not surprising, then, that the greatest and most influential figure in American literary studies should have undergone something roughly comparable. Matthiessen had the good fortune (or the ill fortune, depending on one's perspective) to have attracted a powerful literary mind – William E. Cain – who, whatever his reservations concerning Matthiessen, knows and appreciates him and who, with unusual insight, goes to the heart of Matthiessen's endeavours, his hopes, and his achievements.

Cain accents the political; it is his conviction that the political precedes and determines the rest. He focuses on Matthiessen's similar conviction, his commitment in *American Renaissance* to a 'literature for democracy' and to his five authors' 'devotion to the possibilities of democracy.' Cain observes that the subsequent academic adoption of Matthiessen's position and of his canon derives partly from the fact that his leftist politics are couched in only the most general, idealistic terms. They do not require hard choices or concrete acts. When we look carefully at *American Renaissance*, we see no discussion of slavery in general, or the five writers' opinions on slavery, or the books on slavery that were published during those years. We see no discussion of Melville's *Benito Cereno*, a major text centred on the issue of slavery.[19] Yet slavery was the dominant intellectual and political question of the age.

Cain faults Matthiessen for not including Frederick Douglass or Harriet Beecher Stowe among his Renaissance masters. According to this reading, Matthiessen's canon was shaped yet also circumscribed by race, class, and gender. Today, Cain observes, English departments embrace an enlarged canon that will take into account literary genres and constituencies left out of *American Renaissance*. Jane Tompkins, in particular, argues for the inclusion of sentimental novels authored by women, such as Susan Warner's *The Wide, Wide World* (1851), Harriet Beecher Stowe's *Uncle Tom's Cabin* (1852), and Maria Cummins's *The Lamplighter* (1854).[20] Cain himself protests against the fact that Matthiessen includes no poets from the Harlem Renaissance in his otherwise so innovative *Oxford Book of American Verse*. Had Matthiessen followed his socialist convictions with more energy and integrity, he could have located American writers in a more genuine cultural context and could have grasped more accurately the reality of American history and literary life. Cain believes that had Matthiessen included books by blacks and women, as a believer in democracy should, he could have broadened the cultural context and the very idea of literature.[21]

In my opinion, Cain's critique – insightful, even brilliant – is most compelling with regard to the question of slavery. Cain is right. In *American Renaissance*, Matthiessen curiously avoids the most pressing issue of the day, one which affected, to a greater or lesser extent, all American writers. Similarly, in the very inclusive *Oxford Book of American Verse*, the men of the Harlem Renaissance are totally absent. Even were we to grant that academics today overemphasize the problems of American minorities – problems that went largely unrecognized at Harvard in the 1930s – given the fact that Matthiessen was a Christian socialist, the avoidance of reference to African Americans and to slavery is unsettling. From the perspective of deconstruction, the avoidance of reference is fascinating – an aporia which calls attention to itself, the absence of trace which is the trace of absence, suggesting to us how complex and problematic the idea of democracy must have been in Matthiessen's psyche.

As a Christian socialist, someone whom today we might designate as Old Left, as the American equivalent of Albert Béguin, Matthiessen would perhaps reply to Cain's other critiques that, for him and for the entire liberal tradition in America, democracy meant liberty and equality, that is, equality of opportunity but never proportionate equality of outcome with regard to membership in ethnic groups or, for that matter, with regard to gender. Aesthetic standards have to be given priority over inclusiveness. Matthiessen would say, in his version of Harvard at its best, that he focused in *American Renaissance* on the best and the brightest, and that *Uncle Tom's Cabin* and *The Wide, Wide World*, as works of art, cannot measure up to *The Scarlet Letter* and *Moby-Dick*. The sentimental romances authored by Stowe, Warner, and Cummins are perhaps worthy of study but not necessarily worthy of being included among the greatest books of our heritage. In other words, Matthiessen chose not to include books from every constituency because no constituency, as a constituency, has the right to demand the highest place in the aesthetic canon. For the Old Left, such a demand is not democracy and it is not American. Speaking in my own voice, I would insist upon the importance of the sentimental, domestic fiction of the 1850s and the desirability that it be studied and taught, while conceding that it does not belong on a list of the greatest American classics.

Cain also wants Matthiessen, in the name of democracy, to critique James and Eliot more than he does. Here again, I would suggest that this sort of value judgment grounded in the ideological has nothing to do with democracy; it is, rather, a 1960s offshoot from the vulgar Marxism and the nativism that Matthiessen had been fighting all his life. Although Cain's critique of James's *The American Scene* and of Matthiessen's reading of it proves to be nuanced and subtle, it also anticipates the crude denunciations of old literature by young-seeming ideologues on American campuses who, in the name of race, class, and gender, repudiate our entire cultural heritage to the extent that it diverges from the current consensus on the campuses.[22]

This said, I cannot but agree wholeheartedly with Cain's major point: that all of Matthiessen's work reveals the unresolved tension between Christianity and socialism, and between a purely aesthetic stance and a more engaged one grounded in politics and history. It would be possible, however, to take the opposite stance from Cain and to express reservations with regard to Matthiessen from a conservative perspective. Here one could say that he was misled by the idea of democracy. For example, was it not the principle of democracy that caused him to leave out Edgar Allan Poe and to distort the largely undemocratic ideas of Hawthorne? Was is not the principle of democracy that caused him to make so much of Emerson and to overvalue Melville?[23] One could make a case that, Renaissance aside, the greatest American writers – American classics, if you will – came later: James, Pound, Eliot, and Faulkner are of world-literature standing, beyond the men of the 1850s. And these classics stand on the Right. Theirs is not a democratic literature for a democratic people. Three of the four chose exile from the United States, and all four lived and wrote, in part, in reaction against the American dream.

As I see it, Matthiessen remains a major critic because of his version of inclusiveness, an inclusiveness grounded in aesthetics and not in ideology. As a critic, he pays equal attention to the historical reality – economic and political – and to the work of art as art. Thus he can combine in himself the best of a sociological or semi-Marxist approach and the New Critical approach while avoiding the extremes and the exclusiveness of both.

In 'The Responsibilities of the Critic,' the most important essay in the collection of that title (3–18) and Matthiessen's most important theoretical statement, he urges a wide-ranging, pluralist program for the literary critic: he should know the works of art in our time and also the great works of the past; he should be a literary scholar and also be acquainted with other fields and approaches, and popular culture; and, if an Americanist, he should also be aware of Europe and the European heritage. In sum, this is Matthiessen's credo:

> In proposing an ever widening range of interests for the ideal critic, I have moved from his central responsibility to the text before him out to an awareness of some of the world-wide struggles of our age. We must come back to where we started, to the critic's primary function. He must judge the work of art as work of art. But knowing form and content to be inseparable, he will recognize his duty to both. Judgment of art is unavoidably both an aesthetic and a social act, and the critic's sense of social responsibility gives him a deeper thirst for meaning. (14)

> There is a basic distinction between bringing everything in your life to what you read and reading into a play of the past issues that are not

there ... the critic should freely grant that the artist writes as he must. But for his own work the critic has to be both involved in his age and detached from it. This double quality of experiencing our own time to the full and yet being able to weigh it in relation to other times is what the critic must strive for, if he is to be able to discern and demand the works of art that we need most. (18)

Matthiessen is capable of working on and admiring Hawthorne, Whitman, James, Eliot, and Dreiser. Whether of the Left or the Right, these American writers are worthy of scrutiny not because one agrees with their ideas but because their ideas are given expression in works of art concerning the American experience, works that make the experience live for us today, in somewhat the same way that Balzac – Marx's favourite novelist – makes nineteenth-century France live.

Matthiessen was so extraordinarily prescient, so ahead of his time, in striving for a genuinely literary approach to literature and in locating those writers who could form a tradition of American writing, a usable past for us fifty and seventy-five years after him and a century or a century and a half after them. As Giles B. Gunn observes, as early as 1929 Matthiessen recognized the Puritan heritage, the frontier, and American humour as major factors in the creation of a literature and a culture.[24] And, in what was to be a truncated life, he wrote on so many different writers and strands: Emerson, Thoreau, Hawthorne, Melville, Whitman, Emily Dickinson, Poe, Jewett, James, Dreiser, Eliot, and almost the entire canon of twentieth-century poetry. Matthiessen's range and scope are enormous: he was and is a complete Americanist in the best sense of the term.

No less prescient was Matthiessen's sense that tragedy is the central human experience and the hallmark of most great writing in general and, more specifically, of writing in America. In this he once again differs from the central thrust of the nativists (American optimism, the American dream) and, once again, he exhibits his own adherence to the central tradition of modernism. The sense of tragedy is derived from his Christian socialism or, perhaps more accurately, from the tension between Christian faith and socialism.

It is also derived from his life experience. Although Matthiessen never had to endure, at first hand, the horrors of Nazi Germany and the Nazi New Europe, he had his own demons, private and public. The man's personal tragedy ended in 1950 when, at the age of forty-eight, he committed suicide by jumping from the window of his room in a Boston hotel. Why did he jump? For a combination of reasons, the scholars all agree: depression and despair over the Cold War, the Stalinization of Eastern Europe, the nascent anticommunist hysteria in America (Matthiessen had received a subpoena from the House Committee on Un-American Activities), possible imminent public exposure as a homosexual, loneliness caused by the death of his longtime partner, the painter Russell Cheney, and, not least of all, his own propensity to deep neurosis that had resulted in breakdowns and a previous suicide attempt.[25]

In his sense of Christian tragedy and in his recognition of the tension between it and the idea of socialism, as in so many other ways, Matthiessen resembles Albert Béguin. Both died early, both were passionate Christians, both were fierce patriots (for America and France respectively), both gave witness for their beliefs with a lifetime of commitment; for both of them a vision shines through everything they wrote. Matthiessen shares Béguin's generosity and magnanimity, his ripeness and maturity, his sense of the whole. Perhaps the most succinct way of saying what a humanist critic is, would be Matthiessen's statement to his students in the middle of the Second World War, after he failed his physical examination, that his contribution to the war effort would be a book on Henry James. And the students believed him and made him do it.

8 Northrop Frye's Totalizing Vision: the Order of Words

This book culminates with a chapter on Northrop Frye, arguably the last great humanist critic and the first major theoretician. Frye has probably written more and has had a greater impact on literary studies than any other scholar-critic in our century, in the English-speaking world at least. Between 1947 and his death in 1991 he authored thirty books and edited another sixteen; his collected works, including correspondence, student essays, notebooks, and diaries, in the process of publication by the University of Toronto Press, will add up to more than thirty volumes. As of December 2004, the first fifteen have been published. To give an idea of Frye's output, he published four books in 1963, two in 1965, two in 1967, and three in 1970–1.

For the two decades that followed upon the publication of *Anatomy of Criticism* in 1957, Frye dominated English studies as no one else has, before or since. With the rise of deconstruction and the new historicism, interest fell off. Frye was no longer at the centre of attention, and some of the more recent theoreticians denounced him as they did New Criticism. Nevertheless, he was still cited, commented on, and, more importantly, translated. Then, with the 1990s came a renewal of interest marked by books of commentary and a number of conferences in Australia, China, and Italy as well as in his native Canada, plus the *Collected Works of Northrop Frye* project.[1]

Frye's first book, *Fearful Symmetry*, published in 1947, changed the direction of Blake studies for a generation.[2] He rehabilitated William Blake, considered up to then a minor precursor of romanticism, of interest, to some extent, as a mystic or a madman. Frye also rehabilitated allegory in modern literature, characterizing Blake's long poems as allegories and making a claim that Blake is the quintessential poet.

He treated Blake's opus as a totality and drew from it a general theory of poetry. Central to Blake and to the general theory, Frye located the Bible, with Blake's corpus paralleling the structure of the Bible, the Bible imagined as the greatest work of art, and art as a form that religion can adopt.

Anatomy of Criticism, the volume which made Frye's name and propelled him to the summit of literary criticism in the English-speaking world, appeared in 1957.[3] Characterized as the most important work of literary theory in our century, it is Frye's major single contribution and his one title known to all who follow criticism. In this sense, Frye, like Curtius, Auerbach, Béguin, Rousset, and Matthiessen, is often (falsely) identified with one book. Even though *Anatomy of Criticism* is so well known and has benefited from so much commentary at a very high level, I shall discuss it in some detail, for the benefit of students and of specialists in the Continental literatures.

The first of the 'Four Essays' named in the subtitle relates to a theory of modes. These five fictional modes are determined by the hero's power of action: his superiority or inferiority in kind and in degree to the environment and to other men. They are myth, romance, the high mimetic, the low mimetic, and the ironic. According to Frye's formulation:

> If superior in *kind* both to other men and to the environment, the hero is a divine being, and the story about him will be a *myth* ... If superior in *degree* to other men and to his environment, the hero is the typical hero of *romance* ... If superior in degree to other men but not to his natural environment, the hero is a leader ... This is the hero of the *high mimetic* mode ... If superior neither to other men nor to his environment, the hero is one of us ... This gives us the hero of the *low mimetic* mode ... If inferior in power or intelligence to ourselves, so that we have the sense of looking down on a scene of bondage, frustration, or absurdity, the hero belongs to the *ironic* mode. (33–4)

The five modes, in sequence, depict a shift from the supernatural to the human and from god-like protagonists to people like or beneath ourselves. Frye relates the sequence to the history of Western literature (in the vernacular), by positing that romance is the dominant mode in the Middle Ages, high mimetic in the Renaissance and what today we call the baroque, low mimetic in the eighteenth and nineteenth centuries, and irony in the twentieth century. The mythical would reflect a preliterate, pretextual phase, biblical or early medieval, or it would function as the precondition for the other four modes.

In my opinion, this section is extremely important. Those who critique Frye for ignoring history forget that the entire *Anatomy* is grounded in a theory of literary history, wherein the evolution of modes and forms replaces the usual history arranged according to centuries, intellectual movements, or the reigns of monarchs. Those who critique Frye for being too schematic forget his insistence that in each period and with each great author all five modes will be present, and that in any great book we will find more than one. These are the modes most prevalent in an age but never universal in or unique to it. Given that one mode will be dominant in a given century, its presence helps us categorize the century and place individual works within it. Because of the likelihood of the same pattern occurring elsewhere (in antiquity) and in the future, Frye offers a theory of literary cycles comparable to other such theories: for example the cycle of experimental, high classical, mannerist, and baroque to be found in art criticism. Because of the cycle, he values all centuries and all modes, refusing to envisage history as progressive or regressive, and refusing to view it as organic. Literatures age but do not improve or decline. This is the case, in part, because all the modes reveal the same or similar structures and conventions.

The second essay elaborates a theory of symbols. Here we find the symbol – 'any unit of any literary structure that can be isolated for critical attention'(71) – functioning within four or five phases: as motif and sign, as image, as archetype, and as monad. Each phase represents an opening out from the literary work to the corpus of literature taken in its entirety. The archetype especially insists upon literature as convention and as what today we call intertextuality.[4] It represents structures to be found in all literature, the foundation and, in a sense, the essence of literariness. Each book is related to other books: 'Poetry can only be made out of other poems; novels out of other novels' (97). The conventions enable literature to surpass mere personal experience, to connect one text with others and thus, and only thus, to attain universality. As Robert D. Denham has observed, the five phases correspond to the five historical modes, but in reverse order, the motif relating to the ironic, the sign to low mimesis, the image to high mimesis, the archetype to romance, and the monad to myth.[5] If, on the other hand, one telescopes motif and sign into one phase, the four phases then correspond to and are derived from the four levels of allegory or typology in Christian exegesis so prevalent in the Middle Ages and the Renaissance: the literal, the

typological, the tropological, and the anagogical.[6] Especially impressive
is Frye's effort to conceive a literary equivalent of the anagogic, the
monad relating to the total order of words, as vision, revelation, or
epiphany.

The longest, the most important, and the most influential section in
Anatomy of Criticism is 'Archetypal Criticism: Theory of Myths.' Here
Frye is effective in demystifying the notion that literature is or ought to
be realism and mimesis. Frye is peremptory: 'when the public demands
likeness to an object, it generally wants the exact opposite, likeness to
the pictorial conventions it is familiar with' (132). As he sees it, first of
all, literature adheres to five categories of imagery: apocalyptic (divine)
and demonic, at the limits of expression, and three analogical categories in between that correspond to the displaced world of human existence – romance, high mimesis, and low mimesis. The five categories are
equivalent to the five modes that shape literary history. These five categories can also be perceived as functioning on seven levels: divine,
human, animal, vegetable, mineral, fire, and water.

Secondly, Frye describes four mythoi – broad narrative categories of
literature logically prior to literary genres – that he designates as
spring/comedy, summer/romance, autumn/tragedy, and winter/irony
and satire. Here he profits from medieval symbolism: the structure of
the four seasons, the four tempers or humours, the four elements, and
the four ages of man. The cycle of the year and of life itself relates to the
mythoi and to the cycle of literary modes in history. Frye is at his best on
comedy, which he envisions as a pattern wherein the young, thwarted by
the fathers and their law, either escape from the society of the fathers or,
more often, flee but then return to overcome the obstacle, marry, and
reform the old society in their image. Frye borrows his character types
or functions from Greek and Latin New Comedy: the alazon, eiron, buffoon, and agroikos, among others. The alazon is the blocking character:
an impostor, father (*senex iratus*), *miles gloriosus*, pedant, fop, or *précieuse*.
The eiron is a self-deprecating figure of irony who helps to bring about
the happy ending: a benevolent older man, the hero's friend, or a *dolosus servus*. The buffoon is a parasite who amuses his betters; he can be a
valet (Sganarelle), cook, or host. The agroikos, a churl or rustic,
assumes the function of killjoy, the refuser of festivities.

These functions will reappear, in different guise, in the other three
mythoi. Frye depicts romance as a quest or series of adventures marked
by agon, pathos, and anagnorisis, that is, the journey, struggle, and exaltation. Although perhaps not as illuminating on tragedy, he makes a

valiant effort to account for one of the paradoxes of this mode: the conflict/tension over whether fate or destiny, or a flaw or excess (hamartia) in the protagonist would be the dominant element. Frye takes into account the phenomenon of innocent tragic heroes: Iphegeneia, Socrates, Christ, and Joan of Arc; and he relates tragedy to sacrifice, propitiation, and communion. It is perhaps a flaw in Frye's decision-making to yoke irony and satire in the same mythos of winter. On the other hand, in contrast to most theorists of literature, he makes a place for these relatively neglected literary kinds and includes in his scheme writers (Rabelais, Laurence Sterne, Lord Byron, Franz Kafka, and Faulkner), who elsewhere might appear to be anomalies. And he makes clear the extent to which our modern ironists are grounded in literary culture, for their works act, structurally, as parodies of romance.

The fourth and last section – 'Rhetorical Criticism: Theory of Genres' – is one of the most challenging and innovative. At the same time, in my opinion it is the weakest of the four and of the least use to those who come after. As A.C. Hamilton observes, Frye, reacting against the fashionable criticism of his day which neglected genre theory, strives heroically to include in his *Anatomy* a structure that will account for all genres in all literature.[7] He grounds his categories in the 'radical of presentation' ('the conditions established between the poet and his public' [247]) – that is, how literature relates to the immediate experience of the public in its reception. Frye takes up the three classical Aristotelian and Goethean categories – epic, dramatic, and lyric – and adds a fourth, prose fiction. The four are determined by whether the text is spoken to a group of listeners (epos), acted before a group of spectators (drama), sung or chanted (lyric), or written for a single reader (fiction).

The strengths of this system are many. First of all, Frye proves to be a percipient innovator, pioneering in reader-response theory before it came into being. He can, once again, relate his categories to the history of literature, for each category prevails in a given period of time or in a given literary mode: epos in myth and romance; drama in the high mimetic; prose fiction in the low mimetic; and lyric in irony. Within each category, Frye situates the individual genres. Here, he is especially good in not privileging, for prose, the nineteenth-century novel. He includes, with equal measure, romance, confession/autobiography, and those works (by Lucian, Erasmus, Rabelais, Jonathan Swift, and Voltaire) that can be ranged under the headings 'Menippean satire' and 'anatomy.' Similarly, the category of drama finds a place for opera and the cinema.

This said, Frye's schema also reveals flaws. One flaw is due to the fact that, although he will occasionally mention *Beowulf,* Dante, and Chaucer, Frye's post-biblical consciousness is of English literature from Spenser to Joyce and Eliot. He doesn't really know the Middle Ages. This blind spot inevitably saps the validity of categories that are grounded in a uniquely modern experience of reception. For example, all medieval literature, prose and verse, was sung, chanted, or read aloud to a listening audience. Certain lyric genres were sung, others not. Epos was chanted at one time, and read aloud during subsequent generations. The most important narrative genre of the Middle Ages, romance, was for centuries composed in verse and in prose, and read aloud. And lyric poetry was directed as much to the public in society and, therefore, to the audience as to an individual lady or to God. The rigour of Frye's system is weakened when he assigns romance both to epos and to prose fiction. In addition, how many of us will validate the notion that the lyric is predominant in our age of irony but not in the Middle Ages or the Renaissance or, for that matter, the age of romanticism? For these reasons the radical of presentation, a notion insufficiently grounded in history, cannot serve as the frame for genres that are historical in their evolution.

A second flaw, less serious, occurs because of Frye's very Englishness, the sketchiness of his command of Continental traditions. Thus, in the drama category, he makes a place for the history play, because of Shakespeare, but not for the pastoral or tragicomedy, both more prevalent in French and Italian. The same is true for the various types of *comedia* cultivated in Spain. Although Frye calls one of his genres the *auto,* he has in mind the Franco-British miracle and mystery play, and is apparently unaware of what the *auto sacramental* actually was during the Spanish Golden Age.

All of this aside, and after whatever objections we make concerning details in the scaffolding, *Anatomy of Criticism,* in its totality, remains a structure of unsurpassed richness, elegance, and beauty, a total work of the art of criticism rivalled in our century only by Auerbach's *Mimesis.* Powerfully theoretical and synchronic, whereas Auerbach was so practical and diachronic, Frye nevertheless not only makes a place for history in his anatomy; he offers a rich, complex account, both linear and cyclical, of the history of forms. He anticipates any number of more recent approaches to literature: phenomenology, reader response, intertextuality, and narratology among others. And, Frye's anatomy includes an account of the anatomy as a genre; it is, thus, wilfully self-conscious, metacritical, and metatextual.

Although writing in opposition to the then prevalent school of New Criticism, Frye succeeds in theorizing some of the intellectual positions held by Cleanth Brooks and F.R. Leavis. He insists upon criticism as an independent discipline, free from outside currents (psychology, anthropology, biography, source-hunting, and even history). In this he also resembles Spitzer and Béguin, among others. Criticism of a work of art will not be grounded in the author's intentions (the fallacy of premature teleology) or the reading habits of the public, in either the author's day or our own. From this perspective, the poet has no more innate talent than the critic for the criticism of his own work. Criticism will be properly pluralist (we might say, eclectic), embracing many approaches, all valid and helpful; hence the principle of 'polysemous meaning' (72). It will also eschew the fallacy of the organic analogy, recognizing that great art is to be found in all centuries and periods, and that a cyclical vision of literary history recognizes change but never growth or decline. In other words, criticism will improve with time, but the object of criticism will not. Frye then goes beyond the New Critics in repudiating judgments of value, which he characterizes as illusion to be ascribed to the history of taste, and he demonstrates with brio that criticism offers no tools for determining whether poet A is superior to poet B and why.[8] Finally, he presents a systematic theory of literature that wills the coherence of the total field and, by so doing, makes a claim for the importance of literature and of criticism, both contributing to civilization. However, unlike some later theoreticians, Frye always recognized the primacy of literature itself. He is not one who would refer, with contempt, to mere texts.

Like Curtius, Auerbach, Béguin, Rousset, and Matthiessen, Frye is famous for one major book, the *Anatomy*. Like the others, he produced many other works, undeservedly less known and less appreciated except, of course, by Frye scholars. Some of these took off from and expanded insights in the *Anatomy*. One such work is *The Well-Tempered Critic*, with its analysis of literary language and style.[9] Here Frye proposes a structure of verse (the rhythm of recurrence), prose (the rhythm of semantic logic), and oral speech (the associative rhythm), and sketches out the forms that they can adopt. Perhaps with greater validity, he relates the three primary verbal rhythms to the classical triad of styles – Auerbach's *sermo gravis*, *sermo mediocris*, and *sermo humilis* – further dividing each into two spheres, the hieratic and the demotic, depending on the factor of distance from the spoken vernacular. Thus, the low demotic would relate to Hemingway and Samuel Beckett, the low hieratic to Rabelais and Joyce.

The middle demotic would describe the habitual style of narrative and didactic verse and expository prose, and the middle hieratic, stylized verse including the formulaic style of Homer. The high demotic would be seen in the sublime aphorism and the Gospels, and the high hieratic in moments of epiphany in Eliot, Pound, and Rilke. These pages could have found a place in the fourth essay of the *Anatomy* or, more appropriately, as a fifth essay. In that case, however, the pattern of four would have had to give way to a pattern of five, which would then have weakened the symbolism of the *Anatomy* in its totality.[10]

The most important development or expansion from the *Anatomy of Criticism* is *The Secular Scripture*, the book I consider to be the most important in Frye's *oeuvre* after the *Anatomy* and second only to it in scope and insight.[11] Here Frye expands on the notion of romance, scrutinized primarily as a genre of narrative fiction but also as something more than a genre, a mode embodying the literary – literariness itself, as the Russian Formalists would say. According to Frye, most modern readers and most modern critics consider the novel – the modern novel of realism – to be the norm, and that romance is an aberrant or anomalous form of the novel, a more 'popular' genre that appeals to the tastes of the mass, and, therefore, is lower aesthetically. The novel would be serious because it has ideas; the romance not at all because it only gives pleasure. Historically, however, romance preceded the novel, and, according to the theory of archetypes, the novel is a displaced form of romance, indeed often a parody of romance – the formulaic structure of romance adjusted to a more credible context. Even though all literature, including the modern novel, is grounded in convention and its 'reality' is presented in literary structures, romance would be the most conventional, formulaic, and archetypal of genres, therefore the most literary genre. Romance is not subliterary but, on the contrary, is as 'pure' and undiluted as literature can be.

Just as, in the *Anatomy*, the romance mode follows directly after the mythic, so also, in *The Secular Scripture*, Frye posits that romance is the structural core of all fiction, in a direct line from the folktale, and that it is the mode closest to myth, to ritual (the romance plot is ritualized action), and, therefore, to the unconscious. The history of the genre, and of Western literature, reveals a striking continuity of conventions. Among the repeated elements or functions of romance are the mysterious birth, prophecies, foster parents, disruptions from soldiers or pirates, narrow escapes, and, in the end, marriage and the restoration of identity. The hero and the villain embody two antithetical archetypal worlds: the idyllic (innocence, childhood, spring) vs the demonic (evil, exile, winter). Among these elements or functions we also find the archetype of woman and, in particular, its bifurcation into the dark lady and the lady of light. The one functions as temptress, the other as bride. In his total life experience the romance hero will have both and, by wedding the white lady, bring about a happy ending and the symbolic transformation of winter into spring. Frye suggests a historical evolution from the classical to the Christian, from tragedy to romance, and from violent, heroic masculinity to the more democratic and pacific realm of the feminine. This may help explain, in romance, the exaltation of female virtue, exemplified in the white lady's conserving her virginity against myriad attacks on it and reserving it for the chosen hero; hence the triumph of the weak and the redemption stemming from the feminine. He elaborates also on the notion of four levels of existence – heaven, the earthly paradise (our maternal home), ordinary experience (our fallen state), and hell – and four patterns of the quest, two of descent and two of ascent. One can descend from a symbolic heaven or Eden to earth, or from earth to the nether world; one can rise from hell to earth, or from earth to a higher identity in a higher and better realm.

Romance, as popular culture, can help revitalize high art during 'tired periods.' Here Frye insists upon the fact that the sex and violence seemingly endemic to popular culture today are there only because the perpetrators (Hollywood, the publishing industry) treat the popular audience as if it were only a mob:

> If by popular literature we mean what a great many people want or think they want to read when they are compelled to read, or stare at on television when they are not, then we are talking about a packaged commodity which an overproductive economy, whether capitalist or socialist, distributes as it distributes food and medicines, in varying degrees of adulteration. Much of it, in our society, is quite as prurient and brutal as its worst enemy could assert, not because it has to be, but because those who write and sell it think of their readers as a mob rather than a community. (26)

Finally – here, perhaps, is Frye at his least percipient – according to him, romance stands as a force for social adjustment and conservative values from the past but can also function as a project and ideal for the future, and, therefore, it can be more revolutionary than realism. Frye anticipates the stance of our contemporary specialists in cultural studies who find, in popular culture, a 'site of resistance.'

Frye, like Curtius, has been critiqued for elaborating abstract structures of criticism and history while ignoring the individuality, the textual
uniqueness, of literary works. As with Curtius, the critiques are unfair
and inaccurate, given that Northrop Frye published a relatively vast corpus of studies on the great English writers. He was as much a practical
critic as a theorist.

His most influential book, in this line, is *A Natural Perspective*, a path-
breaking study on Shakespearean comedy that has been a dominant
presence in Shakespeare studies, *the* book to be followed or resisted.[12]
Frye's contribution, as Keir Elam observes, lies in the domain of story
patterns and character types. He introduced and brought about the
acceptance of the actantial categories or functions from Greek and
Roman New Comedy that we saw in *Anatomy of Criticism*: eiron, alazon,
agroikos, *dolosus servus*, etc., demonstrating that these concepts are as
central to Shakespearean comedy as to those writers – Ben Jonson,
Molière – who imitated the ancients more overtly. Secondly, the story
patterns – those from archetypal romance – are such that one can envisage Shakespeare, especially in the late plays, as a creator of romance as
well as of comedy. Due to Frye, it is now the norm to refer to them as
Shakespeare's romances.

By analyzing structure, Frye insists upon the non-realism of Shakespearean theatre, of how the themes – a storm at sea, the separation of
twins, girls disguised as boys, a mysterious father, a calumnied wife,
retreat into the forest – are conventional, how the public is captivated
by the complex, involuted story for its own sake, and how such plots
bring Shakespearean drama much closer to masque and opera than
to, say, Henrik Ibsen or Anton Chekhov. Yet beyond, or rather within,
the involuted story lies a deeper, archetypal structure: the blocking,
tyrannical society, opposed to and empowered over the protagonist(s),
is responsible for confusion, alienation, loss of identity, and exile.
Hence the imagery of storm, insanity, a road of trials, and death. In
the end, however, death yields to a renewed life, the hero's rebirth
symbolized by paradise regained and the vision of the higher world,
harmony, a new identity, self-knowledge, and sexual reintegration symbolized by carnival, festivity, and a wedding. With withdrawal to and
return from the green world, the old society of law is itself reformed
and redeemed.

Frye resembles Lewis in his commitment to a traditional, Protestant
canon of English. It is not surprising that they should revere two of
the great English poets, Spenser and Milton. In my opinion, Frye's

best piece of practical criticism is a superb essay on 'Lycidas.'[13] It accounts for Milton's text as a totality on its own terms: in its partaking of a specific genre, the pastoral elegy of classical and Christian provenance, with its cycle of time and of death and rebirth and its theme of the shepherd poet; and with its connection to all other poems or what Frye calls 'the order of words.' Then, in 1965, he published a brief volume on *Paradise Lost* and *Paradise Regained*, a study comparable to, and equally important and influential as, Lewis's brief *Preface to 'Paradise Lost.'*[14]

Like Lewis, Frye places *Paradise Lost* in its historical and literary context, and never loses sight of it. In particular, he emphasizes the Renaissance notion of the epic genre as a narrative of heroic action that is also encyclopedic and, therefore, functions as a mirror for princes, providing the ruler with a model for royal education, Christian duty, and how to govern the commonwealth. The poet is expected to face up to his responsibility as a Christian and to employ his God-given 'talent' as a sacrifice and offering to God. In a variation on Lewis, Frye seeks to fathom the question of heroism and whether Satan or Adam would be the epic hero. Anticipating the four levels in romance, Frye posits four physical or symbolically topographical orders: heaven, Eden, our physical world, and the realm of sin and death; and the four orders of existence which correspond to them: divine, angelic, human, and demonic. Each of the four orders manifests a particular variety of heroic action. Satan's heroism is a sterile parody of God's; to the extent that Satan functions as the typical hero of epic, Milton is antiheroic. However, other types of heroism can be identified. Christian heroism for Adam would have been to resist evil; in this sense Adam failed to act just as Satan acted badly. Both surrendered the power to act. In fact, by preferring death with Eve to life without her, Adam declares himself to be an anti-Aeneas, as it were, and, therefore, the very image of antiheroism. The genuine hero would be Christ, whose life of heroism is anticipated in *Paradise Lost* and actualized in *Paradise Regained*. The central archetype in Milton is the loss and recovery of paradise, lost by Adam and regained by Christ. Since the Fall humans must seek paradise within, for, created by God with free will, despite original sin they can rise from the third realm to the first two or, as most will do, fall deeper into the fourth. Or, in a somewhat different formulation, by seeking the God and the Holy Spirit to be found within, man will create his new paradise. Frye grounds his reading of Milton in the structure of medieval-Renaissance cosmology and typology. That the same archetypes function in both Miltonian long poems reveals not only his desire as an artist for unity but also the continuity of *Paradise Lost* and *Paradise Regained* as a sequence, and the ways in which 'tragic epic' and 'comic epic' partake of the same structures and are both epic.

Frye resembles C.S. Lewis in his refusal to adopt the New Critical revision of the canon. Neither man could stomach the demotion of Milton in favour of the Metaphysicals; neither could accept the demotion of English romanticism in favour of the modernists. *Fearful Symmetry* was as much a defence of the romantic conception of poetry – and of its execution – as it was a rehabilitation of Blake. I believe the essays contained in *A Study of English Romanticism* to be of equal importance.[15]

The weightiest essay (3–49) is called 'The Romantic Myth.' As Frye sees it, a major shift occurred at the end of the eighteenth century, a shift not just of ideas but of the structures and dominant mythology of literature. It was at this time that the previously dominant pattern of the father-sky god associated with the masculine, reason, harmony, order, and the city gave way to the pattern of the earth-mother goddess associated with the feminine, passion, rebellion, disorder, and man in nature. Behaviour previously ascribed to (displaced onto) God is now open to humans. The old hierarchy is problematized: one can find evil in the stars and good in Satan. The masculine hero, instead of rising to the stars, descends into himself; instead of integration in a community, he prefers exile in nature; and he chooses amorous union with the feminine over masculine command in the city. Since redemption occurs through imagination and an expanded consciousness, so too the new heroism will be found especially in the artist/writer himself adopting the stance of prophet, seer, and rebel. Overall, I find Frye's formulation to be as insightful a synthesis of the birth of modernity as can be found anywhere. I would observe only that the process is perhaps more gradual and more cyclical than Frye admits, for, were he more knowledgeable in French and Spanish, he would have seen the romantic myth also in the late Middle Ages and during the baroque.

The collection reveals a superb essay on Thomas Lovell Beddoes (51–85), a writer whom Frye rediscovers and rehabilitates in the manner of Béguin and Rousset. Frye perceives, in *Death's Jest Book* and two other plays, an early nineteenth-century version of Senecan tragedy that anticipates our more recent theatre of the absurd. In Beddoes's imaginative world the barriers melt between life and death, sanity and madness, and waking and the dream. We find demon lovers, ghosts giving birth to other ghosts, sibling hatred, horror, violence, revenge, multiple murders, and cannibalism. The fool, jester, and skull at a feast, images of death, contribute to an ambience of the grotesque, a dark fusion of the tragic and the comic, as well as hysteria, farce, and the interaction of the living and the half dead. No one in British romanticism could equal Beddoes in his vision of the dark invisible world concealed from our everyday existence.

Immediately following the rediscovery of Beddoes, Frye places a no less insightful rehabilitation of Shelley (87–124). Shelley was the romantic most decried and belittled by Eliot and Leavis, among others. Frye gives battle to the New Critics by praising Shelley both as a poet and as a thinker. He offers a brilliant reading of *Prometheus Unbound*. In terms of ideas, Shelley/Prometheus appears here as a revolutionary, a devotee of secular humanism and man's consciousness. Jupiter embodies chaos and unlawful tyranny grounded in unlawful sexual dominance. Given that it is man who created the gods and their myths, by an act of consciousness Prometheus overthrows Jupiter; this 'revolution' stands as a metaphor for the triumph of Eros, the overthrow of Christianity, and the restoration of a good, Dionysian Greek polis. Archetypally, Frye envisages Shelley's drama as a comedy in which a new, better order replaces the false law of the *senex iratus*. Prometheus is allied to good, unfallen nature; by joining with the Earth Spirit, he becomes a poet. All good comes, not from above, but from below – from caves, oceans, and the expanded consciousness of the rebel poet who weds a sister-bride and attains freedom for all.

In contrast to Lewis, Frye could also include in his system modern writers promoted by the New Critics. He admired Joyce and cited him often in the theoretical books. And he devoted a brief volume, early in his career, to Eliot.[16] As in the case of Shelley, Frye underscores the importance of Eliot's ideas – his social and intellectual attitudes, his poetics and aesthetics – without which we cannot understand our own contemporary literature. At the same time, he separates the ideas from Eliot's permanent achievement as an artist, observing that no major poet stands or falls on what we would today call his ideology. Frye then examines Eliot in the light of archetypal theory. According to Frye, throughout his career Eliot cultivated two genres: the drama and the meditative poem; and he did so in a conversational, common style, not the grand style of rhetoric. Eliot elaborated his own magnificent imaginative world. It is grounded in patterns of opposition: spring vs winter, garden vs waste land, and heaven vs hell. The pattern is played out on two of the four levels of existence: the modern city and the secret garden. Eliot's people are on the outside, on the verge, so to speak, of hell and paradise, beholding them from the city or garden in a vision or in memory. These people are either the young who are betrayed while leading a full life, or the old who live death in life. Frye's reading of *The Waste Land* is especially perceptive. There he sees winter and the unreal city connected to the dying god archetype and to the four elements. The cycle – spatial, temporal, and spiritual – is completed by purgatorial journeys, with a knight reborn along with Christ to redeem the Fisher King so that the sterile barrenness will be nourished and transformed by water.

With *The Modern Century* Frye offers, in a mere 120 pages, a brilliant synthesis on modernity.[17] He accepts the seminal mid-nineteenth century for the birth of the modern world – with Flaubert, Baudelaire, and Marx. Modernity is made manifest in a number of cultural conditions, including the development of technology, the media, propaganda, advertising, and, ideologically, the myth of progress accompanied by the rejection of tradition. Partaking of modernity are the artistic creators who, reacting against their alienation, cultivate an 'international style,' empathize with the young, envisage the writer as rebel, and reject the city as a demonic archetype deemed to be ugly, uniform, and imprisoning, in favour of a new modern pastoral and a return to nature, exalting both the erotic and the primitive. They do this in a literature devoid of traditional rhetoric and often left unfinished or structured as a series of fragments, leaving the reader then expected to put them together, the fragmenting itself being a protest against conformity and wholeness.

The Modern Century contains more than a few examples taken from Canada. The Canadian literary culture illustrates, in Frye's opinion, both yearning after authenticity, grounded in the local and the provincial yet, at the same time, thrusting away from the local and provincial in favour of the international style. This should not be surprising, given the format of the lecture series published as *The Modern Century* and given Frye's lifelong engagement, as a Canadian, with the fortunes of Canadian literature.[18] His first published writings were twenty-six essays and reviews in the *Canadian Forum*, dating from the mid-1930s on. Later, and more importantly, from 1950 to 1959 Frye published an annual evaluation ('Letters in Canada') of Canadian poets for the *University of Toronto Quarterly*. These latter essays and others were collected in *The Bush Garden* and *Divisions on a Ground*.[19] In the 'Letters in Canada' essays Frye was reacting against all that is provincial, derivative, facile, and unprofessional.[20] He named names, denouncing the weak and timid state of Canadian culture and its dismal past eminences – the likes of

Robert W. Service, Bliss Carman, and Charles G.D. Roberts. He condemned regional nostalgia – bad 'naive' or 'primitive' verse – and the no less facile leftist oratory of the 1950s. He condemned, when necessary, the noxious influence of the seventeenth-century Metaphysicals, Eliot's high canon; and he responded, with a qualified critique, to the overrated Leonard Cohen, Irving Layton, and Al Purdy. This said, Frye was open to and personally encouraged all kinds and all styles of writing, eager to accept divergent modes, to situate poetry in the appropriate mode, and to find the excellence therein. He was able to relate to contemporary modernism in all its manifestations, to encourage new poets and applaud the rise of professionalism while never imposing his own preferences. These essays include some superb practical criticism of individual poets (E.J. Pratt, Jay Macpherson, James Reaney, and George Johnston). Above all, they had an impact on the contemporary scene, helping to launch a 'mythopoeic school' of poetry and also setting the precedent that Canadian literature can be taken seriously, that it is a proper topic for study, therefore, that it has to be judged without indulgence and according to international standards.

In a major article of the 1940s Frye reconsiders the history of Canadian verse, recognizing the merits of some early, forgotten figures and condemning, as he was to do in the 1950s, the sentimental and the *faux* primitive.[21] Brilliantly anticipatory as always, Frye observes how difficult it is for a Canadian poet, in his colonial situation, to write anything of quality in either the imperial or the regional frame. And he denounces fallacies – prevalent also south of the border – for example, that, in the makeup of a poet, life is more important than reading and that one ought to privilege the speech of the common man.

Frye's most important article on Canadian literature, which became an immediate classic, the most quoted piece of Canadian criticism, is his 'Conclusion to a *Literary History of Canada*' of 1965, in which he synthesizes 800 pages by thirty-three scholars and offers his own vision of Canadian literature and Canadian specificity.[22] It is here that Frye tries to define the Canadian imagination and the 'myths' that dominate Canadian cultural history. Among these myths – some of which have, as David Staines observes, become part of the critical vocabulary – are the immensity of space and the pervasiveness of the frontier; nature as coldness, silence, desolation, and terror; the garrison mentality; the quest for a peaceable kingdom, made manifest in nostalgia for the pastoral; and the question 'Where is here?' replacing 'Who am I?'[23] Frye's vision was then taken by others, who, along with Frye, launched 'thematic criticism' as a way to make sense of Canadian literature and the Canadian experience.[24] A similar 'myth criticism' defined the first major contributions to post-Matthiessen American studies.[25]

Frye's career encompasses a number of other fields to which he contributed or, to be more precise, other facets of life which find a place in his system. They include social and cultural critique, education, and religion.[26] Of these, religion is the most important. Northrop Frye was ordained a minister in the United Church of Canada in 1936 and devoted much of his first book (*Fearful Symmetry*) to arguing that the Bible is central to Blake and to Western civilization and that it is the greatest work of art in Western civilization. He then lived the archetypal cycle in his own life by devoting his last two major books to a meditation on the Bible and its functioning in both history and civilization.[27]

In *The Great Code*, to begin with, Frye declares irrelevant all questions pertaining to whether the Bible and its revelation are 'real' or 'true'; he also pushes aside historical analysis of the individual books – that is, research into their historical origins. He considers the Bible as a whole, a totality, a unified structure. For Frye, it is wrong to look for something beneath the alleged 'mythical accretions'; the Bible is the mythical accretions. The Bible is metaphor; its truth is metaphoric and centripetal, not empirical, descriptive, and centrifugal. Or, in Aristotelian terms, the Bible has universal/poetic meaning and, therefore, is superior to history, which is only discursive, descriptive, and particular. The Bible is the key to myth, and not the other way around. Finally, the language of the Bible is metaphor, as are the fundamental Christian tenets such as the real presence in the bread and the wine that are Christ's body and blood. The Bible is language just as God is the Word and the Word is God. In the beginning is the Word, and the Word is made flesh.

Frye builds upon these foundations a number of structures, his purpose to recover that earlier metaphoric discourse and mythological universe. Most importantly, he finds seven phases or stages in the biblical narrative taken as a whole that mark the progression from Genesis to Revelation: creation, revolution, law, wisdom, prophecy, gospel, and apocalypse. Structurally, each phase relates to the next one, following traditional Christian allegory, as typology or figura. That is, each foreshadows the subsequent stage and fulfils the preceding stage. Typology in the Bible functions as structure and as history, itself a vision of history that shaped the Western consciousness for centuries.

In this Protestant comprehension of typology and of Scripture, Frye does not see the break between the Old Testament and the New Testament precisely as a Catholic would. Of course, the New Testament fulfils prophecy in the Old Testament, and the Old Testament is proved true because it is confirmed by the New Testament. Christianity is unique among faiths because of its historical process in time and its particular orientation to the past and to the future. In addition, however, the message of the New Testament is also liberating and revolutionary. Because of the break, because of the Good News, Israel gives way to Christ, the law to faith, the social to the individual, and constraint to freedom. Thus, according to Frye, the Bible repudiates tyranny and slavery, crying out for personal liberation. It is radical and utopian and will always appeal to the radical and utopian impulses of the community.

A second structuring of the whole can be envisioned in terms of comedy and romance. The Bible manifests a cyclical or, more accurately, a 'u' structure. The Great Story begins with creation and bliss in the earthly paradise and will end in rebirth and bliss in the celestial paradise. In between occurs a series of descents: the original Fall of Adam and Eve, followed by the fall of the Children of Israel and so many kings and judges. Yet, through so many quests, exiles, and sacrifices, Scripture offers the hope of return from exile, rising from the fall, and finding one's true home. The beast is to be slain, the Babylon to be overcome. First Christ is reborn, and then the people. We fall, we die, yet we shall rise again (metaphorically), at one with the Son in the wedding of the Song of Songs and at one with the Father at his judgment seat.

The Bible is, thus, the most perfect example of mythological writing, one that gives rise to or, rather, creates the archetypes of our mythological discourse and our culture. Biblical narrative revolves around the prince who is persecuted, exiled, and sacrificed yet who, in the end, slays the dragon, weds the maiden, replaces the aged, impotent king, and replenishes the waste land. The comic/romance structure of the Bible is then mirrored in the 'u' pattern of *The Great Code* (Language I, Myth I, Metaphor I, Typology I, Typology II, Metaphor II, Myth II, Language II) and in the 'u' pattern of Northrop Frye's publishing career: from Blake to secular scripture to sacred scripture.

Considerations of space prevent me from considering *Words with Power* and *The Double Vision*. With the latter two books Frye goes beyond treating the Bible as literature or offering a literary reading of the Bible to speculation on the order of words and the ontological function of language. Hamilton is quite right to focus on Frye's obsession with the Bible and its ties to literature, and with the Word at the centre of our verbal universe.[28] Frye discovers (or creates) a Bible-centred mythology from which all literature descends. To this I should only add that Frye's

work on the Bible makes us realize the extent to which he is a philosopher, a philosopher of the Logos, and that it is his biblically charged
philosophy which has drawn the most recent attention from scholars.[29]

As perhaps the most noted literary critic of his age, in an age of rapidly changing methodology, Northrop Frye has been subject to critique
– some of it scathing – both during the glory days of the 1960s and
1970s and in the period since. Unlike C.S. Lewis, who was attacked for
specific readings of one author or book, the assaults on Frye are, quite
often, totalizing, from people who repudiate his system from A to Z.

The critiques can be ranged under three general headings, all of
which relate to Frye's vision of literature, his theory, so to speak, as stated
in the *Anatomy* and in later works. The first series of critiques objects to
the theory and its structure because they are theory and structure. It
states, grosso modo, that the structure is too 'scientific,' systematic, and
absolute. To create the structure and to adhere to it, Frye would have
ignored the specificity of the individual text in order to force it into pre-
existent universal categories. Finally, some have observed that the system
itself reveals flaws, that it is inconsistent and has 'slippage.'[30]

There is, of course, a kernel of truth in these critiques. Frye himself
was aware of the problem. He observed that, in his eyes, literary criticism
is not a science but an independent discipline or field of study in search
of its own paradigms and parameters. Thus, the structures of the *Anatomy*
are meant to be tentative, to be subject to revision or downright repudiation. In his own words: 'the system was for the sake of the insights it contained: the insights were not there for the sake of the system.'[31]

Secondly, it is true that Frye works outwardly, from the individual
book or poem, to its author's total corpus, to (by genre and archetype)
all of Western literature, to the mythical universe and the order of
words. There is nothing wrong with this. After all, we can observe a comparable expansion or progression in Spitzer, Curtius, and the French
structuralists, including Albert Béguin. Like Eliot but in a far more systematic and philosophically grounded manner, Frye contextualizes the
work ('Lycidas') or writer (Milton) in the European tradition, in a
simultaneous existence and order. That in so doing he may have misread individual texts, such as John Keats's *Endymion*, or that his vision of
the Canadian specificity (and the thematic school of Canadian critics to
which it gave rise) is limited temporally and is guilty of reductionism,
takes nothing from his extraordinary achievements as a systematic and
innovative thinker on literature.[32]

The second series of critiques centres on politics and history. As with
Curtius, left-oriented writers attack Frye for his neglect of history – for

an ahistorical reading of the books – which, they believe, results in conservative politics. Here we find primitive pseudo-Marxism in Pauline Kogan, who denounces Frye for an alleged idealistic philosophy and clerical obscurantism that make him a spokesman for the decadent bourgeoisie.[33] As an example, Kogan cites the historical evolution of the five modes which, she believes, runs counter to the Truth of History: the socio-economic development of the West from primitive communism to feudalism to capitalism (early and late) to socialism. In a similar vein, though admittedly a more sophisticated one, John Fekete claims that because Frye denied the historical dimension of literature and promulgated an ahistorical critical praxis, he also denies the purportedly central function of literature to question the status quo and to initiate radical change, and he thereby capitulates to capitalist domination.[34]

It is not difficult to respond to this sort of jeremiad. Frye does history; not all history is social or economic or Marxist. His is a history proper to literature, the history of literary forms, genres, modes, myths, and archetypes. Angus Fletcher has argued that Frye relates criticism and literature to civilization, the latter perceived as the developmental history of mankind; Frye's is a speculative or philosophical historiography, which includes a Utopian history of the future.[35] It is no less true that Frye's literary theory is also cultural theory; from the 1960s on especially, he is eager to bring literature and criticism to bear on present concerns. Indeed, Helen Vendler critiques Frye for having misread Keats because of his (Frye's) belief that literature has social value and can make people better. Frye opposes the conservative myth of concern (ideology) to a liberating myth of freedom, which can help deliver people from bondage. As a number of critics have observed, Frye never neglects the social dimensions of literature, for he insists that all great literature is a symbolic meditation on the destiny of the community.[36]

The third series of critiques is not unrelated to the second. Here we find protest directed at Frye from the perspective of ideology critique. He endures the same fate and largely for the same reasons as Curtius, Lewis, and Matthiessen.

A number of objective, even-handed scholars question Frye's writings on Canadian literature from the vantage point of postcolonial theory. As they see it, Frye embodies the imperialist or settler mentality, content with his Englishness, so that he ignores the French Canadian presence and manifests a cavalier, unproblematic attitude toward the First Nations and their experience of Canada.[37] Eva Mackey, in addition, indicts Frye, Margaret Atwood, and the Group of Seven for having portrayed a gendered Canada that then contributed to the creation of a gendered Canadian nationalism. Finally, the distinguished critics Robert Alter and Harold Bloom object, from a Jewish perspective, to Frye's biblical hermeneutics. According to Alter, the Canadian scholar revives 'Christian suppressionism'; according to Bloom, he is guilty of 'Christian appropriation and usurpation.'[38]

Several responses to this sort of argument come to mind. First of all, Frye is engaged with the history of mentalities. His categories come not from his own imagination but from the world vision of writers and readers over time. Thus, the settler stance vis-à-vis Canada and the settler disregard of the French Canadian contribution and the aboriginal presence may, perhaps, be imputed to Frye. More to the point, they comprise a good part of the mindset of English Canadian writers from the beginning to the 1960s. Frye depicts Canadian reality historically as it was and is, not as progressive intellectuals would like it to have been.

Similarly, Frye's archetypes are conceived, to some extent, in sexual terms, according to a sexual vision of our world and of the cosmos. In this, he follows Freud and Jung. More to the point, he follows the cosmological vision central to Western civilization for two or three thousand years.

Last of all, of course *The Great Code* and *Words with Power* exhibit Christian suppressionism and Christian appropriation. That is what Christianity is all about. Universal religions, such as Christianity and Islam, incorporate the tribal religions from which they have sprung. Derived from Judaism, Christianity incorporated its source; the typological idea of Jewish foreshadowing and Christian fulfilment begins with the Gospels. That has been the history of biblical commentary and of Christian sacred history for at least eighteen centuries.

As I have observed more than once in this chapter. Frye shares a number of attitudes toward literature and criticism with the other humanist critics. He is opposed to value judgments; he is opposed to the notion of organic evolution – the rise and fall of a literature. He believes in criticism as an independent discipline, not beholden for its methodology to history or the social sciences or the sciences of medicine. He speaks out against the 'stock responses' or critical fallacies that hinder understanding: that a work of art is mimetic and, in some sense, an imitation of nature, or a uniquely powerful emotional response to something, or the reflection of history or a pre-historical myth, or the expression of something important in the poet's life – that is, the revelation of something derived from his experience.[39] Literature is literature. As Frye insists, for the writer and for the critic, it is essential to free oneself from mere experience in order to partake of a genuine tradition, to become universal. This means that literature is a construct, made up of words, signs, images, symbols, archetypes, genres, modes, and myths, that it adheres to and develops from conventions, and that these conventions are in fact the workings of literature.

In this way, Frye expands the idea of criticism, defined as 'the whole work of scholarship and taste concerned with literature,'[40] which becomes, in addition, all reflection, philosophical and otherwise, on literature. *The Anatomy of Criticism* and *The Great Code* are coherent and completed systems of the literary, and of the sacred to the extent that it is literary. These systems are multidimensional, in that they are both synchronic and diachronic; they treat the various genres and modes as a structure of potentiality in space and as the structuring of actuality in time. In other words, unlike the other humanist critics, Frye is a theorist, perhaps the first, and he remains one of the most important.

Unlike most of the others, he lived long enough to be aware of the various postmodern critiques of his system and of his beliefs. Joseph Adamson and Imre Salusinszky have sketched, with sensitivity and insight, how Frye can and did respond to the new methodologies.[41] Frye finds, in literature as a social and cultural phenomenon, two myths: the myth of concern and the myth of freedom. Those who see in literature only ideology, or only a cultural site of political warfare and resistance to hegemony, or only questions of race, class, and gender, are cultivating the myth of concern.[42] As Frye sees it, literature also embodies the myth of freedom, which implies an imaginative response that has the authority to separate literature from its ideology and historical background, to grant it meaning and significance in the universal order of words, and to justify its value to succeeding generations. This objective and disinterested element allows literature to outlive the culture of its time and, by its inherent complexity, to make a place for multiple readings and multiple levels of critique, well beyond the less problematic manifestations of the myth of concern.

Frye can help us resist the extremes of ideology and the schools that reduce literature to its ideas or to the social class and gender of its creators. As a secular humanist, Frye insists on the greatness and relevance of the great books, and insists that they, not the ideologues, are emancipatory, and that they help preserve civilization in our age of technology, alienation, and imposed ideology, whether of the Right or the Left. For this I am thankful.

PART TWO

9 Discussion

Eight critics, three languages (German, French, English), and the educational and academic environment of seven national traditions: Austria, Germany, Switzerland, France, the United Kingdom, the United States, and Canada. What do these scholars of literature have in common? How can we place them in literary and cultural history? How are we to differentiate them from their predecessors and their successors?

We find patterns of shared interests. Spitzer and Curtius were impressed by the Spanish Golden Age as a milestone in the history of literature and as a cultural phenomenon that affected both of them emotionally. Spitzer, Curtius, and Auerbach all wrote on Dante. The Dante chapter is one summit in Curtius's *European Literature and the Latin Middle Ages*; Auerbach's *Dante: Poet of the Secular World* anticipates the Dante chapter in *Mimesis*. For both Curtius and Auerbach, the *Commedia* represents a high point in the Middle Ages and in the entire cultural history of the West. For both, no less important is the cultural contribution from medieval writings in Latin over the centuries and the literature in medieval French.

Lewis and Frye published major essays on Spenser and path-breaking books on Milton. For them, Spenser and Milton embody the English tradition at its best. Similarly, on the continent Curtius and Béguin wrote cutting-edge books on Balzac, treating him as a creator of myths rather than as the father of realism. Important Balzac essays come also from Rousset. Lewis and Frye had a predilection for the romance genre, medieval and modern. So also did Matthiessen, with regard to Hawthorne and Melville although he did not often utilize the term.

These critics do not neglect the twentieth century, the writers of their own time. Matthiessen and Frye published sensitive, insightful books on

Eliot, in spite of the fact that they found his politics to be distasteful. Spitzer and Curtius published major studies on Proust. Spitzer and Rousset wrote on the contemporary French *nouveau roman*: Spitzer on Butor, and Rousset on Robbe-Grillet and Simon. Curtius 'discovered' the *Nouvelle Revue Française* writers in France, Béguin 'discovered' Bernanos, and Frye 'discovered' modern Canadian poetry.

All three German-language scholars read widely in and were influenced by some of the major German philosophers: Immanuel Kant, Schelling, Feuerbach, Dilthey, and Heidegger. Béguin and Frye share their passion; so also, although to a lesser extent, does Matthiessen. Auerbach and Frye were inspired by Vico; Auerbach's first important book was a partial translation of the *Scienza Nova*.

And shared dislikes? Curtius, Béguin, and Rousset all reacted against French classicism, condemning not only the narrowness of classicism itself but also the narrowness of a cultural establishment that would exalt one element of the national tradition to the exclusion of the rest. Spitzer and Auerbach made the same statement in a more subtle manner by working on all of French literature without privileging *le grand siècle* in any way.

Lewis and Frye did not, of course, participate in this debate; it was not part of their culture. On the other hand, they objected to the elevation of the English metaphysical poets – John Donne, George Herbert, Richard Crashaw, and their colleagues – to the exclusion of the rest. Although Matthiessen liked the Metaphysicals, he also liked Milton, and he condemned the English eighteenth century, which is in some ways the equivalent of French classicism.

Given these stands, are the eight figures, unlike the American New Critics, in some sense of the term romantics? Frye declared himself, in response to Eliot's classicism, to be a Protestant, romantic disciple of Blake. Béguin declared his preference for the German romantics, the late French romantics, and the French moderns over seventeenth- and eighteenth-century classicism. Lewis, of a romantic temper, loved his Scott and Shelley, and for that matter his Morris and Kipling. All he wrote on literature was in defence of an English canon that the New Criticism had repudiated. And the American Renaissance so prized by Matthiessen – that literature of the 1840s and 1850s – can be designated American high romanticism. On the other hand, Rousset privileges the baroque and the eighteenth century; Auerbach privileges the nineteenth-century novel of realism; Spitzer loves all literature from all the centuries.

Although the eight were influenced by German idealist philosophy, and although they share certain aesthetic presuppositions with the European romantics, especially the cult of the work of art, many of their beliefs are not romantic at all. Among these other beliefs are to be found the impersonality of the poet and the functioning in literary creativity of rhetoric, stylistic register, genre, and convention. In the last analysis, they rebelled against the literary orthodoxies of their age. They undermined the institutional academic dogma upheld by their teachers and their colleagues. In this respect they are rebels and nonconformists, rather like the antihumanist postmodernists today.

One reason, perhaps, for the nonconformity can be derived from the historical events that shaped their lives. Just as much of academic postmodernism can be ascribed to the student revolts of the 1960s, the humanist critics were defined by more staggering events: the First World War, the rise of Hitler, and the Second World War. Spitzer and Curtius fought against the rise of cultural anarchy and violence in Weimar Germany; Curtius protested against Germany's then narrow, stultifying, provincial cultural nationalism. The Second World War disrupted their lives totally. Curtius changed his field of research and wrote his best book. Auerbach was forced into exile and wrote his best book. Spitzer was forced into exile and onto a world stage in America. Off in Basel, Béguin joined the intellectual Resistance, became a Catholic and a French cultural nationalist, eventually moved to Paris, and changed his field of research. The war and the postwar developments in America, including the anticommunist witch hunts, helped orient Matthiessen's political and aesthetic commitments and, in the end, led to his suicide. As for Lewis, the war offered the occasion for his first Christian talks on radio. The talks made him famous and changed the course of his life.

Postmodernist opinion tells us that the predecessors were reactionary elitists in their politics or that they were hypocritically and cowardly apolitical, which amounts to the same thing. The accusation is accurate, in part but only in part, for the New Critics. It is totally off for the eight discussed in this book. Béguin was a Christian socialist, a man of the Left active in the public sphere as a writer and journal editor. Matthiessen was a Christian socialist, a man of the Left active in the public sphere as a labour union organizer and representative. Frye was a man of the Left – let us say the Centre-Left – who wrote and spoke out on any number of social issues. All three believed passionately in, and devoted a part of their lives to, the struggle for democracy and creating a better world. Michel Jeanneret informs me that his colleague, Jean Rousset, the most discreet of men, was also a Christian socialist. On the other side, Lewis despised the post-1945 Labour Party and all it stood for, especially the welfare state. He rebelled against what he thought was a new tyranny, the tyranny of demagogic extremism. He was also reacting against the snobbish, complacent, upper-class leftists who nested in Oxbridge and who were the academic Establishment. Curtius was a Christian conservative and a public intellectual who wrote against demagogic extremism, on the Left and on the Right, denouncing the harm to German intellectual life represented by the Nazis. *Persona non grata* during the Hitler years, he published no books and gave no lectures abroad. And he nominated Auerbach ahead of himself for a university chair at Basel. Finally, Spitzer and Auerbach were victims of the Nazi terror; they behaved with dignity and courage during their years of exile in Turkey and in North America. They, along with Rousset, let their scholarship speak for them. With all three, it radiated a passion for the human spirit. With all three – with all eight – there was never cowardice or hypocrisy or the mean-spirited defence of institutional power for its own sake.

With regard to religion, we find a strong Christian presence, as was the case for the New Critics. Curtius was a deeply committed Protestant, Béguin a fervent convert to the Catholic Church, Lewis a fervent convert to the Protestant Church, Matthiessen a deeply committed Anglican, and Frye an ordained minister in the United Church of Canada. Lewis was perhaps the leading Christian apologist in the twentieth century; Béguin and Frye wrote extensively on religious topics. Rousset was a non-practicing Catholic. Spitzer and Auerbach were Jews; we would say, nowadays, that they were of Jewish descent. Both felt a powerful attraction for European Catholicism, Spitzer for the Spanish tradition and Auerbach for the French. Both deemed Dante to be their poet. No one did more to understand, to interpret, and to present, with sympathy, the history and cultural contributions of Christianity to Europe, the fact that, over the centuries, European civilization was and still is (culturally) a Christian civilization.

As a consequence, some of the humanist critics were public intellectuals who functioned in the public sphere. This was certainly the case for Curtius, Béguin, Lewis, Matthiessen and Frye. Spitzer and Auerbach, in spite of themselves, also participated if only by their presence in America at a particular time under particular circumstances. Jean Rousset alone was able to limit his persona to his scholarly writings. The other seven all addressed, in one way or another, contemporary issues. All were concerned, during and after the Second World War, with the future of culture and, for that matter, the future of society itself. Without ever seeking to impose their own ideology or the ideology of a party or a clique, they posed so many important questions and offered a number of important answers. And they did it with authenticity, courage, dignity, and what I would call nobility, in contrast to some of the successors such as the one-time fascist journalist Paul de Man and the one-time Nazi Waffen SS officer Hans Robert Jauss.

From a strictly critical perspective, what, if anything, do the humanist scholars have in common? With the partial exception of Auerbach, all proclaimed the autonomy of literary study: that it is a discipline with its own rules and goals, and that it must not be made tributary to external disciplines such as psychology, anthropology, biography, and history. All eight, including Auerbach, were committed to the close reading of the text itself, to privileging the text, especially its language and style, over extratextual questions concerning, for example, the author's life or his intentions. In this they resemble the Anglo-American New Critics, the French structuralists, and the Russian Formalists. The end of agency and the death of the author are notions scarcely invented by postmodernists. On the contrary, they are the central tenets of all significant schools of criticism – except for the Marxist – in the twentieth century.

The humanist critics and the others arrived at their respective positions by reacting against – rebelling against – the literary studies in vogue during their formative years. For the Middle Ages, these were a dry, narrow philology limited to the editing of texts and to language study: the linguistic analysis of Old French or Middle English and, more particularly, the putative dialect of the author and the putative dialect(s) of the scribe(s). For more recent works, these were a dry, narrow literary history, concentrating on the author's biography, his intellectual formation, and, above all, his sources. In other words, they were reacting against a series of academic disciplines which, whatever their value otherwise, never came to grips with literature itself, never addressed actual novels and poems. Secondarily, the humanists distanced themselves from general, impressionistic literary essays, written often outside the academy by gentlemen of taste or conviction. In the United States it was the progressive, nativist convictions of a Parrington and a Brooks and Brooks's genteel impressionism that form the backdrop to *American Renaissance*.

It is nonetheless true, however, that even though Spitzer, Curtius, Auerbach, Béguin, Rousset, Lewis, Matthiessen, and Frye rebelled against the *Literaturwissenschaft, histoire littéraire,* and literary history of their day, they had been formed by the philologists and historians, had learned from them, and, often, paid them respect. Unlike some adherents of the recent schools, they were themselves solidly grounded in philology and history, and they knew their colleagues' work. One reason for their success and the lasting power of their books is the scholarship, the fact that they were innovative critics and, at the same time, men of erudition, true scholars.

Because of the past scholarship, which was largely historically oriented, and because of their philosophy of the autonomy of the text, the humanist critics held a problematic, ambiguous stance toward history. As we saw earlier, Rousset's position was that history is a helpful and perfectly respectable ancillary discipline, worthy of esteem, with which the critic should be familiar. Yet it is not criticism. The critic must be a critic and not a historian. Rousset and the others lived the distinction even though some of them might have objected to so broad and all-inclusive a formulation. What a Rousset or a Frye meant by such a statement is the following: the sources, the genesis, and the *composition* of a work of art are largely irrelevant to our criticism of it; irrelevant also the details of the author's biography; irrelevant the author's intention in writing; and irrelevant the contemporary public's interpretation in listening or reading. Once again, the humanist critics' procedure does not differ markedly from those of the Russian Formalists, the New Critics, and the structuralists.

A significant difference can be observed with regard to the results. All eight men studied in this book were indeed historians, but of a kind foreign to standard literary history and to Marxist dialectical materialism. Their contributions fall into two categories: the history of literary tropes, genres, and conventions over the centuries, and the history of *mentalités*, mental structures or mindsets over the centuries. (More on this later.) This is not social or economic history, nor is it the *ressentiment* of minorities. It is nevertheless history and, because of its scope and range, as important as the others to interpreting our culture.

Because of the autonomy of the text and the critic, a direct personal relationship exists between the critic and the book he is reading. Spitzer's movement toward the 'inward life-centre' and the subsequent 'click,' and Auerbach's *Ansatzphänomen* bear witness to a scholar's personal and, yes, emotional, immediate response to a book, or to an increment, stylistic or other, in the book. Curtius also speaks of the critic's personal, sympathetic, intuitive commitment to what he reads. The response can be scholarly and intellectual; it is also intuitive. We see the passion, the love, on most pages of Béguin and Lewis. Even Frye, so averse to value judgments, is a man of sympathy and empathy, a follower of Blake and not Valéry. He, like Spitzer, performs a *critique des beautés*, as do all eight, a *critique des beautés* and not a reading for evil, one penchant today. Therefore, it follows that all eight hold to the value of the texts they study; they believe in the great books and their tradition.

Also unlike the postmodernists, except for Frye, the humanist critics were not philosophers and not theoreticians. Spitzer, Auerbach, and Matthiessen devoted an article or two, in their later years after they had become famous, to accounting for their methodology. A preliminary chapter in more than one book served the same purpose in Béguin and Rousset. Lewis, the most pragmatic of all, authored two brief volumes which I have called theory though they can also be deemed personal polemic.

Although, as cultured, well-educated people, the humanists knew philosophy and owed much to philosophers (Vico, Kant, the German Idealists), they felt little need to justify what they were doing or to question the fundamental principles of culture and life. Vico, Dilthey, and Benedetto Croce played a much smaller role in their lives than do Friedrich Nietzsche, Jacques Derrida, Michel Foucault, and Jürgen Habermas in ours.

Current theoretical sophistication marks an advance over the critics and scholars of earlier generations. We cannot go back to a pretheoretical age, nor would we want to. On the other hand, the humanists' relative neglect of philosophy, plus the fact that they lived in a less compartmentalized world, gave them one advantage over a number of our theorists today. They wrote for a general cultured and intellectual public, not just for other scholars in the field. The scope and range of their work caused them to transcend any one narrow field. Béguin and Lewis, and perhaps also Curtius and Frye, wrote a beautiful, arresting, high literary prose. All eight wrote with clarity and precision, with force and elegance. This is one reason why most of them became, at one time in their lives, intellectuals in the public sphere, whereas most of us today are not.

What do they share in terms of achievement? First of all, with the exception of Spitzer, each published at least one major book, a big book we might say, a Fryvian anatomy, massive, authoritative, all-encompassing, like an ornate and highly structured work of art. Such are *Europäische Literatur und lateinisches Mittelalter, Mimesis, L'âme romantique et le rêve, La littérature de l'âge baroque en France, The Allegory of Love* and

English Literature in the Sixteenth Century, American Renaissance, and *Anatomy of Criticism* and *The Great Code.* Such also would be one of the major article collections by Spitzer. Such books remade the entire field of literary studies. In a sense, they were oppositional books, demystifying clichés and the critical dogmas of the moment, opening windows and bringing fresh air into the academy. They were supremely innovative, as innovative as the best work of the structuralists, deconstructors, and new historicists.

Given these critics' belief in the autonomy of literature, and given their personal, emotive, intuitive response to the text, we can understand that practical criticism – the reading of an individual work of art as a work of art – looms large in their perspective and will always play a significant role in their work. This is true, obviously, for Spitzer, Auerbach, and Lewis. But, as I have insisted, the others – Curtius, Béguin, Rousset, Matthiessen, and Frye – accused of having sacrificed the close reading of texts to the elaboration of a system, either in the systematic book or elsewhere, nonetheless contributed superb interpretations of individual works. Although Spitzer is unique in the quantity of articles that remain the best on the topic, studies by the others endure also and are discussed and profited from today.

As we have seen, the humanist critics developed a number of approaches to literature which anticipate more recent developments, making them pioneers of New Criticism, structuralism, and poststructuralism. Among the later methodologies anticipated or actually practiced by the humanists can be listed the sociology of literature (*sociocritique*) (Auerbach, Lewis, Matthiessen), reception theory (Auerbach, Lewis, Frye), Freudian criticism (Spitzer), Jungian criticism (Béguin, Frye), rhetorical criticism (Curtius, Auerbach), structuralism (Curtius, Rousset, Frye), narratology (Spitzer, Rousset, Frye), stylistics (Spitzer, Curtius, Auerbach), phenomenology (Spitzer, Curtius, Béguin, Rousset, Matthiessen, Frye), and, for all eight, intertextuality, the history of mentalities, and, in some sense of the term, cultural studies. This offers one explanation for the fact that the eight are quoted and footnoted all the time and that some of them are prized by a number of our foremost critical minds today: Said on Auerbach, and Jameson and Kermode on Frye, to give two examples.

The anatomies these men created are works of extraordinary scope and range. Think of literature from Homer to Proust (Auerbach), from late antiquity to Diderot (Curtius), from late antiquity to Spenser (Lewis), and from the early Middle Ages to the twentieth century (Spitzer), in a handful of languages. The seemingly more modest endeavours – two centuries of German romanticism and French modernism (Béguin), one century of the French baroque (Rousset), ten years of the American nineteenth century (Matthiessen) – are comparable in knowledge, imagination, and authority. As for Frye, from one vantage point he 'covers' literature, largely English, from *Beowulf* and Chaucer to Eliot and Joyce; from another perspective, he conceptualizes all literature everywhere, a cosmology or ontology of literature. These critics bring to us a sense of time and history (*longue durée*), a vastness of erudition and culture, which, in comparison, make even the most prominent advocates of the more recent schools a trifle thin.

Their work offers new visions of literature in its evolution over time, therefore new ways of configuring literary history. From Curtius we have a centuries-old continuum of rhetorical topoi, the alternation of periods of classical style and of mannerist style, and the transmission of culture from antiquity to us through the medium of Latin. From Auerbach we have the separation of styles and the figural reading of history leading to renewed ways of representing reality, with a first summit in Dante and a second in Balzac, Stendhal, Flaubert, and Zola. From Béguin we have the authors of German romanticism as pioneers in mental attitudes (the dream experience) and in writing that are the origin of French and European modernism. From Rousset we have a baroque literature, located after Renaissance classicism and before Louis XIV classicism, to be accounted for by its own unique structures, images, and phenomenology; also a rich, exciting, and narratologically innovative eighteenth-century novel prior to Balzac and Stendhal. From Lewis we have a revalorized medieval and Renaissance universe, largely the same, notable for its practice of allegory, courtly love, chivalry, and the high courtly mode of writing; the Renaissance goes wrong when it abandons the medieval heritage. From Matthiessen we have a Renaissance of American literature, in the nineteenth century, that exhibits high aesthetic ideals and the exploration of democratic values, tempered and enriched by its vision of Christian tragedy. From Frye we have the entire Western tradition grounded in the Bible, with comedy and romance the dominant forms and with a series of dominant modes over the centuries. Whether or not their original formulations have been modified, whether or not we agree with them, because of these scholars we cannot envisage entire centuries and movements as we used to. No writer studied by Spitzer can be the same to us. We cannot think of literature or of history in the same way.

The broad view and the new visions apply especially to the canon. The eight figures all brought to light and caused to be taken seriously writers previously neglected, from the past and the present. With Béguin we think of Bloy, Bernanos, and at least half a dozen modern French Catholic poets. With Frye we think of Blake, Beddoes, and at least half a dozen modern Canadian poets. In addition, entire traditions are brought back and raised to the forefront of our attention: literature in medieval Latin and in Old French, the Scots Makars, the French baroque, French eighteenth-century fiction, the German romantics, the age of Hawthorne and Melville, and modernism in all its guises. The canon is expanded, not contracted as was the case with the New Critics; unlike the New Critics and the poststructuralists, no works and no periods have to be sacrificed to make way for the newly discovered and the newly prominent.

On the one hand, most of the eight critics proclaim the centrality of the Middle Ages and the Renaissance; Western culture is perceived to be an incomplete, ongoing project, with the Middle Ages vital to its development and to our understanding of it. During a century when, because of *Historismus*, we could appreciate for the first time the cultures of the past, and when, at the same time, ignorance of and contempt for the past was just arising, these men struggled to understand and to maintain our culture and civilization, all that makes up, inevitably, a past and a history.

At the same time, as we have seen, most of the eight also engaged with their contemporary literature, the literature of modernism and modernity. They knew the modern and worked with it. They recognized that the past cannot exist without the present just as the present cannot exist without the past. While readily accepting some sort of *Alterität* (Otherness) between, for example, the mental structures of the Middle Ages and ours (Spitzer and Lewis are peremptory in this regard), they believed no less passionately in the continuity of culture and the human condition, in a sense the continuing, perennial centrality of the culture of the past, contemporaneous with us in our culture. Culture can be seen as a bulwark for us in an age of technology and alienation. Curtius, Auerbach, and Béguin saw it as their response to the Nazis and what Nazi Germany stood for. It was a European response, the hallmark of a millennium-old high culture, a tribute to the greatness and the uniqueness of the West.

Given the call, at the Stanford conference, for looking at Auerbach in his time instead of being timeless, I wish to follow their example and consider our eight critics as they relate to the greater historical and intellectual movements of our age, specifically humanism, modernism, and postmodernism. The humanism will be especially apt, given the title of this book and, therefore, one of the assumptions under which it is written.

A first difficulty lies in fact that the three terms – humanism, modernism, and postmodernism – are *surcodés*: they account for a myriad of differing phenomena, and scholars have written on them from a myriad of differing perspectives. Let us begin with a brief sketch of humanism.

Humanism refers, first of all, to a historical phenomenon of the Renaissance. Here also, the scholarship on Renaissance humanism is enormous and has given rise to divergent interpretations.

There is what can be called the traditional view of Renaissance humanism and the 'Renaissance man,' largely of nineteenth-century origin. This view states that the humanists read the Greek and the Latin classics, for the first time, as literature, and that they brought the classics back into the European mainstream. Responding to the decline of the Church and to an atrophied medieval metaphysics, they sought ethical standards directly from human experience, that is, a lay morality with ethical conduct conceived as an end in itself. They even proclaimed the autonomy and dignity of man and of man's reason, valid apart from metaphysics, a new radical freedom from the constraints of the past. In sum, they invented modernity, they are the ancestors of modern man; our faith in human freedom and the rights of the individual come from them.

Although this traditional view is still taught in the schools and holds sway as a commonly accepted fact of history, especially among those who today attack humanism, the scholars have revised it almost out of recognition. At the same time, they disagree among themselves over any number of other questions. Given constraints of time and space, rather than sketch out a number of conflicting scholarly positions, I shall attempt my own brief synthesis relying primarily on three leading authorities, themselves in disagreement: Hans Baron, Paul Oskar Kristeller, and William J. Bouwsma.[1]

There was no humanist revolution in the Renaissance. The humanists were, first and foremost, schoolteachers. They taught grammar, rhetoric, poetry, history, and ethics as the increments of a general education rather than for professional training. The concentration was on grammar and, especially, rhetoric. Although the *cursus* was meant to prepare students for verbal communication, the techniques of *persuasio* were oriented toward Latin and not the vernaculars. After 1400, for a brief period in Florence, the *umanisti* contributed to civic humanism, reaching out toward the active life of the citizen. The assumption was always that humanistic studies will develop virtue, will make one a better and more truly Christian person.

Throughout the Middle Ages people venerated the literature and culture of antiquity. Throughout the Middle Ages people believed in man's dignity and his ability, through reason, to know the universe and even to know God. The Renaissance humanists were all Christian; a number of them were ordained priests. They were, except for that period in Florence, apolitical; they relished the contemplative life and endorsed a hereditary or elective monarchy. Oriented toward the past rather than toward the future, to the extent that they held a personal philosophy, they tended to be Christian Platonists. And they were text-centred, book people. In sum, the humanists embodied a broad cultural movement centred on classical and Christian education, proclaiming the value of the humanities, with a consciousness of the Graeco-Roman past, therefore of change over time, and a program of civic Christian virtue best expressed through rhetoric.

The term *studia humanitatis* dates from antiquity, and *umanista* dates from the fifteenth century. The term for humanism itself was first coined by Friedrich Niethammer in 1809. *Humanismus* meant a secondary school and university curriculum grounded in the study of the classics – Greek and Latin language, literature, and culture. The goal, supported by G.W.F. Hegel, Wilhelm von Humboldt, and others, was the cultural development of the North German bourgeoisie. This *Bildung* entails a process of the individual's inner, personal, spiritual growth; the growth, it was assured, would then support the mission of a new Germany.

A still more recent development is the humanism espoused by the American Humanist Association as explained by writers associated with the movement, especially Corliss Lamont and Paul Kurtz.[2] From their perspective, humanism is atheism, materialism, faith in science and technology, the belief in progress, and a commitment to philanthropy and social justice. Rebelling against the then standard orthodoxy of the Protestant denominations, especially the Evangelicals, and against Roman Catholicism, these humanists proclaimed a naturalistic metaphysics, the denial of supernatural religions, the scientific method applied to all domains of human endeavour, an ethical system aiming at happiness, freedom, progress, common decency, compassion, altruism, and personal excellence – in sum, a life-affirming, positive alternative to the repression they thought was inherent in supernaturally based systems. Significantly, according to James Hankins, one motivation for Kristeller's life work was his desire to rescue genuine Renaissance humanism from this American distortion.[3] He may have also been concerned that the Americans, fetishizing science and progress, were hostile to a classical education.

Ever since Flaubert and Nietzsche, great writers have attacked human-ism. The humanism they attack is neither the doctrine and practice of the Middle Ages or the Renaissance or German romanticism. It corre-sponds to the doctrine of some nineteenth-century philosophers, Auguste Comte and Herbert Spencer among others, who subscribe to the notion of man as an end in himself and as the measure of all things; of a fixed, static, universal human nature; and of the necessary better-ment of society through science and technology. (Comte and Spencer also stand behind twentieth-century American humanism.) This humanism corresponds also to the practice of the nineteenth- and twen-tieth-century bourgeoisie, with its insufferably complacent espousal of a feel-good optimism or vague humanitarianism, plus again the bland, automatic faith in science, technology, progress, evolution, and peace; this in contrast to what the writers thought was the reality of the bour-geoisie: rapacious, intolerant, and domineering, using their classical education as one weapon among many to maintain their privileges and their hegemony. In other words, humanism was assimilated to the modern condition, and the protest against modernity included denun-ciation of what writers believed to be the underlying intellectual founda-tions for modernity.

This said, so many who denounce bourgeois humanism offer their own, personal, revisionist humanism in its stead. Hence, the radical Sartrean humanism that conceives a human condition wherein each person is free to construct his humanity, for man is always a process with, at the centre, his subjectivity and the consciousness of his freedom, subjectivity, and the process.[4] Hence, the Christian humanism of Jacques Maritain, according to whom, because of the Incarnation, man is redeemed in God by God.[5] Given his Christ-centred conscience and consciousness, he finds the justification for freedom and fulfilment, his own and that of society as a whole. Hence, Heidegger's antihumanism, which, although it proclaims that he is in no way a humanist, nonethe-less, like the modern humanisms, takes a stance against metaphysics and metaphysical certitude and proclaims that man is the site where Being is revealed and made manifest.[6] Eventually, Heidegger commits to his own *Kehre* from ontology to meditations on poetry and language. Hence, a radical Marxist humanism centred on human beings with no fixed or given human nature, who, conscious of the reality of technology and also of class struggle and the central role of the working class, will create a better world through world revolution.[7] According to this doctrine, man differs from all other animals by his work and by the fact that he works in society; these are the fundamental elements that cannot be explained other than by dialectical materialism. The goal of Marxism is a society that will enable each person to flourish and to fulfil himself to his greatest capacity.

There are other humanisms, some of which respond to the assaults on humanism from postmodernists and some of which, sympathetic to the postmodernist vision, seek to negotiate a new humanism, one that will respect the cultures of the non-European peoples and not attempt to impose universalist transcendent values.[8] The great intellectual Edward W. Said argues, in what may well have been his last book, published posthumously, for an enlightened humanism that will retain the best of the old humanisms and also be open to and embrace the new.[9] One conclusion to be drawn is that, no matter what anybody says, humanism is a charmed term that scholars and philosophers will not abandon. A second is that more than one humanism functions today in the Zeitgeist and that humanism can also be defined as the contest between current humanisms.

It is easier to approach modernism, even in so brief a sketch. Although the opposition between *antiqui* and *moderni* goes back to Cicero, as does the notion of *studia humanitatis*, the sundry historical manifestations over the centuries of the new and contemporary are largely irrelevant to my purpose. The theoretical debates of the last fifty years concern our *moderni*, the modernism that defines so much of twentieth-century high culture. Scholars as far apart as Hugo Friedrich and Northrop Frye agree that the new international style begins in the 1860s with Baudelaire, Flaubert, and perhaps Marx, and that it extends up to the Second World War and beyond.[10]

One problem arises from the fact that some professors of English (especially in the United States), familiar only with the Anglo-American tradition, make general statements about modernism based on this restricted corpus.[11] Drawing their argument from Eliot, Pound, Lawrence, Yeats, and Joyce, a number have claimed that modernism is inherently reactionary and elitist, if not 'objectively fascist.' Had they been familiar with Russian futurism and French surrealism, with Vladimir Mayakovsky, Éluard, and Aragon, plus Bertolt Brecht, the young André Malraux, Salvatore Quasimodo, Federico García Lorca, and Pablo Neruda, they would have recognized the emancipatory-revolutionary strain in modernism.

We might begin by making the clear distinction between modernity – the historical reality of life from 1860 to 1960 – and modernism – the central thrust in the arts, especially literature, during that period.

Modernity is seen by the modernists to be embodied in science, technology, industry, materialism, capitalism, imperialism, instrumentalism, the belief in progress, and the belief in democracy. With the exception of a handful of writers who joyed in modernity – F.T. Marinetti and Whitman, for example – the vast majority of modernists rebelled against, indeed repudiated, the ills of modern life, and they did so from both the Left and the Right.

We find, among the great moderns, masters of tragic realism whose works reflect the political, social, and economic structures of contemporary life, grounded in history, with the middle and the lower classes treated seriously and awakening to consciousness. Such are, each in his own way, Thomas Mann, Heinrich Mann, Anton Chekhov, Maxim Gorky, Zola, Malraux, Dreiser, and Hemingway. This is certainly true. At the same time, I should make the case that, in our modernist century, all the arts repudiate the conventions of Western mimesis since the Renaissance – that is, they break with visual perspective, the box stage, and the traditional coherent plot, rounded characters, and social commentary to be found in the modern novel.

Therefore, in terms of form, the majority of modernists created fragmented, disjointed, and tormented texts that reflect, as objective correlatives, the fragmentation, disjointedness, and torment of modern life. These texts testify to a frankly elitist stance vis-à-vis the literary public: hence the fact that some of them are intentionally arcane and obscure, and hence also a stylistic register that sometimes diverges enormously from the demotic. Such texts make special demands on the reader or audience, who are obliged to work in order to understand and enjoy. The aesthetic stance includes extraordinary artistic self-consciousness in the subject-author and a will to the artistic autonomy of the object-text, which becomes self-reflexive and, as we say nowadays, metatextual. An extreme manifestation of the modernist aesthetic has been categorized as the avant-garde, which, in Dada and surrealism, reveals a powerful sense of antagonism, agonism, and nihilism, directed toward all other contemporary art including the modernist and which, consequently, gives rise to rich formal experimentation.

Critics on the Left, such as Wilson and Lukács, accuse the writers of an imagination severed from reality, the refusal of the real world and its history, a pathological subjectivity, and a concentration on pure form to the exclusion of content.[12] On the other hand, it can be maintained, with greater validity, that the fragmentation and distortion, the pathology and angst, reflect the reality of reification and alienation in the twentieth century and do so in the same way that Picasso paints his reality. With this understanding, readers can empathize with the pain and ugliness that emanate from so many modernist works, the crisis of the subject and of individual personality, their shock value, impersonality, dehumanization, sadomasochism, and irrationality.

Edmund Wilson argues that the movement he calls symbolism, what today we call modernism, embodies a second romantic reaction against classicism. Renato Poggioli points to romanticism as a precedent for the avant-garde, listing the traits that they have in common.[13] In addition, the repudiation of reason, rationality, and social decorum associates one facet of modernism with romanticism. The same is true for modernism as protest, and especially the protest of the young against a repressive, bourgeois social order, resulting in the modernist cult of young people and their *cénacles* of rebellion. Here also can be situated the modernist infatuation with evil and with criminal elements, a theme launched by Baudelaire and Rimbaud which culminates in Céline and Jean Genet. This is certainly true. I should argue, at the same time, that the modernist writers also rebel against certain strands in late romanticism: its cult of the personality, its sentimentality, its roots in folklore, and its fetishizing genteel domesticity.

I restate then, the notion that modernist writers, whether of the Left or the Right, are, almost by definition, oppositional and contestatory. On the one hand, they celebrate the New. On the other hand, because of their oppositional, contestatory stance vis-à-vis the contemporary modern, they develop a complex, problematic attitude toward the past. We find nostalgia for an idealized past, the mythical premodern organic society, in some of the conservative modernists: Pound, Eliot, Claudel, and Hofmannsthal, among others. More common is the practice of intertextuality. While repudiating the relatively recent past culture cherished by the bourgeoisie – situated in figures such as Shelley and Tennyson or Hugo and Anatole France – the modernists do not hesitate to incorporate vast elements of the preceding culture, classical, medieval, and modern, largely European but also African and Asian, in works that revel in and are the modern manifestation of Goethe's *Weltliteratur.* They reject the narrow bourgeois *Bildung* while, at the same time, declaring their own cultural antecedents, a tradition wider, broader, and more authentically universal than had ever been the case previously. They create a cosmopolitan style, what Frye calls the international style, antagonistic to provincialism and to narrow nationalisms, therefore excoriated by totalitarian regimes, communist and fascist alike.[14]

Postmodernism is surely the most problematic of the three movements, in part because we are contemporaneous with it, and accounting for a contemporary phenomenon poses quite special problems; secondly, because postmodernism proclaims itself to be in a 'post' situation vis-à-vis modernism, in some sense dependent on modernism, and, therefore, our understanding of it has to rely on our understanding of the 'pre' phenomenon. Scholars have quite rightly asked whether we should conceive postmodernism to be a crisis or revolt within modernism, a break from and the conscious rejection of modernism, the extreme form of modernism (a late modernism), the necessary and inevitable outcome of modernism, the commercialization and domestication of modernism, or an entirely independent phenomenon that just happened to come into being chronologically after the modernist one. They also question whether postmodernism manifests greatness or decline, positive values or nihilism, a new vision or the same old thing, and whether it is a serious cultural phenomenon or merely a fad or a joke. Furthermore, one person's postmodernism is another person's modernism, and vice versa.

A good place to start would be to distinguish postmodernism from postmodernity, often called the postmodern condition, as we did with modernism and modernity. According to the most influential theorists, we now dwell in a series of interlocking structures dependent on and rising from the phenomenon of globalization, an all-powerful international capitalism, and its all-pervasive technology, especially the technology of communication. It is impossible to escape these structures. Hence the notion of the simulacrum: our sense of reality is replaced by multiplying signs and representations. The only reality is virtual reality. Since all of our contemporary culture simulates, we can perceive no reality behind the simulacrum other than itself. Our being functions uniquely in signs and simulacra. From another perspective, because the economic has invaded all domains of culture, our culture is now pervasively economic, nothing other than a commodity. Cultural production is economic production offering a commodity of signs that, once again, no longer reflect reality. Given this situation, the grand narratives of the past which made a claim for universality – Christian faith, socialist or democratic emancipation, social justice, and for that matter progress and the truths of science – prove to be invalid. On the contrary, these grand narratives and metanarratives are delegitimized because of capitalist technoscience and because their very discourses are tied to the forces that hold power and exert hegemony.[15]

Although Jean-François Lyotard and Jean Baudrillard provided theoretical confirmation of postmodernity, it can be argued that postmodernism as an aesthetic and critical movement is of American origin, the only international period style that occurred first or was first discovered in the United States.[16] Rather like the baroque, it appeared first in the arts, and more specifically in architecture. Linda Hutcheon observes that, whereas the high modernist international style (Ludwig Mies van der Rohe, Walter Gropius, Le Corbusier) was, to some extent, authoritarian, elitist, antihistorical, and totalizing, American postmodernism is eclectic, historically aware, hybrid, and inclusive.[17]

In terms of literature and, for that matter, of criticism, postmodernism can be conceived as a semipopulist reaction against high modernism. This means, in narrative fiction, a return to something like the more traditional representation of reality. I do not mean, of course, a return to realism in the Balzac-to-Zola mode. Scholars agree that central to postmodernism is the belief that there exists no direct access to the real, only the problematic mediation of language and textuality. Reality is constructed through language and transformed into textuality. This said, I am convinced that the vast majority of postmodernist novels employ a more traditional narrative technique – often in the picaresque mode or as magical realism – to explore such questions. We also discover the acknowledged role of personal experience – pseudoautobiography – as an important element in the new fiction, along with a greater simplicity of form and of intertextual reference, and a strain of anti-intellectualism accompanied by the return of the sentimental.

One element in postmodernism is the questioning and undermining of the boundaries between literary registers and genres, and between high and low, mass, or popular culture. As the boundaries melt, the notion of hierarchy, of the superiority of x to y, is delegitimized. On the one hand, we find validated a number of genres previously consigned to the category 'paraliterature' if given recognition at all: detective stories, science fiction, fantasy, horror, 'romance novels,' children's literature, and for that matter film and television. The texts are studied in the university; the authors are treated with respect. Entire schools of American poetry and French prose choose to write in a counterdiscourse, that is, the demotic slangy speech of everyday life, especially as it is spoken by the young. Along with this, we see a culture of surfaces, what Jameson calls depthlessness, and the absence of striving for the masterpiece, the aesthetically supreme work of art. Given these factors and given the belief that the distinction between high and low or elite and mass is ideologically grounded, many postmodernists arrive at the conclusion that mass culture is to be treated with as much respect as classical culture. As they say, all cultural artifacts are textual, and all texts are cultural.

In historical terms, postmodernism implies much more than a writer's freedom from tradition, that is, a break with the past. Modernism also called for freedom from tradition but then re-established other, richer traditions. However, whereas modernism valued the old and the new, postmodernism values only the new, relishing and even fetishizing the ephemeral; hence critiques from various quarters that the postmodern culminates in the semiliterary or kitsch or the crudely primitive or leftist philistinism.

There are those, especially the Marxists, who accuse some contemporary thinkers of a naive and unproblematic acceptance of the world as it is, and even of revelling in the dehumanizing, alienating simulacra of a commodified mass culture.[18] There is some truth to the accusation, especially concerning those individuals of the 'professional-managerial class' who, for all intents and purposes, are familiar only with popular culture. However, the Marxists fail to take into account the elements of parody, irony, mockery, insult, transgression, and all facets of the ludic and the performative, common to so much postmodernist creation – the ludic in contemporary culture that critiques the world, the text, and the author, all three, in complex and problematic ways.

From this we can comprehend the disagreement over whether postmodernism repudiates history or brings it back, and whether postmodernists are committed to a form of left-wing political engagement or are inherently reactionary. The postmodernist fixation on what Jameson calls 'new social movements,' the plight of blacks, Latinos, feminists, and homosexuals, ought to be strong evidence for engagement on the Left, unless one maintains that such concerns are ephemeral and provincially American, and that they distract from the genuinely authentic historical struggles on the planet. Ultimately, I follow Jameson in placing writers both on the Left and on the Right in both modernism and in postmodernism. I should add only that such is the case in all literature, going back at least to the chansons de geste and romans courtois, and in all languages.

Many postmodernist critics claim a philosophical grounding for postmodernism: the crisis in representation, the primacy of ontology over epistemology, and the denial of a universalist metaphysics, transcendent signifiers, and a historical teleology – notions associated with Heidegger and Derrida. Similarly, other critics seek literary figures who would have inspired the postmodernists or who were their predecessors, postmodernist *avant la lettre*. According to Matei Calinescu, postmodernism can be thought of as an extension of the avant-garde, Dada, and surrealism.[19] Richard Murphy finds postmodernism in the German expressionist avant-garde.[20] Ihab Hassan and William V. Spanos cite a number of authors who would be protopostmodernist or postmodernist in spirit.[21] These include the marquis de Sade, Friedrich Hölderlin, Dostoevsky, Rimbaud, Mallarmé, comte de Lautréamont, Nietzsche, Kafka, Rilke, Luigi Pirandello, Antonin Artaud, Maurice Blanchot, Genet, Beckett, and Eugène Ionesco. Most scholars would, of course, cite these worthies, from Rimbaud on, as modernist. A disagreement occurs over the French *nouveau roman*, with some claiming the genre to be postmodernist and Hutcheon, correctly in my opinion, ascribing it to late modernism. Although a number of critics take umbrage at poaching in the modernist and premodernist fields for big names, I do not. It is perfectly legitimate for scholars working on a period style to want it to be more than a single, discrete current isolated in space and time. Therefore, they look beyond chronological boundaries for traits, elements, attitudes, for mental structures or a phenomenology to be found as a recurring phenomenon in modern literature or even in world literature. This makes postmodernism something other, and much more, than the mere extension of or rebellion against high modernism. It is a valid notion, one with which I am in agreement.[22]

It comes as no surprise that the eight critics studied in this book can be identified as humanists; they can be associated with the late medieval-Renaissance *umanisti* and with early nineteenth-century *Humanismus*.

They all were schoolteachers; that is, in our modern times, university professors, the lone semi-exception being Béguin, who gave up his chair at Basel to become a public intellectual – writer, editor, and translator – in Paris. All eight, as university professors and spokesmen for the humanities, were committed to higher education in the old manner and not training for a trade or profession.

All eight were shaped by a classical education or something approaching it, the standard of their era. Auerbach's statement that his great book was unthinkable in any other domain than that of classical German culture could also have been said by Spitzer, Curtius, and Béguin. This reference alludes to the European training in the classics and, still more, to the intellectual climate created by the great German philosophers from Kant to Heidegger. The Anglo-Saxons – Lewis, Matthiessen, and Frye – however much they differ in other respects, are all three grounded in the English equivalent, Protestant humanism in a line that includes Sidney, Milton, Blake, Coleridge, and Arnold.

The eight scholars, with the exception of Matthiessen, all worked on old texts, restoring them to our purview. Although Curtius and Lewis made definitive statements on Virgil and the Virgilian heritage, these critics embodied a new humanism appropriate for their times. Auerbach and Frye grounded Western civilization in the Bible, both the Old and the New Testaments. Spitzer, Curtius, Auerbach, Béguin, and Lewis allotted a new role, central and seminal, to the Middle Ages and to medieval literature in Latin, French, and Italian as a dominant force that shaped our culture. Spitzer thought of himself as a 'philologian,' as the heir to the medieval clerks, just as Curtius thought of himself in the tradition of the medieval scribes copying manuscripts so that culture will live in the future. (Here, the exception is Matthiessen, who sought classics in America and writers who would have been the founding fathers of American culture.)

Their concern was with literature and culture but also with language. Language and style are central to the work of Spitzer, Curtius, Auerbach, Lewis, and Frye. For Spitzer, the investigation of literary language was central to everything he wrote, and everything he wrote can be entitled *Stilstudien*. Lewis published *Studies in Words*, in which he insisted on the importance of historical semantics and textual criticism for reading all literature.[23] Auerbach and Frye had much to say on the various registers of language, once again a domain of culture without which it is impossible to read the classics, ancient and modern.

Their ideal of reading was for the individual, in the tradition of *Bildung*. This meant growth in the individual, intellectual, and other than intellectual. I think that Lewis and Frye expressed openly what the others took for granted. For Lewis, we learn from books and become better people on account of them. Literature takes us out of ourselves, it expands our horizons and consciousness. For Frye, although literature doesn't improve over the centuries, readers do. Literature makes us more humane, and the myths of freedom embodied in literature contribute to our emancipation.

What is good for the individual is good also for the nation. Matthiessen devoted his life to the defence and illustration of an American usable past, a classical American culture that could contribute a sense of tradition and of progressive values to his fellow citizens in the twentieth century. Béguin fought to defend and illustrate French culture during and after the Second World War, to provide old and new models for his fellow citizens in a time of crisis. Spitzer, Curtius, and Auerbach, while proud of their German-language heritage, recognized the relative narrowness and provincialism of German civilization in their day and sought to enrich it with the French and Italian, and thus to bring it and its spiritual life into a greater Europe. Ultimately, all eight were committed to a vision of Western civilization as a whole, whether centred on Virgil (Curtius) or on the Bible (Frye), and, in Frye's case, a vision of all literature, in his 'order of words.'

It is obvious, from the preceding paragraphs, that the eight humanist critics do not adhere to, and should not be associated with, the bourgeois humanism so reviled by Marx, Nietzsche, Sartre, and Adorno, nor with the atheistic American Humanist Association. Among so many areas of divergence, I would note the following three:

1 Of the eight critics, five were Christians, two were men of Jewish descent oriented toward Christianity, and one was a non-practicing Catholic oriented toward Christian socialism.
2 They were committed passionately and with fervour to the humanities and, especially, to the old books in an old humanist culture.
3 Far from subscribing to a simplistic model of progress, these men held complex, nuanced, problematic visions of history; they were conscious of the tragic in modern times and of the failure of one-dimensional ideologies throughout history.

In one domain, however, they do partake of the modern humanistic mindset: their celebration of the human spirit and of the achievement of mankind throughout history and also today.

This brings us to the question of modernism. A number of the humanist elements to be found in the eight critics are also elements inherent in modernism. As I said before, it is hardly a coincidence that some postmodernists denounce humanism and modernism in the same terms and for the same reasons.

Our eight critics, each in his own way, rebelled against the prevailing academic orthodoxy, an orthodoxy that can be envisaged as part and parcel of modernity. Romance and Germanic philology and the congruent, more modernly-oriented history of literature (*Literaturwissenschaft*) were created in the later nineteenth century to make literary studies as impersonal, empirical, scientific, and self-validating as the natural and physical sciences. As Spitzer and the others observed, the 'sciences of literature' were all that they set out to be, except that they had nothing to say about literature itself. In individual, specific cases, Curtius was attacked for concentrating on contemporary writing; Rousset, for 'inventing' a baroque that challenged French classicism; Matthiessen, for combining New Critical techniques with cultural history in order to explain nineteenth-century American writers; and Frye, for imagining his own totalizing system to replace literary history and the New Criticism.

In addition, we find a number of the critics aware of the crisis within modernity that was to bring about its downfall. Such are Curtius, eager to defend high culture against the demagogic populism of the Left and the Right; Auerbach, in anguish over a postwar simplistic, undifferentiated, and levelling world; Béguin, implicitly applauding his writers – Bloy, Péguy, and Bernanos – who cried out against modern materialism and decadence; and Frye, who, in the Arnoldian tradition and in partial agreement with Leavis, saw literature and criticism as unique phenomena that work to assist the emancipation of people in an age dominated by radical and reactionary ideology.

Secondly, with the exception of Lewis, the humanist critics devoted part of their energy to studying and explaining the great modernist writers, their contemporaries. Among those studied and explained are Proust, Gide, Valéry, Péguy, Bernanos, postwar French poetry, and the *nouveau roman* (Butor, Robbe-Grillet, Simon); and James, Woolf, Eliot, Joyce, Stevens, and postwar Canadian poetry; plus a few major writers from Italy and Spain. Even Lewis, uncomfortable in his twentieth century, helped launch the fortune of Charles Williams. Furthermore, Curtius, Béguin, and Frye knew contemporary modernist writers personally and worked with them.

A certain number of critical options taken by the humanist critics are shared by the modernists, so much so that it is difficult to say who influenced whom. Such are: the autonomy of both literature and literary criticism, free from totalizing systems, political and religious, so that criticism has to be conceived as an independent discipline. We concentrate on the book not the author, on the tradition not originality, or, as Lewis and Frye both insist, we free the book and the reader from mere personal experience. Finally, all literature is intertextual, partaking of and harking back to other works of literature, conventions, genres, and modes over the centuries.

In reaction to the late nineteenth- and twentieth-century infatuation with science and with a purportedly detached scientific response to texts, all eight critics underscore the role of sympathy, intuition, *Erlebnis*, *présence*, and passion in their criticism and in their personal makeup. We observe this phenomenon in all who arrive at a phenomenology – the pattern of mind of the author or the structural patterns of the text. This is as true of Spitzer as it is of Béguin, of Auerbach as it is of Rousset and Matthiessen. A second response to *Literaturwissenschaft* can be located in the re-emergence of myth, the fact that Béguin and Frye posit myth – as origin, the past, a higher reality, the verbal imitation or embodiment of ritual, or the shaping principle of literature – to be the central element in and category for the scrutiny of texts. Questioning reason and the rational and finding a place for the emotions and the body are hardly the invention of postmodernists. They go back to Rousseau and the romantics and are central to our twentieth-century modernism under the aegis of Freud, Jung, and Marx.

Like the great literary modernists – Proust, Mann, and Joyce – and for that matter like the surrealists, the humanist critics displace the narrow bourgeois high culture prevalent in their time, substituting for it a richer, older, enlarged, and enhanced transnational literary culture. They repudiate the local in favour of the international and universal. They also rediscover any number of old books and open the canon to previously unrecognized authors and texts, indeed to entire literary periods, in particular the Middle Ages. For all of them, with the partial exception of Rousset, literature and a vibrant, living high culture from the past, a usable past, are marshalled as weapons against the new barbarisms, especially fascism and the Nazi New Order.

One result, which some contest today, is the valorization of Europe and of Western civilization as the supreme manifestation of Europe, its gift to the world. This stance implies the unique greatness of Western culture and the supreme importance of the aesthetic, focusing on high art – the great books and the literary experience – in the creation of a universal world vision, whether it be Curtius's Western culture springing from Virgil, a rhetorical *ordo* extending from Homer and Virgil to Goethe and beyond, or Auerbach's *ordo* of the representation of reality in its ups and downs extending from the Old Testament and Homer to Proust and Woolf, or Frye's totalizing, encyclopedic conceptualization, historical yet also ontological and cosmological, of the order of words everywhere. In this sense, for Spitzer, Frye and the others, as modernists, as the children of Goethe and of Arnold, literature and its criticism function much as theology did in an earlier time, and literary study, in some ways, becomes one element to replace religion in a partially post-Christian age.

With modernism and postmodernism occurring congruently during the postwar decades, with postmodernism functioning in part as an extension or an extreme culmination of modernism, and with multiple conflicting definitions of both currents, it is inevitable that some characteristics I have ascribed to the humanist critics as ties to modernism could be interpreted as anticipating the postmodern. To simplify, I shall simply list a few of these difficult-to-ascribe elements:

1 historical relativism (Auerbach's historicism) ensuring that no one single aesthetic or historical position can judge or account for all the art in all the centuries;
2 the belief that Western culture, or any culture, is an incomplete process and not a finished or even formulated product;
3 the comprehension of a reified, alienating, undifferentiated world that threatens the certitudes and the very existence of traditional humanism;
4 with Béguin, Matthiessen, and Frye, a measure of political engagement aimed at contemporary issues including those relating to hegemony and exploitation;
5 the refusal to lock step in any one discipline or academic field or to limit oneself to any one methodology, with the result that all eight critics create their own imaginative and interpretive worlds.

The eight humanists do anticipate some elements of postmodernism in a number of related areas, in ways that would not normally be ascribed to the modernists. One such area concerns the function of pedagogy. I am thinking of Béguin's abandoning a university chair in order to make his ideas live with and for ordinary people in the French-speaking world. Critics seemingly as far apart as Spitzer and Frye or Curtius and Matthiessen aimed at taking the study of literature away from the pedants and from a social elite, and making it available to students and the general public. Lewis, Matthiessen, and Frye, each in his own way, sought, if not to break the barriers between high culture and popular culture, at least to make them more flexible and more problematic. Significantly, *An Experiment in Criticism* and *The Secular Scripture* both respect the books that average people read and insist on the average person's capacity to read as intelligently as the specialized intellectual; Lewis and Frye do this, in part, in an endeavour to ·revalue modern romance, a genre at the time decried by the academic intelligentsia yet central to their new vision of literature. Matthiessen's interest in frontier

American humour follows a similar line. So, also, Auerbach and Frye study impartially the full range of literary registers – *sermo gravis, sermo mediocris,* and *sermo humilis,* or the high, middle, and low hieratic and demotic – according as much value to the low as to the high, and in Auerbach's case, making Christian *sermo humilis* the central seminal force in the history of Western culture.

Frye, who lived through the beginnings of postmodernism, read a number of poststructuralist thinkers, especially Derrida. Those who berate myth criticism and its first proponent will perhaps be pleasantly surprised to discover that Frye insisted that reality exists for us only as it is embodied in literary structures, that is, in language, and that the reality and the history to be found in the Bible are uniquely metaphorical. In addition, Frye and the others did work that predates today's cultural studies. For example, Spitzer's analysis of the Sunkist orange juice advertisement remains a classic, and in much of his later critical writing he sought to relate the text under discussion to the historical culture of the time in which it was written. Curtius's *The Civilization of France* was an extraordinarily prescient study not of French culture in the abstract but of how the French see themselves, his findings always grounded in the history of the past and the historical understanding of the present. Finally, Matthiessen's *American Renaissance* would not be the book it is without his masterful integration of a full range of non-literary cultural manifestations into the study of literature.

Auerbach has been praised for the self-reflexivity, the metacritical self-consciousness of his great book, and how the figural method allows twentieth-century modernism to fulfil nineteenth-century realism and to prefigure the more recent postmodernism.[24] We find a similar self-consciousness and awareness in Frye, whose later studies of culture make a place for the various ideologies that emanate from myths of concern. Both Frye and Matthiessen, as North Americans, are conscious of the colonial heritage of their nations; the colonial experience, in relation to the older culture in old Europe, is a constant in their writings on Canada and the United States. Still further, Frye can discuss the more recent colonial situation of Canada vis-à-vis the United States. Spitzer, Auerbach, and Béguin lived the transnational, nomadic, hybrid experience to the full. A similar problematic governs Curtius, who lived the 'inner emigration' at home, and, perhaps also, C.S. Lewis from Ulster, who never fitted in nor was accepted at Oxford. It is not surprising, then, that such reserved academic gentlemen do reveal some of their personal lives in their writing, that autobiographical elements enter in, and always for the good.

Once this is stated, and assuming that it is valid, nevertheless the humanist critics are not postmoderns, not at all. In some very important ways their convictions and the convictions of the postmodernist world are in conflict.

As I have said before, except for Frye and, perhaps also Lewis, the humanists are not theoreticians; they do not do theory. They did not problematize or historicize their own cultural work nor were they cognizant of the social and historical forces that helped shape it. For the most part they accepted, consciously or unconsciously the (bourgeois?) values of their generation.

Secondly, with the exception of Béguin, they were all lifelong university professors, mandarins if you will, who reaped the highest academic honours open to them. For Spitzer and Auerbach it happened twice: once in Germany then, later, in America. Although they questioned and refuted their predecessors' methodology, they readily accepted the academic structure and hierarchy. In part because they were mandarins, four of them – Spitzer, Curtius, Auerbach, and Lewis – each believed to some extent in scholarly objectivity and that he alone had made the correct reading of a text. Academic authority thrived! And Frye, the proponent of polysemous meanings and critical pluralism, also did not suffer fools gladly.

Each proposed a unique, all-encompassing vision of literature and civilization – eight grand narratives. Despite their relative openness to popular culture and the average reader, they all believed, as a matter of course, that the great books, the masterpieces of Western literature, are superior to other kinds of writing. Similarly, despite the valorization of *sermo humilis* and the low demotic, they all believed, Spitzer especially, that the discourse of great writers is inherently creative and superior to the standard spoken vernacular. There is no particular reason to believe that they would have been interested in the claims made by the new social movements – the assertion by women and visible minorities that their voices are silenced and that they are not sufficiently represented in the cursus. Finally, and this is perhaps the most important, although all eight recognized the presence in literature of ideology, its inevitable presence, they all believed that it is the duty of the critic and, for that matter, the intelligent reader to separate literature from ideology and to scrutinize it value-free or, as Frye says, to liberate literature from ideology, its own and that of the critic.[25]

It is easy to critique the humanist scholars from the vantage point of postmodernism. It is no less easy to critique postmodernists from the humanist vantage point. One need only recall Curtius's 'barbarization of education,' Auerbach's 'levelling, standardization, and imposed uniformity,' Lewis's 'misreading by the literary,' and the sundry manifestations of Frye's 'myth of concern.'

To do so would be unprofitable. We must not forget that postmodernism is a period style, a cultural attitude, and an approach or a bundle of approaches. The postmodernist current is as varied, as multiple, as the preceding currents. Also, as I suggested in the 'Introduction,' these mindsets coexist in the same chronological frame, much as, say, in 1570 we can find coexisting elements of the Renaissance, mannerism, and the baroque, or, in any single moment or in a single author we find coexisting elements of Frye's romance, the high and low mimetic, and irony. Conservative publicists claim that our campuses are deluged by a tidal wave of antihumanist and anti-intellectual ideology called deconstruction, the new historicism, feminism, postcolonialism, multiculturalism, and queer theory. As I see it, the truth is less apocalyptic and much more stimulating. The above-mentioned approaches stand side by side and compete with any number of the older schools. Those of us who subscribe to New Criticism, or the psychoanalytic approaches, or classical Marxism, or the various formalisms, or for that matter philology and literary history, are equally represented. Few English or modern language departments are totally committed to much of anything, for good or ill. The legacy of the humanist critics remains strong, both when they are lauded (by Jameson and Said) and when they are denounced (by Fekete and Nerlich).

I propose, therefore, to conclude this chapter with something quite different. I should like to speak directly with my own voice and to offer a meditation on one of the problems which most divides colleagues in literary studies: the question of the canon, or, which books should we read, teach, and privilege in cultural terms. In so doing, I speak as one who reveres the humanist critics and who also partakes of the other currents, ancient and modern. I should like to negotiate a position between or, rather, among the competing mindsets. The reader should also note that I am an American academic and that, in this section, when I speak of students, the university, popular culture, and the culture wars, I refer to a specifically American context, one which is, of course, by no means confined to the United States.

Quite often, nowadays, to address the phenomenon of marginality and the function of the literary canon implies discussing race, class, gender, and ethnicity. It also implies exploring from a cultural studies perspective the extent to which the canon has been shaped by social, political, and ideological forces, and whether these forces are inherently conservative and contribute to the imposition of hegemonic values and, concurrently, to the marginalization of non-traditional voices. Finally, it questions even the notion of a canon and a list of great books. I speak, instead, as a perverse postmodern Averroes. I believe in the Two Truths. On the one hand, unlike some conservatives, I am fascinated by the new scholarship and its insights, especially narratology, intertextuality, post-colonialism, gender-related approaches, and cultural studies. I recognized the artificiality of the classical French academic canon and of a newer, Mallarmé-oriented poetic canon, and saw through them to their social and ideological roots.[26] Surely everyone who studies literature of the past has to be a historian of cultures as well as a philologist or critic.

On the other hand, unlike some on the Left, I maintain the humanist vision of my parents and teachers (including Erich Auerbach), their commitment to the great books and to the 'great chain of civilization' extending, Auerbach and Curtius would say, from Homer to Proust, kindred spirits over the ages who pass on the torch of civilization. Like many of us, born American, I am culturally half-European (French actually), a hybrid, a *métis*, distanced from as well as ingrained in both European and American issues. People like us are so very American, for, throughout our history, we Americans separate into two camps: the Whitman-Dreiser-Sandburg people, and the James-Eliot-Pound people. Those joying in progress, democracy, populism, materialism, and technology; and those others who seek, as Truman Capote would say, but meaning something else, other voices in other rooms.

There are those, on the Right and on the Left, who believe that the current disagreement over what constitutes the study of literature and which books (the so-called canon) should comprise the object of study, is startlingly new, unique to our American culture wars of the 1980s and 1990s. Nothing could be further from the truth. In literary life such quarrels go back at least to Aristophanes and his defence of old values (Aeschylus) against dangerous innovation that can corrupt the public (Euripides). European universities introduced programs in the national languages on the belief that Germanic and Romance philology was or could be as legitimate a field of scholarship as classical philology. They did it over fierce and righteous indignation. At various times efforts were needed to convince the powers that be that postmedieval books are worthy of study, or that contemporary books are worthy of study, or that literary criticism, as opposed to philology and history, deserves a spot in academe.[27]

Two of the major schools of criticism in English offered a methodology but also a revision of value judgments concerning the tradition as a whole: the New Critics denigrated Milton, the romantics, and the Victorians while exalting the Metaphysicals and the poets of modernism; then the myth critics rehabilited Spenser, Milton, and the romantics while denigrating no one, at least in principle. Matthiessen contributed to the first revision, and Frye, preceded by Lewis, launched the second. This means that students of English had to come to terms with the evolution of literature from Chaucer to Eliot, in its totality, and that the 'mighty dead,' for good or ill, were seen to be present in the living, forming an uninterrupted cultural continuum.

Comparable revisions occurred in America and on the Continent. Matthiessen led the way in proclaiming an American Renaissance – a classical generation if you wish – around Emerson, Thoreau, Hawthorne, Melville, and Whitman. He also pioneered in the valorization of the American moderns: James and Eliot. Others added to the 'modern classics' Pound and Faulkner. A more recent generation then decentred both traditions by adding black writers and women and by ceasing to privilege New England.

In France and Germany questioning the canon meant, in the last analysis, questioning the pre-eminence of French and German classicism and the bourgeois values attributed to them. In the case of France, Spitzer, Curtius, and Auerbach rehabilitated the Middle Ages; Rousset rehabilitated the baroque and the eighteenth century; Spitzer, Curtius, Béguin, and Rousset rehabilitated the moderns. In all these endeavours the humanist critics did not stand alone; the revisions were made and unmade by the entire scholarly community. This said, compared to ours, the Continental canon wars were more gradual, occurred on a smaller scale, and, to some extent, were limited to specialists in the field.

One reason, perhaps, for the slower pace of revision in France, Germany, Italy, and Spain is that these nations take culture seriously; differing from the Anglo-Saxons, national identity is determined, in part, by the accepted cultural tradition. Hence, the promulgation of 'le grand siècle,' 'el siglo de oro,' and 'die Goethezeit,' the last a model or element which, for well over a century, was the determining factor in *Geist* and *Kultur.*

Cultural historians often state that the claim to canonicity and to the status of high culture by a regime or an academy – the institution of literature – serves to empower the regime or the academy and to repress those elements in society which do not participate in the hegemony.

This is partially true for the phenomenon of French classicism. Barthes has written on 'classico-centrism,' the tendency to conceive the evolution of literature as a slow rise to, then falling away from, the summit, a high point that purportedly corresponds to the genius of the nation and its language.[28] Several of us, including Frye, have commented on the organicist analogy, that nineteenth-century men of letters assimilated a nation's literary history to the course of human life, with birth, growth, maturity, decline, and, presumably, senescence.[29]

We are also aware of the politics inherent in the assumption of a past golden age and present decadence. Ever since the fetishization of the age of Louis XIV in the eighteenth century (in Harold Bloom's terminology,[30] Voltaire was an ephebe cowering before Strong Fathers, the likes of Boileau and Racine), the classical ideal has been employed to combat new contemporary writing – romanticism, realism, naturalism, symbolism, surrealism, and for that matter *nouveau roman* – and to combat the anti-Establishment contestatory politics that each of these movements embodied. The classical canon and its claim to universality also helped to smother vital cultural life in the provinces, whether it was given expression in French or in the regional languages including Basque, Breton, Catalan, and Occitan. This is why Éluard and Aragon, great poets of Communism, fought to enlarge the national canon to include the hypermodern and the Middle Ages.

It is not an accident that the ideal of French classicism is invented at a time when literary self-consciousness becomes associated with linguistic and cultural nationalism. Nor is it an accident that the ideal occurs when, for the first time, Paris becomes the literary capital of the realm. What is accidental, however, is the fact that the traits proclaimed by Voltaire's century to be typically French – and therefore, accepted and rebelled against by the nascent English, German, Italian, and Spanish cultural nationalisms – are simply the traits that characterized one sequence of French literature extending from 1650 to 1800. A passion for things Greek and Roman, psychological analysis, social observation, the rebellion of the secular, the mastery of form, clarity, harmony, and order, the virtues of great prose – these are perhaps endemic to French writing from Molière to *Les liaisons dangereuses*. They are not typical of French literature or of the French people taken as a whole.

It should also be pointed out that, in many French departments and for a number of trendy French intellectuals, the old golden age of Louis XIV and Versailles has simply been transferred to a new golden age of modern Paris: the succession of writers that extends from Baudelaire to

Proust. The result is the same sort of stereotyping – that is, a patronizing condescension toward those who preceded Flaubert and Baudelaire and the willingness to downgrade contemporary writers to the extent that they differ from the giants of modernism.

It should not be imagined that repressive ideology is the monopoly of the Right. Goethe, Schiller, and Hölderlin were embraced with equal fervour by Wilhelmine conservatives, Weimar Social Democrats, Nazis, and GDR Communists. In France, from the heyday of the Third Republic on, Catholic and aristocrat-oriented writers of the classical seventeenth century were misread and distorted, from a progressive, free-thinking bias, with the result that they were then and are now taught in the French schools as if they were the rough contemporaries and comrades of Victor Hugo and Anatole France.

This moderate-left republican and free-thinking bias contributed also to the marginalization of the French Middle Ages and the French baroque. This is because the organicist analogy allows a nation to have one summit of classical perfection, not two or three or six, and because everyone believed that the Middle Ages was very Christian. Molière, Racine, and La Fontaine could, with a little violence, be co-opted by the progressive, secularist, and militant *maîtres* of the Republic's schools. Chanson de geste and roman courtois, the quest for Jerusalem and the quest for the Grail, Reynard the Fox and the allegories of love, and for that matter baroque Christian epic, pastoral romance, and devotional sonnet sequences could not. Therefore, a vital dimension of the national heritage was and is marginalized in the consciousness of the educated French *honnête homme*. To some extent the Middle Ages and the baroque in their entirety are or were marginal. As my old teacher Henri Peyre would have said: they were not classical, therefore not really French; or they were not really French, therefore not classical.[31]

Since 1960 we have been in the process of shaping what I call the enlarged scholarly canon. The enlarged scholarly canon includes, for the French Middle Ages – in addition to the acknowledged twelfth-century masterpieces – late epics and romances, the fabliaux and the beast epics, saints' lives, miracles, and mystery plays, sacred and secular allegory, *dits amoureux* by Machaut, chronicles by Froissart, and the whole range of lyrics from the first trouvères to the grands rhétoriqueurs by way of Christine de Pizan. We can treasure *Renaut de Montauban* as much as the *Chanson de Roland* and the *Prose Lancelot* as much as Chrétien de Troyes; we can rate convention as high as originality and playful, mannered experimentation as high as straightforward storytelling.

The enlarged canon can be identified as medieval, humanist, and postmodernist. It is medieval to the extent that it respects medieval judgments of their own contemporary works and makes a place for those books – the *Prose Lancelot, Renaut de Montauban,* Machaut's tales of love, Froissart's *Chroniques,* and the mystery plays – that the medievals themselves respected and loved. It is humanist in that it endorses the notion of a canon, a treasury of great books, and the ideal of high culture. It is postmodernist in that it expands the canon to include any number of great texts not recognized to be great in their own day or by the romantics or by the moderns – *Girart de Roussillon* written in Occitan and the debate poems and prose treatises of Christine de Pizan written by a woman. It so opens up the canon that our field of specialization can be conceptualized as having vastly expanded margins and no centre at all or, if you prefer, having a frame with a vastly expanded centre in which *Roland* has to share the honours with a dozen other epics, and *Tristan* with two dozen other romances. Similarly, in the Splendid Century (now the Age of Louis XIII as well as Louis XIV) Molière and Boileau have to share the centre with at least a dozen masters of baroque epic and baroque lyric. Would Molière have minded? Probably not, but it would make Boileau very, very unhappy.[32]

For those of us who participated in this endeavour, our purpose was never to mock or undermine the notion of great books or the culture to which they contribute. On the contrary, we strove to make them more exciting and more worthy of study by scholars or general readers today, and, of course, to speak of them in the hundreds not just five or six, and to speak of all the centuries and not just one or two.

When I was in graduate school, students and faculty had a relatively solid command of the national tradition over the centuries, from a scholarly if not always an aesthetic vantage point. And they were largely ignorant of and/or downgraded what today we call world literature in English, Francophone literature, and even the literature of Latin America. They were temporally sophisticated and spatially impaired. Today the tables are turned. Today far too many students and their professors are spatially sophisticated and temporally impaired. This means the loss of a sense of history. For many of our students and for American society as a whole, history means nostalgic movies about the 1960s. Ultimately, whether our students are white or black, male or female, is perhaps of less significance than the fact that they are American teenagers. They will have read very little of anything, and their cultural empathy will normally occur with movies or television serials about American teenagers.

Hence the popularity of *Starwars* and of J.D. Salinger. *Starwars* and Salinger have their uses. They are not, however, Racine, Shakespeare, and Sophocles. If African Americans and white young women have problems identifying with King Oedipus, so do white young men, including the sons of the professional classes. All our students are ignorant of the past.

The situation in Europe, although less spectacular, is slowly evolving in much the same direction. We can call it creeping presentism. The German classics are attacked in the public sphere, and attention shifts from Goethe and Heine to cultural studies or to the literatures of the Weimar Republic, the Third Reich, the GDR, and writing by contemporary minorities.[33] In France some of the most brilliant intellectuals have reinforced a Parisian belletristic inclination to neglect the past altogether. Sartre and Barthes contrasted negatively what they consider to be neoclassicism (for them that is the past) with what they call the birth of true *écriture*, the latter coinciding with the crisis in bourgeois society, ca. 1850.[34] Similarly, since 1968 less Molière is read in the French secondary schools; however, Molière is replaced by Mayakovsky, Hemingway, and Boris Vian, not by writers from the Middle Ages and Renaissance. Whatever the causes, if anything, the importance, the perceived value of 'early literature' (pre-Flaubert), has declined as both students and faculty recognize the living vitality of the contemporary and concentrate on it.

The languages that we teach, the literatures and cultures that we teach and on which we publish, go back for centuries if not for millennia. It is impossible to understand the contemporary culture of any of our nations, enriching, contextualizing, and problematizing them, without our having mastered the centuries of history behind contemporary culture. French villages are shaped by the medieval church and castle as well as by the Third Republic schoolhouse and town hall.

In strictly literary terms, therefore, it is harder to specialize in the twentieth century than in any preceding period, first of all, because of a naturally expanding canon – new books are published daily – but also because, to do one's job properly, one ought to know the past centuries as well as one's own. The theory of intertextuality makes us aware of the extraordinary cultural richness of modern literature, and especially of writers in the line of Proust, Mann, and Joyce, Rilke, Aragon, and Pound. In addition, a vital living command of the tradition helps us place our contemporary cultural production including its innovations. Knowing medieval epic and quest romance, and late medieval allegory and the Renaissance picaresque, will make us realize that *nouveau roman* and surfiction are less a unique phenomenon of rebellion against Balzac than the return to a long tradition of archetypal and picaresque narrative, so that Gustave Flaubert and Leo Tolstoy are seen not as the rule but the exception, almost an anomaly. Similarly, command of poetry from the Greeks to, say, Alexander Pope and Voltaire, will help us realize the extent to which modern and postmodern verse – whether in the high, middle, or low registers – is less a unique rebellion against the romantic cult of sincerity and its plunging into the abyss than a return to the old tradition of imitation and convention or of the free play of language, so that Shelley and Hugo are to be seen not as the rule but the exception, almost an anomaly. Frye's modes, symbols, and mythoi are more the result of pragmatic, historical observation than they are abstract intellectual structures imposed on a recalcitrant artistic creativity. Today, for the first time in history, because of our sense of historicism (Auerbach's *Historismus*) and because of our technology (photographs, slides, and the Internet; records and compact discs; translations and paperbacks; for that matter, the airplane that takes us to Ispahan and Kyoto), we can seize, devour, and be nourished by all the great cultures of the present and the past, to know and love them all.

Apparently in opposition to this, apparently negating it, would be postmodernist theory and, in particular, cultural studies that states, as we saw above, the importance of studying all cultural artifacts, and that these artifacts, of popular culture as well as of a privileged canon, grant insights into society. The more extreme formulations insist upon the historical construction of all high culture and upon the artificiality and arbitrariness of erecting a barrier between high and popular culture. According to this view, all books are related to their historical contexts, which are political. The great books in the Western canon are inherently conservative; they indoctrinate their readers, offer no role models for women and minorities, and function to exclude the masses from intellectual life.

My brief response proposes that we recognize how complex and problematic such questions are and that we avoid clichés – from the Right and from the Left – that, because they distort our respective positions, have brought us to the culture wars.

To begin with, the study of cultural artifacts – of all cultural artifacts – is enriching. This is especially true for contemporary American popular culture which, for the reasons we all know, is spreading and is rapidly becoming world popular culture. The structures of paraliterary genres are fascinating in their own right and in their ties to high culture in its historical dimension. One quite trivial example among so many: my personal experience. At one time I analyzed the American soap opera as a petty bourgeois, low mimetic reworking of the conventions and archetypes to be found in medieval courtly romance and baroque pastoral romance; the soap opera and also science fiction are the direct heirs of honoured modes of narrative, centuries old, yet now forsaken by the practitioners of high culture. Far more important are the number of scholars devoting their careers to these studies, plus the associations that have been founded to support them. For instance, the Society for the Study of Medievalism, with its journals *Studies in Medievalism* and *The Year's Work in Medievalism*, scrutinizes the medieval presence as a creative cultural force in subsequent periods including our own. Some of the best work concerns manifestations of the Middle Ages in contemporary popular culture. Finally, popular culture offers us a unique pedagogical means of relating to today's undergraduates, to be disdained at our peril.

This said, it would be a mistake to glorify these cultural artifacts and to revel in their contribution to American globalization, because such American-centred narcissism is not a symptom of intellectual health and because our planetary cultural hegemony ought to be seen as one manifestation of imperialism, late capitalistic and technological. In any case, a number of people I know who do popular culture also do the great books; they teach and research both domains. Furthermore, if for nothing but pragmatic reasons they distinguish between them, both intellectually and in terms of value.

Similarly, I am convinced that the new scholarship – feminist, postcolonial, queer, and new historicist – is exciting. These ways of looking at texts and looking at history grant insights into texts, their audience, their composition, and their ideology that, otherwise, we would not have. There are those shocked and outraged by Said's reading of *Mansfield Park* (the social economy of Sir Bertram's great house is derived from the repressive political economy of his plantation in Antigua) or Gayatri Chakravorty Spivak's reading of *Jane Eyre* (Jane's triumphant emergence is posited upon the degraded occulting of Rochester's wife, a white Creole from the Indies treated as a colonized female subject).[35] I find them exciting and illuminating; such readings are possible only in our time. Again, I personally profited from the insights of postcolonial criticism in my study of the European minority literatures written in Scots, Breton, and Occitan, an approach justified by those minority-language writers who proclaimed the colonial or postcolonial condition of their regions.[36]

Still, we are not obliged to accept that the Said-Spivak interpretations are the only or the most important ones relating to these texts, or that, because of them, we ought to think less highly of Jane Austen and Charlotte Brontë and/or of their novels. In other words, we must avoid what Jeffrey Wallen calls a 'reading for evil,' both simplistic and reductionist.[37] Said himself is most eloquent in this regard. In *Culture and Imperialism*, while arguing that Western literature since 1800, especially the English, participated in and helped create a mindset conducive to and accepting of imperialism, he also insists that 'understanding that connection does not reduce or diminish the novels' value as works of art: on the contrary, because of their *worldliness*, because of their complex affiliations with their real setting, they are more interesting and more valuable as works of art' (13).

I should only add how historically inaccurate is the assumption that great works of literature are politically regressive and ought to be condemned because of this purported regression. From the eighteenth to the twentieth century we find any number of writers who rebel against oppression, exclusion, and fanaticism. Examples from France alone are Voltaire, Diderot, Rousseau, Hugo, Zola, Anatole France, Romain Rolland, Malraux, Éluard, and Aragon. From the international current of European modern writers can be cited, among so many on the Left: Brecht, Heinrich Mann, Günter Grass, and Anna Seghers; Gorky and Mayakovsky; Alberto Moravia, Elio Vittorini, and Quasimodo; and Benito Pérez Galdós, Rafael Alberti, and Lorca. Yet, what about the writers of reaction? That Aristotle defended the notion of slavery and that only ten percent of the inhabitants (free Athenian men) participated in Hellenic democracy should indeed cause us to reflect on the fetishizing of classical Greece as a source or model. However, this in no way diminishes Aristotle's stature or the stature of classical Greek literature. The same is true for the nineteenth-century Russian classics, including liberal and emancipatory writers from Pushkin to Gorky, and also the czarist, Holy Orthodox, Slavophile Dostoevsky, all of whom flourished in an age of autocracy. One does not have to be Catholic to appreciate Dante or to be a member of the Party to appreciate Brecht and Neruda. In other words, in a truly civilized society the ideal is for readers to read, profit from, and exalt Protestants, Catholics, and atheists, feminists and misogynists, writers on the Left and on the Right. This does not mean that a writer's ideology is to be considered irrelevant to our appreciation of his work or that we prize it for its form alone. Great committed poets are great because of, not in spite of, their commitment. Because of the commitment, they arrive at insights into the human condition that transcend their own immediate conscious reasons for writing and ours for reading. In this respect as in others, the postmoderns can take a lesson from Marx. Marx loved Balzac, who was Catholic and a monarchist.[38] He loved Shakespeare and Greek tragedy, which he thought avoided class issues altogether. Those of us who believe in social justice would do well to heed the Marxist reminder that bringing about concrete social change requires something more than consciousness-raising about old books in a handful of students or colleagues.

One of the worries to us in the James-Eliot-Pound camp is the notion that the curriculum and the canon should be redefined in terms of ethnicity or gender – that is, determined by the ethnic background ascribed to our students or to the American people taken in their entirety. On the one hand, this praxis of reading assumes and encourages the immediate, superficial identification (empathy?) between the student/citizen and the author and/or character, an identification that, as teachers and critics, we ought perhaps to problematize and to decentre. From a European perspective, we ought to recognize that some form of alienation or estrangement or otherness (*Verfremdung, Alterität*) is as inherent in the perception of a work of art as it is in the human condition generally.

Some problematizing and decentring of ethnicity and group identity can also contribute to the new *Bildung*. At the very least, students can be offered the choice of culture and identity – the capacity to choose between a determined group identity and free affiliation. In Alain Finkielkraut's terminology, the choice is between the German or Eastern notion of cultural identity whereby one is born into a *Volksgeist* and bound to it forever; and the French or Western vision whereby one enters into an implicit social contract and one has the right to choose freely and to change one's religion, culture, and personal allegiance.[39] I opt for the Western model. And I insist that women and visible minorities can, if for no other reason than that they speak English or another European language, partake of and identify with all of Western civilization, literary and artistic.

In response to the Maoist notion that the culture of the masses is of supreme value and ought to be studied and embraced by ci-devant elites in need of re-education, I prefer the orthodox Marxist-Leninist view that one of the crimes of capitalism is to have deprived the masses of high culture; therefore, it is the duty of intellectuals to bring culture to the people, to help them realize that it is their inheritance as well as ours, and to help enrich their lives with the beauty, truth, and wisdom that emanate from the great works in the tradition. It is unfortunate that the love and dissemination of classical culture – one of the few genuine successes of the Soviet regime – should now be rejected by professors in North America.

Indeed, the majority of feminists and queer theorists of my acquaintance teach the great books with affection and esteem, not hatred. Furthermore, feminism and queer theory manifest a richness and complexity of schools and currents, in powerful disagreement among themselves. It is the richness and complexity, the divergence, within theory which contributes to its value. Surely we can proclaim as wide, rich, and varied a domain for schools of criticism as for kinds of texts, and a comparable decentring so that no one methodology is privileged over the others. All the major twentieth-century currents – from Russian Formalism to the new historicism and beyond – all have something to contribute. Just as it is methodologically unacceptable to presume that French classical tragedy or nineteenth-century fiction or the lyric from Baudelaire to Valéry is superior or more central or more French than other genres in other centuries, so also scepticism is surely the appropriate response to partisans of a critical or theoretical approach, on the Right or on the Left, who declare that their approach is superior to all others, and therefore that those colleagues who brazenly and shamelessly persist in the practice of other approaches are patently dinosaurs or fools. In practice this means (as I wrote in the C.S. Lewis chapter) a colleague five years out of date being denounced as a dinosaur or a fool by one only two years out of date. The ferocity of academic thrust and parry is curious to behold – especially in English studies, although we on the Continent do our best.

From the perspective of the canon, however, we are not faced with an either/or situation. William E. Cain chooses the best road: 'My argument calls for greater inclusiveness – not the elimination of the old canonical texts, but, instead, the addition of new texts that are valuable in themselves and that lead to a deepening understanding of the more familiar, widely known ones.'[40] In this he is not alone. Were it not for the new scholarship from Cain and others, we would never have learned to appreciate Frederick Douglass and W.E.B. DuBois. Were it not for Nina Baym and Jane Tompkins, I would never have heard of the domestic, sentimental strain in the nineteenth-century American novel, the strain exemplified by Susan Warner, Harriet Beecher Stowe, and Maria Cummins.[41] These works are fascinating and deserve eminently the attention they have received. Whether Warner and Cummins or Alice Walker and Maya Angelou are 'major,' 'great' writers is another question altogether. Probably not. However, I am not convinced that it is all that helpful to grade the newcomers (Toni Morrison A–, Maya Angelou C+ ...), a practice which, according to Frye, is in any case methodologically untenable.

It would nevertheless be an error to presume that women's writing was consciously and wilfully excluded from the canon by the male Establishment. As John Guillory demonstrates so convincingly, in past centuries women were, instead, excluded from access to the means of cultural production.[42] In practical terms, as I see it, this means the access to education in Latin, the assumed prerequisite for literary production and a literary career. When women did write and their works were disseminated, for the most part they received acclaim and rewards roughly comparable to the men. Any number of previously excluded or unrecognized older writers have been rediscovered and are now included in the enlarged scholarly canon. They were originally excluded for reasons of ideology, including politics and religion, or for aesthetic reasons – their way of writing went out of favour sometime in the past or it simply did not conform to the presuppositions of the late nineteenth- and early twentieth-century professoriat. They were not excluded for reasons of race, class, or gender.

The present is not all bad. We ought not to berate the present or ignore the past. For me, the continuity of high culture, from two thousand or three thousand years of the past into the present, constitutes much of its excitement. Books from the past have value only to the extent that they live in and shape our present. For, whenever we declare, with whatever good intentions and esoteric pride, that the contemporary world is the Self, and we and our life's work are the Other, we condemn ourselves and our life's work to the margins, forever. We also lose our students. Burckhardt and Jules Michelet propagated a modern, bourgeois myth (reformulated by Robertson and in his way by Zumthor) that the Middle Ages was simple, archetypal, very Christian, communal, other, and, in some sense of the term, non-literary, whereas the modern world manifests complexity, diversity, individualism, secularism, subjectivity, and is very literary. Such formulations are simplistic, reductionist, antihistorical, and more than a century out of date. On the contrary, because our Freudian, Jungian, structuralist, intertextual, audience-response, and gender-related readings of medieval texts are successful, can we not attribute the success in part to the fact that those approaches correspond to, and sometimes consciously mirror, a Middle Ages (and Renaissance) that believed so powerfully in archetypal patterns, levels of meaning, registers of style, rhetoric, and all the symbolism and sexual overtones inherent in dreams, the four elements, and the pilgrimage of man?

The enlarged scholarly canon and critical pluralism can join in criticism and history that transcend the individual text: the study of genres, forms, and modes over the centuries. This criticism, by its very nature, refuses to consider in isolation any one period in our culture including the medieval. *Fin' amor* persists in sonnet sequences of the Renaissance, with the romantics, with the great tradition of novelists treating passion and adultery – Rousseau, Laclos, Goethe, Balzac, Stendhal, Flaubert, Tolstoy, Fontane, Proust, and Mann – and, as surrealist *amour fou.* The desire for epic, the longing for a committed poetry of war, is fulfilled in the centuries of chanson de geste and roman courtois, again in Renaissance and baroque epic, again with romanticism, and in the poetry of the Resistance and the American long poem from Whitman to today. Writing centred on narratological play, the unreliable narrator, and the non-mimetic, metatextual stylization of reality is found in Machaut and Chaucer, then in Diderot and Sterne, and today in Vladimir Nabokov and Nathalie Sarraute. Modern creators of myth renew with the old mythmakers, those who bequeathed to us Roland and his horn, the Four Sons of Aymon and their horse Bayard, Tristan, Isolt, and the philtre, Lancelot, Guinevere, and the Grail, the Cid, the Nibelungs, and, more recently, Faust, Don Juan, and Don Quixote.

One interpretation of the phenomenon would be a cyclical shift, movement, or recurrence in style over the centuries between mannerist or baroque or romantic or *trobar ric* or *trobar clus,* dominant in certain periods, and classical or *trobar plan,* dominant in other periods. The shift from the troubadours and singers of geste to Chrétien, Guillaume de Lorris, and Machaut, and then back to Villon is repeated constantly in literature. Another possibility would be a more inclusive pattern that tries to make sense of *longue durée,* something akin to the cyclical theory proposed by art historians for the Renaissance. The notion of a romanesque experimental achievement (the early trouvères of epic and lyric) leading to the high gothic classical perfection of Chrétien, Guillaume de Lorris, and the *Prose Lancelot*; leading to the *rayonnant* mannerism of Jean de Meun, Juan Ruiz, Machaut, Froissart, Chaucer, Gower, and the *Pearl*-poet; leading to a flamboyant, baroque-like synthesis in the century of Villon and the mystery plays will be repeated twice and perhaps three times subsequently in the history of letters. In which case, postmodernism could be our mannerism and would help explain our fascination both with our immediate modernist predecessors and with the masters of mannerist play and narratological experimentation today and in earlier centuries.

It is also possible, from a quite different perspective, to envisage our twentieth century as a return to the Middle Ages, a century of medievalism when the medieval achievement can be better appreciated than at any time since Ariosto and Spenser. To the extent that our age contains partial repudiation of the notions of progress, technology, materialism, and secularism; that it embodies a return to symbolic thinking, religious anguish, myth making, and even, with film, radio, and television, to a partially oral culture; and that, in our fine arts, theatre, and narrative, we have gone beyond the striving for mimesis prevalent in the previous two or three centuries – it is no longer, then, romanesque sculpture or the mystery plays or the *Canterbury Tales* which are other.

For all these reasons I am convinced that, whatever our political options, we must emphasize the continuity and embrace the present with the past, for either, alone, separated like the honeysuckle vine and the hazelnut tree in Marie de France, will wither and perish. And, because we live and love the present and the past, we can radiate (modest?) optimism concerning the future.

It would appear that the researcher convinced that Western culture has been in steady decline since, say, the Middle Ages, must be a rather unhappy person – how much further down can we go? – as is the critic convinced that Western writing is in steady decline since, say, Mallarmé. Both are to be pitied. We have the technology, as never before, to devour all the masterworks from all the lands and all the centuries. We have critical approaches to enrich our reading of all the books, past and present, as never before. Yes, so many of the young, the gifted young – our students and our children – are held captive by their computers, television, video games, contact sports, what they call music, and their unique, never seen before, eternally riveting love life. We are not Lancelot. We cannot free them. Yet, for most of them and most of us, for all of us who come from the lower classes, however defined – everyone does sooner or later – this is the first time in history that we can benefit from culture, that the books, art, and music are ours. After all, in the golden age – say, the twelfth century – how many people were literate: two percent? five percent? At the lowest ebb of Western civilization, in the midst of barbarian invasions and all-but-total anarchy – say the

seventh century – how many people were literate: one percent? Many
more than one percent of our young are culturally literate. They read,
they major in humanities, they tell me I am not the last dinosaur. We
survived back then. We will survive now.

Yes, literature is a historical and social construct. Yes, it mirrors and
creates reality. It is also that which embodies and manifests literariness.
This means that all literature, the great works of the past but also the
masterpieces of the present, is grounded in a tradition of image and
archetype, of topos, convention, and rhetoric; therefore that the work of
art is a text subject to the laws of textuality, due to a person (genius or
craftsman) working within the tradition, imitating, refashioning, and
restating what the *auctores* have done for centuries. This fundamentally
intertextual practice in writing is then transmitted to us, readers and
critics, who read in a comparable intertextual matrix as we recreate the
books for ourselves, our students, and our readers.

Therefore, something in that literariness, and the reality that the text
mirrors and creates, makes it perennial and universal. The *Odyssey*
moves us as much as Joyce does, and vice versa; the *Aeneid* as much as
Hermann Broch, and vice versa. When the baron de Charlus, in Proust,
confesses that the greatest tragedy in his life was the death of Lucien de
Rubempré, a character in Balzac, I – junior year abroad – knew what he
meant. In a flash I knew that the greatest tragedy in mine was when
Albertine left, and I would never get over it.

I close with an *exemplum* and a parable, both brief. The *exemplum*.
Consider the *Song of Roland*, arguably the first masterpiece of modern
Europe. Woman is a prize to be seized or a token to be displayed that
reinforces the homosocial bond and testifies to the hero's greatness.
The Muslim Orient is a menace – the incursion of hordes of semihu-
man adversaries. Vanquished in Holy War, they are offered the choice
of conversion or annihilation. No reader today is expected to share the
feudal-aristocratic-crusader values of pre-Gothic France, although they
are fascinating (rather like Klingon) and they do tell us much about
the structures of and tensions within feudalism. The literariness of the
Song of Roland is something else. It is the mimesis and mythos of heroism, duty, responsibility, sacrifice, and atonement. It is a youth choos-
ing to die in expiation for his pride, and a surrogate father weeping
over the son's body, forced to carry on, old and tired, without the son.
It is tragedy and coming to terms with tragedy. At these moments of
anagnorisis – ours as well as the characters' – pity and terror are
purged and we the (implied) readers-audience are taken outside of

ourselves. We are enchanted, spellbound, and, in the leap of aesthetic faith and the throes of an aesthetic vision, we (if only for an instant) resemble the gods.

The parable. Once upon a time, in what was to become Clermont-Ferrand, Sidonius Apollinaris dreaded his enforced contact with the Goths. They were so big, and their grunts were so loud. Yet he taught them Latin and, in his spare time, wrote his own poetry. And then he died. Centuries later Auvergne was to be covered by churches and castles, was to be a land of troubadours. In the 1940s Louis Aragon, poet of the Resistance, hiding in the South, evoked medieval courtly love and chivalry as the first vital modern literary creativity in France and Europe and a counterweight of civilization to the barbarism and misogyny of self-proclaimed supermen. In the 1960s Jean Boudou, the greatest novelist in Occitan, wrote a novel about a man dying from cancer in Clermont-Ferrand, in despair because no one anymore, in the city of troubadours, spoke his language. And then Aragon and Boudou died. But, you see, the books endure. The books live.

Notes

1 Leo Spitzer

1 E. Kristina Baer and Daisy E. Shenholm, *Leo Spitzer on Language and Literature: A Descriptive Bibliography* (New York: Modern Language Association, 1991).

2 David Bellos, 'Leo Spitzer: An Introduction,' in *Leo Spitzer: Essays on Seventeenth-Century French Literature*, ed. David Bellos, xi–xxix, esp. xxi (Cambridge: Cambridge University Press, 1983).

3 Discussed especially in 'Linguistics and Literary History,' in Leo Spitzer, *Linguistics and Literary History: Essays in Stylistics*, 1–39 (Princeton: Princeton University Press, 1948); and in 'Sviluppo di un metodo,' *Cultura Neolatina* 20 (1960): 109–28, trans. 'Development of a Method,' in *Leo Spitzer: Representative Essays*, ed. Alban K. Forcione, Herbert Lindenberger, and Madeline Sutherland, 421–48 (Stanford: Stanford University Press, 1988).

4 Spitzer, 'Linguistics and Literary History,' 19–20, 23.

5 See, among others, Jean Hytier, 'La méthode de M. Leo Spitzer,' *Romanic Review* 41 (1950): 42–59; Harry Levin, 'Two *Romanisten* in America: Spitzer and Auerbach,' in *The Intellectual Migration: Europe and America, 1930–1960*, ed. Donald Fleming and Bernard Bailyn, 463–84 (Cambridge, MA: Harvard University Press, 1969); Geoffrey Green, *Literary Criticism and the Structures of History: Erich Auerbach and Leo Spitzer* (Lincoln: University of Nebraska Press, 1982); James V. Catano, *Language, History, Style: Leo Spitzer and the Critical Tradition* (Urbana: University of Illinois Press, 1988); Baer, 'Leo Spitzer on Philology: An Introduction,' in *Leo Spitzer on Language and Literature*, 1–12; Hans Ulrich Gumbrecht, *Vom Leben und Sterben der grossen Romanisten* (Munich: Hanser, 2002), 72–151.

6 Yakov Malkiel, 'Necrology: Leo Spitzer,' *Romance Philology* 14 (1960–1): 362–4.

7 Stephen Gilman, 'A Rejoinder to Leo Spitzer,' *Hispanic Review* 25 (1957): 112–21, esp. 116, 112; in response to Spitzer, 'A New Book on the Art of *The Celestina*,' *Hispanic Review* 25 (1957): 1–25. Also in defense of Gilman, see J. Richard Andrews and Joseph H. Silverman, 'On "Destructive Criticism"': A Rejoinder to Mr. Leo Spitzer,' *Modern Language Forum* 42 (1957): 3–24.

8 Green, *Literary Criticism and the Structures of History*, 88–94. See also René Wellek, *A History of Modern Criticism: 1750–1950*, vol. 7: *German, Russian, and Eastern European Criticism, 1900–1950* (New Haven: Yale University Press, 1991), 134–53.

9 Spitzer, 'Development of a Method,' 447.

10 Green, *Literary Criticism and the Structures of History*, 1–7.

11 Spitzer, 'Development of a Method,' 448.

12 Spitzer, '*Geistesgeschichte* vs. History of Ideas as Applied to Hitlerism,' *Journal of the History of Ideas* 5 (1944): 191–203, in response to Arthur O. Lovejoy, 'The Meaning of Romanticism for the Historian of Ideas,' *Journal of the History of Ideas* 2 (1941): 257–78.

13 Spitzer cited by Wellek, *History of Modern Criticism*, 7: 144.

14 Spitzer, 'El barroco español,' *Boletín del Instituto de Investigaciones Históricas* 28 (1943–4): 12–30; and *Romanische Literaturstudien, 1936–1956* (Tübingen: Niemeyer, 1959), 789–802.

15 Erich Auerbach, *Mimesis: dargestellte Wirklichkeit in der abendländischen Literatur* (Berne: Francke, 1946), trans. Willard R. Trask, *Mimesis: The Representation of Reality in Western Literature* (Princeton: Princeton University Press, 1953); Ernst Robert Curtius, *Europäische Literatur und lateinisches Mittelalter* (Berne: Francke, 1948), trans. Willard R. Trask, *European Literature and the Latin Middle Ages* (New York: Pantheon Books, 1953); Karl Vossler, *Die göttliche Komödie*, 2 vols. (Heidelberg: Winter, 1907–10), trans. William Cranston Lawton, *Medieval Culture: An Introduction to Dante and His Times* (New York: Harcourt, Brace, 1929).

16 Wellek, *History of Modern Criticism*, 7: 136; Spitzer, *Die Wortbildung als stilistisches Mittel exemplifiziert an Rabelais, nebst einem Anhang über die Wortbildung bei Balzac in seinen 'Contes drôlatiques'* (Halle: Niemeyer, 1910).

17 Spitzer, *Linguistics and Literary History*, repr. (New York: Russell, 1962).

18 Spitzer, *Stilstudien* (Munich: Hueber, 1928); *Romanische Stil- und Literaturstudien* (Marburg: Elwert, 1931).

19 Spitzer, *Studien zu Henri Barbusse* (Bonn: Cohen, 1920); 'Pseudo-objektive Motivierung (Eine stilistisch-literaturpsychologische Studie),' *Zeitschrift für Französische Sprache und Literatur* 46 (1923): 359–85; 'Der Unanismus Jules Romains' im Spiegel seiner Sprache,' *Archivum Romanicum* 8 (1924): 59–122; 'Zum Stil Marcel Prousts,' in *Stilstudien*, 2: 365–497.

20 Spitzer, *Betrachtungen eines Linguisten über Houston Stewart Chamberlains Kriegsaufsätze und die Sprachbewertung im allgemein* (Leipzig: n.p., 1918); *Fremdwörterhatz und Fremdvölkerhass: Eine Streitschrift gegen die Sprachreinigung* (Vienna: Manzsche, 1918). Curtius's essay is *Deutscher Geist in Gefahr* (Stuttgart: Deutsche Verlags-Anstalt, 1932).

21 Spitzer, 'American Advertising Explained as Popular Art,' in *A Method of Interpreting Literature*, 102–49 (Northampton: Smith College, 1949).

22 Spitzer, 'Le style "circulaire,"' *Modern Language Notes* 55 (1940): 495–9; 'Note on the Poetical and Empirical "I" in Medieval Authors,' *Traditio* 4 (1947): 414–22; and *Classical and Christian Ideas of World Harmony*, ed. Anna Granville Hatcher (Baltimore: Johns Hopkins University Press, 1963).

23 E.M.W. Tillyard and C.S. Lewis, *The Personal Heresy: A Controversy* (London: Oxford University Press, 1939).

24 The seminal volumes from this approach are Durant Waite Robertson, Jr., *A Preface to Chaucer: Studies in Medieval Perspectives* (Princeton: Princeton University Press, 1962); Bernard F. Huppé and D.W. Robertson, Jr., *Fruyt and Chaf: Studies in Chaucer's Allegories* (Princeton: Princeton University Press, 1963); Huppé, *A Reading of the Canterbury Tales* (Albany: State University of New York Press, 1964); John V. Fleming, *The 'Roman de la Rose': A Study in Allegory and Iconography* (Princeton: Princeton University Press, 1969).

25 Spitzer, *L'amour lointain de Jaufré Rudel et le sens de la poésie des troubadours*, University of North Carolina Studies in the Romance Languages and Literature (Chapel Hill: University of North Carolina Press, 1944).

26 Spitzer, 'Marie de France – Dichterin von Problem-Märchen,' *Zeitschrift für Romanische Philologie* 50 (1930): 29–67.

27 Spitzer, 'The Prologue to the *Lais* of Marie de France,' *Modern Philology* 40 (1943–4): 96–102; 'La "lettre sur la baguette du coudrier" dans le lai du *Chievrefueil*,' *Romania* 69 (1947): 80–90.

28 Spitzer, 'Sobre el carácter histórico del *Cantar de myo Cid*,' *Nueva Revista de Filología Hispánica* 2 (1948): 105–17.

29 Spitzer, 'Speech and Language in *Inferno* XIII,' *Italica* 19 (1942): 81–104.

30 Spitzer, 'The Farcical Elements in *Inferno* XXI–XXIII,' *Modern Language Notes* 59 (1944): 83–8; 'The Addresses to the Reader in the *Commedia*,' *Italica* 32 (1955): 143–65.

31 Spitzer, 'Zur Literaturgeschichte: Zur Auffassung der Kunst des Arcipreste de Hita,' *Zeitschrift für Romanische Philologie* 54 (1934): 237–70.

32 Spitzer, '*Explication de texte* Applied to Three Great Middle English Poems,' *Archivum Linguisticum* 3 (1951): 1–22, 157–65.

33 Spitzer, 'Étude ahistorique d'un texte: "Ballade des dames du temps jadis,"' *Modern Language Quarterly* 1 (1940): 7–22; 'Zur sprachlichen Interpretation

von Wortkunstwerken,' *Neue Jahrbücher für Wissenschaft und Jugendbildung, Leipzig* 6 (1930): 632–50.

34 *Leo Spitzer: Representative Essays,* 422.

35 Benjamin Bennett, 'The Politics of the Mörike-Debate and Its Object,' *Germanic Review* 68 (1993): 60–8.

36 Emily Apter, 'The Human in the Humanities,' *October* 96 (Spring 2001): 71–85.

37 Spitzer, 'Development of a Method,' 432.

38 Donald H. Hook, 'Spitzer and Key Revisited: The Artfulness of Advertising,' *Language and Style* 19 (1986): 184–95; Roger Pensom, 'Form and Meaning in *Aucassin et Nicolette,*' in *Littera et Sensus: Essays on Form and Meaning in Medieval French Literature Presented to John Fox,* ed. D.A. Trotter, 63–72 (Exeter: University of Exeter, 1989); Orrin N.C. Wang, 'Allegories of Praxis: The Reading of Romanticism and Fascism in A.O. Lovejoy and Leo Spitzer,' *CLIO* 20 (1990–1): 39–51; Amy Wygant, 'Leo Spitzer's Racine,' *MLN* 109 (1994): 632–49; Jules Brody, 'Lire La Fontaine: la méthode de Leo Spitzer,' *Papers on French Seventeenth Century Literature* 23 (1996): 15–21; Richard Klein, 'The Object of French Studies: *Gebrauchkunst,*' *Forum for Modern Language Studies* 37 (2001): 405–15; Apter, 'The Human in the Humanities,' and 'CNN Creole: Trademark Literacy and Global Language Travel,' *Sites* 5 (2001): 27–46.

39 Spitzer, 'Linguistics and Literary History,' 22.

2 Ernst Robert Curtius

1 Tübingen: Niemeyer, 1983; Richards's Introduction (pp. 1–19) is invaluable. I also recommend Arthur R. Evans, Jr., 'Ernst Robert Curtius,' in *On Four Modern Humanists: Hofmannsthal, Gundolf, Curtius, Kantorowicz,* 85–145 (Princeton: Princeton University Press, 1970).

2 Walter Berschin and Arnold Rothe, eds., *Ernst Robert Curtius: Werk, Wirkung, Zukunftsperspektiven, Heidelberger Symposion zum hundertsten Geburtstag 1986* (Heidelberg: Winter, 1989); Wolf-Dieter Lange, ed., *'In Ihnen begegnet sich das Abendland': Bonner Vorträge zur Erinnerung an Ernst Robert Curtius* (Bonn: Bouvier, 1990); Jeanne Bem and André Guyaux, eds., *Ernst Robert Curtius et l'idée d'Europe: Actes du Colloque de Mulhouse et Thann* (Paris: Champion, 1995). See also two recent intelligent, well-informed book-length studies: Christine Jacquemard-de Gemaux, *Ernst Robert Curtius (1889–1956): Origines et cheminements d'un esprit européen* (Berne: Lang, 1998), and Karl Thönnissen, *Ethos und Methode: Zur Bestimmung der Metaliteratur nach Ernst Robert Curtius* (Aachen: Aquamarine, 2001).

3 Westra, review of *Werk, Wirkung, Zukunftsperspektiven, Canadian Review of Comparative Literature* 19 (1992): 642–5 passim.

4 Peter Jehn, 'Ernst Robert Curtius: Toposforschung als Restauration,' in *Toposforschung: Eine Dokumentation,* ed. Jehn, vii–lxiv (Frankfurt: Athenäum, 1972); Michael Nerlich, 'Romanistik und Anti-Kommunismus,' *Das Argument* 14:1 (1972): 276–313, 'Sur les différences nationales dans la capacité de deuil: à propos de Ernst Robert Curtius et Paul de Man,' *Lendemains* 59 (1990): 5–15, and 'Curtius trahi par les siens: Annotations aux actes d'un colloque sur "le grand Européen cosmopolite,"' *Romanische Forschungen* 109 (1997): 436–74; Hans Ulrich Gumbrecht, '"Zeitlosigkeit, die durchscheint in der Zeit": Über E.R. Curtius' unhistorisches Verhältnis zur Geschichte,' in *Werk, Wirkung, Zukunftsperspektiven,* 227–41, repr. in Gumbrecht, *Vom Leben und Sterben der grossen Romanisten,* 49–71 (Munich: Hanser, 2002); Hans Manfred Bock, 'Die Politik des "Unpolitischen": Zu Ernst Robert Curtius' Ort im politisch-intellektuellen Leben der Weimarer Republik,' *Lendemains* 59 (1990): 16–61; Mark Anderson, 'La restauration de la décadence: Curtius et T.S. Eliot,' in *Curtius et l'idée d'Europe,* ed. Ben and Guyaux, 167–81; and Peter André Bloch, 'Curtius visionnaire idéaliste de la littérature contemporaine,' ibid., 107–18.

5 Their major works are: Robertson, *A Preface to Chaucer,* and Paul Zumthor, *Essai de poétique médiévale* (Paris: Seuil, 1972).

6 Curtius, *Li quatre livre des Reis: Die Bücher Samuelis und der Könige in einer französischen Bearbeitung des 12. Jahrhunderts* (Dresden: Gesellschaft für Romanische Literatur; Halle: Niemeyer, 1911).

7 Curtius, *Ferdinand Brunetière: Beitrag zur Geschichte der französischen Kritik* (Strasbourg: Trübner, 1914); *Maurice Barrès und die geistigen Grundlagen des französischen Nationalismus* (Bonn: Cohen, 1921); *Balzac* (Bonn: Cohen, 1923).

8 Potsdam: Kiepenheuer, 1918.

9 Stuttgart: Deutsche Verlags-Anstalt, 1925.

10 Leo Spitzer, *Studien zu Henri Barbusse* (Bonn: Cohen, 1920); 'Pseudo-objektive Motivierung (Eine stilistisch-literaturpsychologische Studie),' *Zeitschrift für Französische Sprache und Literatur* 46 (1923): 359–85; 'Der Unanismus Jules Romains' im Spiegel seiner Sprache,' *Archivum Romanicum* 8 (1924): 59–122; 'Zum Stil Marcel Prousts,' in *Stilstudien* (Munich: Huebner, 1928), 2: 365–497.

11 Curtius, *Marcel Proust* (Berlin: Suhrkamp, 1952).

12 Curtius, 'T.S. Eliot,' *Neue Schweizer Rundschau* (April 1927): 348ff.; *James Joyce und sein 'Ulysses'* (Zürich: Verlag der Neuen Schweizer Rundschau, 1929). These are brilliant essays in modern criticism and in the appreciation of modern literature.

13 When Anderson, 'La restauration,' and Bloch, 'Curtius visionnaire,' state that Curtius was indifferent to the literature of modernity or that he found it repugnant, they allude to his relative neglect of literature in German. Even though *Germanistik* was not his field, Curtius nevertheless admired enormously George, Rilke, Hofmannsthal, and Hesse.

14 The repudiation or, rather, *dépassement* of nationalism (both French and German) in favour of French-German understanding and a mutual striving for European unity is one of the themes most emphasized in recent scholarship on Curtius. See, for example, *Ernst Robert Curtius et l'idée d'Europe*, Jacquemard-de Gemaux, *Ernst Robert Curtius*, and Manfred S. Fischer, '*Europa' und 'das Nationale' bei Ernst Robert Curtius* (Aachen: Fischer, 2000).

15 This is the generally accepted view, nuanced however by Hans Helmut Christmann, 'Ernst Robert Curtius und die deutschen Romanisten,' in '*In Ihnen begegnet sich das Abendland*,' ed. Lange, 65–84. See also Stefan Gross, *Ernst Robert Curtius und die deutsche Romanistik der zwanziger Jahre: Zum Problem nationaler Images in der Literaturwissenschaft* (Bonn: Bouvier, 1980).

16 Curtius, *Deutsch-französische Gespräche 1920–1950: La correspondance de Ernst Robert Curtius avec André Gide, Charles Du Bos et Valery Larbaud*, ed. Herbert Dieckmann and Jane M. Dieckmann (Frankfurt: Klostermann, 1980). On the correspondence, consult Raimund Theis, *Auf der Suche nach dem besten Frankreich: Zum Briefwechsel von Ernst Robert Curtius mit André Gide und Charles Du Bos* (Frankfurt: Klostermann, 1984).

17 Curtius, *Die französische Kultur: Eine Einführung* (Stuttgart: Deutsche Verlags-Anstalt, 1930), vol. 1 of *Frankreich* by Ernst Robert Curtius and Arnold Bergsträsser, trans. Olive Wyon, *The Civilization of France: An Introduction* (New York: Macmillan, 1932).

18 Charles Du Bos, 'Ernst Robert Curtius,' in *Approximations, cinquième série*, 107–39, esp. 112 (Paris: Corrêa, 1930).

19 Curtius, *Deutscher Geist in Gefahr* (Stuttgart: Deutsche Verlags-Anstalt, 1932) was attacked by Hermann Sauter in the Nazi *Völkischer Beobachter* no. 83 (24 March 1933).

20 Attacked by Anderson, Bloch, Gumbrecht, and Nerlich; see note 4 above. More judicious, in my opinion, and more cognizant of the historical situation at the end of the Weimar Republic are the following: Evans, 'Ernst Robert Curtius'; Richards, *Modernism, Medievalism, and Humanism*, and 'La conscience européenne chez Curtius et chez ses détracteurs,' in *Ernst Robert Curtius et l'idée d'Europe*, 257–86; Christoph Dröge, 'Avec Goethe, contre Berlin: l'image de l'Allemagne chez Curtius et Gide,' ibid., 199–215; Joseph Jurt, 'Curtius et la position de l'intellectuel dans la société allemande,' ibid., 239–55; Jacquemard-de Gemaux, *Ernst Robert Curtius,*

161–80; and, finally, the response to Nerlich's allegations by four scholars involved in the Mulhouse/Thann conference, 'Réponses à Michael Nerlich: "Curtius trahi par les siens,"' *Romanische Forschungen* 110 (1998): 478–90.

21 For the Sauter review in *Völkischer Beobachter*, see note 19 above. According to Sauter, among other things, Curtius fails to understand the true German spirit because of his contacts with Jews and with people misled by the Jewish way of thinking, and because he knows so little of the biological [racial] foundations of the German spirit. On Curtius's plight under the Nazis, see Richards, 'La conscience européenne,' with the illuminating results of his research into the National Socialist archives.

22 Curtius, *Europäische Literatur und lateinisches Mittelalter* (Berne: Francke, 1948), trans. Willard R. Trask, *European Literature and the Latin Middle Ages* (New York: Pantheon Books, 1953).

23 See Peter Jehn, ed., *Toposforschung: Eine Dokumentation* (Frankfurt: Athenäum, 1972); and Max L. Baeumer, ed., *Toposforschung*, Wege der Forschung 195 (Darmstadt: Wissenschaftliche Buchgesellschaft, 1973).

24 On Curtius's ties to Aby Warburg and to the Warburg Institute from 1928 to the postwar years, see Dieter Wuttke, ed., *Kosmopolis der Wissenschaft: E.R. Curtius und das Warburg Institute, Briefe 1928 bis 1953 und andere Dokumente* (Berlin: Koerner, 1989).

25 Bernard Cerquiglini, *Éloge de la variante: Histoire critique de la philologie* (Paris: Seuil, 1989).

26 Northrop Frye, *Fearful Symmetry: A Study of William Blake* (Princeton: Princeton University Press, 1947); *Anatomy of Criticism: Four Essays* (Princeton: Princeton University Press, 1957).

27 Frye, *T.S. Eliot* (Edinburgh: Oliver and Boyd, 1963); *A Natural Perspective: The Development of Shakespearean Comedy and Romance* (New York: Columbia University Press, 1965); *The Return of Eden: Five Essays on Milton's Epics* (Toronto: University of Toronto Press, 1965); *Fools of Time: Studies in Shakespearean Tragedy* (Toronto: University of Toronto Press, 1967); *A Study of English Romanticism* (New York: Random House, 1968); *The Myth of Deliverance: Reflections on Shakespeare's Problem Comedies* (Toronto: University of Toronto Press, 1983); *Northrop Frye on Shakespeare*, ed. Robert Sandler (New Haven: Yale University Press, 1986).

28 Curtius, *Kritische Essays zur europäischen Literatur* (Berne: Francke, 1950, rev. ed., 1954), trans. Michael Kowal, *Essays on European Literature* (Princeton: Princeton University Press, 1973).

29 Curtius, 'Henri Bremond und die französische Mystik,' in *Französischer Geist im zwanzigsten Jahrhundert*, 437–512 (Berne: Francke, 1952).

30 Curtius, *Gesammelte Aufsätze zur romanischen Philologie* (Berne: Francke, 1960),
106–304. See Wolf-Dieter Lange, 'Antiromantische Philologie in Deutschland: E.R. Curtius im Gespräch mit Philipp August Becker (1935–1947),'
in *Werk, Wirkung, Zukunftsperspektiven*, 37–48; Ursula Hillen, *Wegbereiter der
romanischen Philologie: Ph.A. Becker im Gespräch mit G. Gröber, J. Bédier und E.R.
Curtius* (Frankfurt: Lang, 1993).
31 Jean Rychner, *La chanson de geste: Essai sur l'art épique des jongleurs* (Geneva:
Droz, 1955).
32 Curtius, *European Liturature and the Latin Middle Ages*, vi–viii. The original
German text was first published in 1946: 'Vorwort zu einem Buche über das
lateinische Mittelalter und die europäischen Literaturen,' *Die Wandlung* 1:11
(November 1946): 969–74.
33 Curtius was a Christian conservative, rather like C.S. Lewis. That is all.
Actually, more progressive than Lewis, he supported the Weimar Republic's
introduction of modern literature as a school subject, and he approved
of the separation of church and state in France. More on this topic in
chapter 9.
34 In *Essays on European Literature*, the two essays on Virgil (3–26, esp. 9) and the
three on Goethe (27–91).

3 Erich Auerbach

1 Erich Auerbach, *Mimesis: dargestellte Wirklichkeit in der abendländischen
Literatur* (Berne: Francke 1946), trans. Willard R. Trask, *Mimesis: The
Representation of Reality in Western Literature* (Princeton: Princeton Univer-
sity Press, 1953). See also Seth Lerer, ed., *Literary History and the Challenge
of Philology: The Legacy of Erich Auerbach* (Stanford: Stanford University
Press, 1996); Walter Busch and Gerhart Pickerodt, eds., *Wahrnehmen,
Lesen, Deuten: Erich Auerbachs Lektüre der Moderne* (Frankfurt: Klostermann, 1998); and 'Fifty Years after Auerbach's *Mimesis*: The Representation of Reality in Literature,' selected papers in *Poetics Today* 20:1
(Spring 1999): 1–91. The proceedings of the Stanford conference are a
tribute to Auerbach and a touchstone to critical opinion in our postmodern age.
2 My term, 'Tis sixty years since,' alludes, of course, to the subtitle of Walter
Scott's *Waverley; or, 'Tis Sixty Years Since*, a novel that commemorates a time of
transition in the history of Scotland no less momentous than the period following the Second World War for us.
3 Charles Muscatine, review of *Mimesis, Romance Philology* 9 (1955–6): 448–57,
esp. 448.

4 René Wellek, *A History of Modern Criticism: 1750–1950* (New Haven: Yale University Press, 1991), 7: 113–34, esp. 113. See also the tribute from Edward W. Said, 'Introduction to Erich Auerbach's *Mimesis*,' in *Humanism and Democratic Criticism*, 85–118, esp. 85–6 (New York: Columbia University Press, 2004): '*Mimesis* is the greatest and most influential literary humanistic work of the past half century … an example of humanistic practice of its highest.'

5 Marc Escola, 'Vrai caractère du faux dévot: Molière, La Bruyère et Auerbach,' *Poétique* 98 (avril 1994): 181–98; Margaret Drabble, 'Mimesis: The Representation of Reality in the Post-War British Novel,' *Mosaic* 20:1 (Winter 1987): 1–14. Scholars have proposed that Auerbach anticipates Bakhtin, the aesthetics of reception, the new historicism, and cultural studies.

6 For general studies on Auerbach, see Klaus Gronau, *Literarische Form und gesellschaftliche Entwicklung: Erich Auerbachs Beitrag zur Theorie und Methodologie der Literaturgeschichte* (Königstein: Forum Academicum, 1979); and Geoffrey Green, *Literary Criticism and the Structures of History: Erich Auerbach and Leo Spitzer* (Lincoln: University of Nebraska Press, 1982).

7 Auerbach, *Literatursprache und Publikum in der lateinischen Spätantike und im Mittelalter* (Berne: Francke, 1958), trans. Ralph Manheim, *Literary Language and Its Public in Late Latin Antiquity and in the Middle Ages* (New York: Bollingen Foundation, 1965).

8 W. Wolfgang Holdheim, 'Auerbach's *Mimesis*: Aesthetics as Historical Understanding,' *CLIO* 10 (1980–1): 143–54, and 'The Hermeneutic Significance of Auerbach's *Ansatz*,' *New Literary History* 16 (1984–5): 627–31; Michael Holquist, 'The Last European: Erich Auerbach as Precursor in the History of Cultural Criticism,' *Modern Language Quarterly* 54 (1993): 371–91.

9 Leo Spitzer, 'Development of a Method,' in *Leo Spitzer: Representative Essays*, ed. Alban K. Forcione et al. (Stanford: Stanford University Press, 1988), 425–48, esp. 446.

10 Auerbach, 'Vico and Aesthetic Historism,' in *Scenes from the Drama of European Literature*, 181–98, esp. 183–4 (Minneapolis: University of Minnesota Press, 1984; first published 1959).

11 Lee Patterson, *Negotiating the Past: The Historical Understanding of Medieval Literature* (Madison: University of Wisconsin Press, 1987).

12 Although the change of fashion in English studies has proved to be so rapid that nowadays Robertson is neglected, his impact was enormous and, in the long run, beneficial.

13 Hayden White, 'Auerbach's Literary History: Figural Causation and Modernist Historicism,' in *Literary History and the Challenge of Philology*, 124–39. Given all this, I question the statement by Aamir R. Mufti in 'Auerbach in Istanbul: Edward Said, Secular Criticism, and the Question of Minority

Culture,' *Critical Inquiry* 25 (1998–9): 95–125, esp. 99–100: '*Mimesis* is in at least one important sense a fragmentary work, literally, consisting of a series of close readings of small fragments of texts with no overall argument or theoretical perspective ... the work lacks ... an explicit frame or argument.'

14 Scholars such as Holquist ought not to simplify the pre-Dantean medieval culture as categorically religious and Christian. Its variety and complexity are, as Auerbach knew so well, comparable to those of the postmedieval and the modern.

15 William Calin, *A Muse for Heroes: Nine Centuries of the Epic in France* (Toronto: University of Toronto Press, 1983), chaps. 7–10, 18. The French poet Pierre Emmanuel informed me that, although he had never heard of figural typology, my reading of him was accurate; he said he must have picked up *figura* indirectly, from his immersion in a particular, quasi-underground tradition of Catholicism which surfaced in Léon Bloy and Georges Bernanos. He was also a passionate reader of Agrippa d'Aubigné.

16 Calin, *A Muse for Heroes,* chap. 13; 'What *Tales from a Wayside Inn* Tells Us about Longfellow and about Chaucer,' *Studies in Medievalism* 12 (2002): 197–213; 'Aubanel's *Mióugrano* and the Romantic Persona: A Modern Reading,' *Tenso* 3 (1987–88): 43–57; 'Dante on the Edwardian Stage: Stephen Phillips's *Paolo and Francesca,*' in *Medievalism in the Modern World,* ed. Richard Utz and Tom Shippey, 255–61 (Turnhout: Brepols, 1998).

17 Auerbach, *Zur Technik der Frührenaissancenovelle in Italien und Frankreich* (Heidelberg: Winter, 1921); trans. of Giambattista Vico, *Die neue Wissenschaft über die gemeinschaftliche Natur der Völker* (Munich: Allgemeine Verlags-Anstalt, 1924); *Dante als Dichter der irdischen Welt* (Berlin: de Gruyter, 1929), trans. Ralph Manheim, *Dante, Poet of the Secular World* (Chicago: University of Chicago Press, 1961). All of Auerbach's writings on Dante were translated into Italian and published under the title *Studi su Dante* (Milan: Feltrinelli, 1963).

18 Auerbach, *Introduction aux études de philologie romane* (Frankfurt: Klostermann, 1949), trans. Guy Daniels, *Introduction to Romance Languages and Literature* (New York: Capricorn, 1961). On *Literary Language and Its Public,* see note 7.

19 Auerbach, *Scenes from the Drama of European Literature* (Minneapolis: University of Minnesota Press, 1984; first published 1959). Five of the six essays in this collection were published earlier in two of Auerbach's collections in German: *Neue Dantestudien* (Istanbul: Horoz, 1944) and *Vier Untersuchungen zur Geschichte der französischen Bildung* (Berne: Francke, 1951). They are also to be found in his *Gesammelte Aufsätze zur romanischen Philologie* (Berne: Francke, 1967).

20 Robert Gorham Davis, 'The Imitation of Life,' *Partisan Review* 21 (1954): 321–6; Wellek, *A History of Modern Criticism,* 7: 114–15. In a magisterial review

article on *Literary History and the Challenge of Philology*, Holquist quite properly rebukes those who, critiquing Auerbach, are guilty of 'special pleading for their own periods,' cf. 'Erich Auerbach and the Fate of Philology Today,' *Poetics Today* 20:1 (Spring 1999): 77–91, esp. 86.

21 This was already the response by the great Helmut A. Hatzfeld, reviewing Auerbach in *Romance Philology* 2 (1948–9): 333–8.

22 For a most legitimate 'correction' of the *Roland* chapter in *Mimesis*, see William D. Paden, 'Tenebrism in the *Song of Roland*,' *Modern Philology* 86 (1988–9): 339–56.

23 David Perkins, *Is Literary History Possible?* (Baltimore: Johns Hopkins University Press, 1992).

24 Among those who have demystified shoddy scholarship in this domain, see Astradur Eysteinsson, *The Concept of Modernism* (Ithaca, NY: Cornell University Press, 1990), and Joseph Frank, *The Idea of Spatial Form* (New Brunswick, NJ: Rutgers University Press, 1991).

25 Perkins himself wrote an outstanding piece of literary history: *A History of Modern Poetry*, 2 vols. (Cambridge, MA: Harvard University Press, 1976–87).

26 In *Literary History and the Challenge of Philology*, Auerbach is seen as a modernist by White, 'Auerbach's Literary History,' and Carl Landauer, 'Auerbach's Performance and the American Academy, or How New Haven Stole the Idea of *Mimesis*,' 179–94. Green, 'Erich Auerbach and the "Inner Dream" of Transcendence,' ibid., 214–26, deems the German scholar to be both modernist and postmodernist.

27 Terry Eagleton, review of Green, *Literary Criticism and the Structures of History*, *Modern Language Review* 79 (1984): 385–6; Herbert Lindenberger, 'On the Reception of *Mimesis*,' in *Literary History and the Challenge of Philology*, 195–213. Lindenberger's essay is indispensable for all who work on Auerbach and his legacy.

28 Green, *Literary Criticism and the Structures of History*; Jesse M. Gellrich, '*Figura*, Allegory, and the Question of History,' in *Literary History and the Challenge of Philology*, 107–23. See also Gert Mattenklott, 'Erich Auerbach in den deutsch-jüdischen Verhältnissen,' in *Wahrnehmen, Lesen, Deuten*, 15–30.

29 I was Auerbach's last student and, during the year 1956–7, his research assistant.

30 The studies in question are Northrop Frye, *The Great Code: The Bible and Literature* (New York: Harcourt, Brace, Jovanovich, 1982), and *Words with Power: Being a Second Study of 'The Bible and Literature'* (New York: Harcourt, Brace, Jovanovich, 1990). I will address this problem in chapter 8.

31 Martin Elsky, 'Erich Auerbach's *Seltsamkeit*: The Seventeenth Century and the History of Feelings,' in *Reading the Renaissance: Ideas and Idioms from*

Shakespeare to Milton, ed. Marc Berley, 176–204 (Pittsburgh, PA: Duquesne University Press, 2003).

32 See Karlheinz Barck, 'Walter Benjamin and Erich Auerbach: Fragments of a Correspondence,' *Diacritics* 22: 3–4 (Fall–Winter 1992): 81–3. Also, Hans Ulrich Gumbrecht, '"Pathos of the Earthly Progress": Erich Auerbach's Everydays,' in *Literary History and the Challenge of Philology,* 13–35.

33 Auerbach, 'Epilegomena zu *Mimesis,' Romanische Forschungen* 65 (1954): 1–18.

34 Mufti, 'Auerbach in Istanbul'; Said, 'Introduction to Erich Auerbach's *Mimesis.'*

35 Paul A. Bové, *Intellectuals in Power: A Genealogy of Critical Humanism* (New York: Columbia University Press, 1986), 79–208.

36 See also Thomas Docherty, 'Anti-Mimesis: The Historicity of Representation,' *Forum for Modern Language Studies* 26 (1990): 272–81, who calls for historicity within representation and the chrono-politics and geo-politics of representation. He concludes with the hope of 'a more revolutionary form of democracy' (281).

37 Holquist, 'The Last European,' 384, 391.

38 Arthur R. Evans, Jr., 'Erich Auerbach as European Critic,' *Romance Philology* 25 (1971–2): 193–215; Paul Zumthor, 'Erich Auerbach ou l'éloge de la philologie,' *Littérature* 5 (février 1972): 107–16; Wellek, *A History of Modern Criticism,* 7: 122; Jan M. Ziolkowski, 'Forward' to Auerbach, *Literary Language and Its Public,* ix–xxxix, esp. xxii–xxiii. I consider Evans's and Ziolkowski's essays to be especially insightful readings of Auerbach.

39 Auerbach, 'Philology and Weltliteratur,' *Centennial Review* 13 (1969): 1–17, esp. 5.

40 Auerbach, 'Philology and Weltliteratur,' 2.

4 Albert Béguin

1 The standard book in English on the Geneva school remains Sarah N. Lawall, *Critics of Consciousness: The Existential Structures of Literature* (Cambridge, MA: Harvard University Press, 1968). Amidst a myriad of studies, the reader should also consult René Wellek, *A History of Modern Criticism: 1750–1950,* vol. 8: *French, Italian, and Spanish Criticism, 1900–1950* (New Haven: Yale University Press, 1992), chapter 7, 'The Genevan School,' 94–129; Henryk Chudak and Alain Grosrichard, eds., *Bilan de l'École de Genève: Actes du colloque polono-suisse ... Varsovie, mai 1992* (Warsaw: Éditions de l'Université de Varsovie, 1995); and the articles in *Œuvres et Critiques* 27:2 (2002) devoted to the theme 'La critique littéraire suisse: Autour de l'École de Genève,' especially Olivier Pot, 'Jalons pour une critique en mouvement (autour de l'École de Genève),' 5–46.

2 Pierre Grotzer has done massive work on Béguin: a biography, *Existence et destinée d'Albert Béguin: Essai de biographie* (Neuchâtel: Baconnière, 1977); a study of his intellectual evolution, *Albert Béguin ou la passion des autres* (Paris: Seuil, 1977); and two bibliographies: *Les écrits d'Albert Béguin: Essai de bibliographie* (Neuchâtel: Baconnière, 1967), and Béatrice and Pierre Grotzer, *Les Archives Albert Béguin: Inventaire* (Neuchâtel: Baconnière, 1975). See also Dorothée-Juliane Franck, *La quête spirituelle d'Albert Béguin* (Neuchâtel: Baconnière, 1965), and the very interesting, innovative study by Gerd Lemke, *Untersuchungen zu Zitat und Zitiermethode im Werk des Literaturkritikers Albert Béguin* (Frankfurt: Lang, 1973). A number of conferences and issues of journals have been devoted to the man and his work. Consult Julien Green et al., *Albert Béguin: Étapes d'une pensée; Rencontres avec Albert Béguin* (Neuchâtel: Baconnière, 1957); *Esprit* 268 (décembre 1958); *Cahiers du Sud* 360 (avril–mai 1961); *Esprit* 361 (juin 1967); *Civitas* 11 (juillet 1973); Pierre Grotzer, ed., *Albert Béguin et Marcel Raymond: Colloque de Cartigny* (Paris: Corti, 1979); Gastone Mosci, ed., *Albert Béguin: Letteratura e impegno* (Rome: Gruppo di Presenza Culturale, 1979); Maria Teresa Puleio et al., eds., *L'avventura intellettuale ed umana di Albert Béguin: Atti del Convegno internazionale … Catania 20–24 maggio 1981* (Rome: Bulzoni, 1984); Martine Noirjean de Ceuninck, ed., *De l'amitié: Hommage à Albert Béguin (1901–1957)* (Neuchâtel: Université de Neuchâtel, 2001).
3 Albert Béguin, *L'âme romantique et le rêve: Essai sur le romantisme allemand et la poésie française*, 2 vols (Marseille: Éditions des Cahiers du Sud, 1937; repr. Geneva: Slatkine, 1993).
4 Wellek, *A History of Modern Criticism*, 8: 101.
5 Lawall, *Critics of Consciousness*, 60.
6 Wellek, *History of Modern Criticism*, 8:115.
7 See Grotzer, *Existence et destinée*, 65–100.
8 I discuss this issue, with regard to poetry, in *In Defense of French Poetry: An Essay in Revaluation* (University Park: Pennsylvania State University Press, 1987), 99–123.
9 Béguin, *Balzac visionnaire: Propositions* (Geneva: Skira, 1946); *Balzac lu et relu* (Paris: Seuil, 1965). The second volume (which appeared after Béguin's death) is comprised of the first volume plus much additional material. In this respect also, Béguin resembles Edmund Wilson.
10 Béguin, *Gérard de Nerval*, suivi de *Poésie et mystique* (Paris: Stock, 1937); *Gérard de Nerval* (Paris: Corti, 1945). Here also the second volume is comprised of the Nerval portion of the first volume plus five more recent essays.
11 Béguin, *Léon Bloy, l'impatient* (Fribourg: Egloff, 1944); *Léon Bloy, mystique de la douleur* (Paris: Labergerie, 1948).

12 Béguin, *La prière de Péguy* (Neuchâtel: Baconnière, 1942); *L' 'Ève' de Péguy: Essai de lecture commentée* (Paris: Labergerie, 1948); the third volume is his masterly reconstituted edition of Péguy's *Le mystère de la charité de Jeanne d'Arc* (Paris: Club du meilleur livre, 1956).

13 Béguin, *Pascal par lui-même* (Paris: Seuil, 1952).

14 Béguin, *Bernanos par lui-même* (Paris: Seuil, 1954).

15 Béguin, *Poésie de la présence, de Chrétien de Troyes à Pierre Emmanuel* (Neuchâtel: Baconnière, 1957); *Création et destinée: Essais de critique littéraire* (Paris: Seuil, 1973); *Création et destinée II: La réalité du rêve* (Paris: Seuil, 1974).

16 For all these reasons, I find it difficult to accept Stéphane Michaud's comment in 'Le moment Béguin,' *Œuvres et Critiques* 27:2 (2002): 91–104, esp. 98: 'Il rejoint cependant trop une forme d'intolérance au monde moderne ... pour qu'on ne s'en inquiète pas.'

17 J. Hillis Miller, 'The Geneva School: The Criticism of Marcel Raymond, Albert Béguin, Georges Poulet, Jean Rousset, Jean-Pierre Richard, and Jean Starobinski,' in *Theory Now and Then*, 13–29 (New York: Harvester Wheatsheaf, 1991); Gaëtan Picon, 'Balzac surnaturel,' *Esprit* 268 (décembre 1958): 841–52; Georges Poulet, 'Albert Béguin,' in *La conscience critique*, 129–58 (Paris: Corti, 1971), and 'De l'identification critique chez Albert Béguin et Marcel Raymond,' in *Albert Béguin et Marcel Raymond*, ed. Grotzer, 13–39; Marcel Raymond, 'Sur *L'âme romantique et le rêve*,' in *Être et dire: Études*, 209–16 (Neuchâtel: Baconnière, 1970), and 'Albert Béguin,' in *Albert Béguin et Marcel Raymond*, 269–74; Jean Rousset, 'Albert Béguin et l'Allemagne,' in Green, *Albert Béguin: Étapes d'une pensée,'* 157–64; Jean Starobinski, 'Le rêve et l'inconscient: la contribution d'Albert Béguin et de Marcel Raymond,' in *Albert Béguin et Marcel Raymond*, 41–63. See also Jean-Jacques Demorest, 'Albert Béguin, le salut par les poètes,' *Modern Language Notes* 78 (1963): 453–70; and Grotzer, *Albert Béguin ou la passion des autres*, passim.

18 Béguin, 'La rencontre des livres,' in *Création et destinée*, 13–18. Béguin adopts Albert Thibaudet's terminology against both Thibaudet and Barthes, who privilege the professional reader with his professional or 'scientific' approaches. Albert Thibaudet, *Le liseur de romans* (Paris: Crès, 1925).

19 Béguin, 'Critique externe et critique interne,' in *Création et destinée*, 170–6, esp. 174.

20 Béguin, 'Propositions,' in *Création et destinée*, 167–9, esp. 167.

21 Béguin, 'Note sur la critique littéraire,' in *Création et destinée*, 179–83; 'Gaston Bachelard,' 234–7; 'Georges Poulet,' 238–44, and 'Roland Barthes: Précritique,' 245–51.

22 For example, Bernard Böschenstein, 'Albert Béguin face aux poètes du
romantisme allemand,' in *Albert Béguin et Marcel Raymond*, 85–93; and
Stéphane Michaud, 'Le moment Béguin.' The Benjamin text is cited by
Michaud, 92–3.
23 Joanna Zurowska, 'Albert Béguin comparatiste: une relecture de *L'âme
romantique et le rêve*,' in *Bilan de l'École de Genève*, 65–74.
24 Alfred Kazin, *Writing Was Everything* (Cambridge, MA: Harvard University
Press, 1995).
25 Béguin, 'Critique et engagement,' in *Création et destinée*, 189–93, esp. 193.
26 Grotzer, *Existence et destinée*, chap. 6, 'Le choc des événements,' 57–64 and
114, n. 7. Thus we can appreciate Béguin's quoting twice a memorable passage from Bloy: *Léon Bloy, l'impatient*, 83 and 151: 'L'antisémitisme, chose
toute moderne, est le soufflet le plus horrible que notre Seigneur ait reçu
dans sa Passion qui dure toujours, c'est le plus sanglant et le plus impardon-
able parce qu'il le reçoit *sur la Face de sa Mère* et de la main des chrétiens.'
27 Grotzer, *Existence et destinée*, 67.
28 Cited by Grotzer, *Existence et destinée*, 73.
29 Béguin, 'La fonction du critique,' in *Création et destinée*, 184–9, esp. 184.
30 On Béguin the Christian socialist, his relations with Emmanuel Mounier,
and their legacy from Péguy, consult Gastone Mosci, *Mounier e Béguin*
(Urbino: QuattroVenti, 1983).

5 Jean Rousset

1 Born in Geneva, Rousset taught at the Université de Genève from 1949 to
1976, when he retired. He began as Marcel Raymond's *assistant* and succeeded to Raymond's chair of French literature in 1962.
2 The only full-length study on Jean Rousset was published as recently as 2001:
Roger Francillon, *Jean Rousset ou la passion de la lecture* (Geneva: Zoé, 2001),
a judicious, well-informed book.
3 Jean Rousset, *La littérature de l'âge baroque en France: Circé et le paon* (Paris:
Corti, 1953).
4 Significantly, Gustave Lanson, in his *Histoire de la littérature française* (Paris:
Hachette, 1895), the book which determined literary history for much of
the French-speaking world, relegated the preclassical, pre-Louis XIV writers
to the category 'attardés et égarés' (pt. 4, bk. 1, chap. 2).
5 See the very intelligent article by Michel Jeanneret, 'La forme et la force:
Rousset, le baroque et les structures mobiles,' in *Bilan de l'École de Genève: Actes
du colloque polono-suisse … Varsovie, mai 1992*, ed. Henryk Chudak and Alain
Grosrichard, 75–82 (Warsaw: Éditions de l'Université de Varsovie, 1995).

6 A generation of scholars followed in his wake, exploring, defending, and illustrating the baroque. Two of the most eminent testify to a direct personal impact from the Swiss scholar: Gisèle Mathieu-Castellani, 'Marcel Raymond et Jean Rousset, maîtres-pilotes en baroquie: La critique séminale de Marcel Raymond; Portrait de Jean Rousset en critique amoureux,' *Œuvres et Critiques* 27:2 (2002): 153–68; and Claude-Gilbert Dubois, 'Le prospecteur et son suiveur: une promenade à pas rapprochés dans les labyrinthes du baroque,' ibid., 169–78.

7 Jean Rousset, ed., *Anthologie de la poésie baroque française*, 2 vols. (Paris: Colin, 1961).

8 William Calin, *Crown, Cross, and 'Fleur-de-lis': An Essay on Pierre Le Moyne's Baroque Epic 'Saint Louis,'* Stanford French and Italian Studies 6 (Saratoga, CA: Anima Libri, 1977); *A Muse for Heroes: Nine Centuries of the Epic in France* (Toronto: University of Toronto Press, 1983), 191–257.

9 Rousset, *L'intérieur et l'extérieur: Essais sur la poésie et sur le théâtre au XVIIe siècle* (Paris: Corti, 1968).

10 Rousset, *Forme et signification: Essais sur les structures littéraires de Corneille à Claudel* (Paris: Corti, 1962). Derrida's review article, 'Forme et signification,' *Critique* 19 (1963): 483–99, 619–36, which includes his own meditation on the ontology of reading, writing, and the book, praises Rousset's theoretical introduction, 'une remarquable introduction méthodologique qui deviendra sans doute ... une partie importante du discours de la méthode structuraliste en critique littéraire' (488). He also states that structuralism fails to capture the depths, force, tension, power, and movement in a work of literature and that Rousset himself fails to grasp 'l'historicité interne de l'oeuvre elle-même' and 'son *opération*' (498). Curiously, Derrida adopts the intentional fallacy and a version of neopositivism when he praises Rousset's readings of Claudel and Proust, because his approach mirrors their conscious aesthetic, and then faults the Genevan scholar for having employed the same approach to authors from the more distant past. Francillon, on the contrary, denies that Rousset is a structuralist at all, because he makes no effort to be 'scientific' (*Jean Rousset*, 24, 139, 174).

11 The seminal texts, from roughly the decade 1965–75, are: Roland Barthes, *S/Z* (Paris: Seuil, 1970), trans. Richard Miller, *S/Z* (New York: Hill and Wang, 1974); Claude Brémond, *Logique du récit* (Paris: Seuil, 1973); A.-J. Greimas, *Sémantique structurale: Recherche de méthode* (Paris: Larousse, 1966), trans. Danièle McDowell et al., *Structural Semantics: An Attempt at a Method* (Lincoln: University of Nebraska Press, 1983); Roman Jakobson, *Questions de poétique* (Paris: Seuil, 1973); Tzvetan Todorov, *Grammaire du Décaméron* (The Hague: Mouton, 1969.)

12 Rousset, *Le mythe de Don Juan* (Paris: Colin, 1976). Francillon, *Jean Rousset,* 73–6, observes, pertinently, that this volume continues and develops further the critic's studies in the baroque.

13 Rousset, *Leurs yeux se rencontrèrent: La scène de première vue dans le roman* (Paris: Corti, 1981); *Passages: Échanges et transpositions* (Paris: Corti, 1990).

14 Philippe Carrard, 'Starobinski, Rousset et la question du récit,' *Swiss-French Studies* 1:2 (November 1980): 24–61.

15 John E. Jackson, 'L'École de Genève,' in *Histoire de la littérature en Suisse romande,* ed. Roger Francillon, 3: 519–35 (Lausanne: Payot, 1998), esp. 529.

16 Francillon, *Jean Rousset,* 149, 18.

17 Rousset, *Narcisse romancier: Essai sur la première personne dans le roman* (Paris: Corti, 1973).

18 Wayne C. Booth, *The Rhetoric of Fiction* (Chicago: University of Chicago Press, 1961); Gérard Genette, *Figures III* (Paris: Seuil, 1972), trans. Alan Sheridan, *Figures of Literary Discourse* (New York: Columbia University Press, 1982); Franz Stanzel, *Die typischen Erzählsituationen im Roman* (Vienna: Braumüller, 1955), trans. James P. Pusack, *Narrative Situations in the Novel* (Bloomington: Indiana University Press, 1971).

19 Francillon, *Jean Rousset,* 146–7.

20 Rousset, *Le lecteur intime, de Balzac au journal* (Paris: Corti, 1986).

21 See Genette, *Figures III,* and Gerald Prince, *Narratology: The Form and Functioning of Narrative* (Berlin: Mouton, 1982).

22 The seminal texts are Wolfgang Iser, *Der implizite Leser: Kommunikationsformen des Romans von Bunyan bis Beckett* (Munich: Fink, 1972), trans. *The Implied Reader: Patterns of Communication in Prose Fiction from Bunyan to Beckett* (Baltimore: Johns Hopkins University Press, 1974); and *Der Akt des Lesens: Theorie ästhetischer Wirkung* (Munich: Fink, 1976), trans. *The Act of Reading: A Theory of Aesthetic Response* (Baltimore: John Hopkins University Press, 1978).

23 Rousset, *L'intérieur et l'extérieur,* 241.

24 Rousset, *Forme et signification,* i–xxvi.

25 As in the title of Francillon's book: *Jean Rousset ou la passion de la lecture.*

26 As in the title of her article: 'Marcel Raymond et Jean Rousset … Portrait de Jean Rousset en critique amoureux.'

27 See also the suggestive remarks by Carrard, 'L'École de Genève et la rhétorique de la circonspection,' *Stanford French Review* 13 (1989): 267–82, esp. 273–4: 'Les "je" [Rousset the critic as *énonciateur*], on le voit bien, n'appartiennent pas ici à ces shifters d'organisation … que Barthes considérait comme l'un des signes autorisés du locuteur dans le discours à prétention de vérité. Ils ne renvoient pas non plus – toujours dans la terminologie de Barthes – à la "personne passionnelle" d'un critique qui prendrait partie par rapport aux textes envisagés.'

Le "je," dans ces formules, est celui du chercheur qui note, retient, cite ou
emprunte.'

28 Rousset, *Forme et signification*, 22
29 J. Hillis Miller, 'The Geneva School: The Criticism of Marcel Raymond,
Albert Béguin, Georges Poulet, Jean Rousset, Jean-Pierre Richard, and Jean
Starobinski,' in *Theory Now and Then*, 13–29 (New York: Harvester Wheatsheaf, 1991).
30 Georges Poulet, *La conscience critique* (Paris: Corti, 1971), 159–64.
31 Rousset, *Forme et signification*, xi, n. 16.
32 Rousset, *Passages*, 131–214, and *Dernier regard sur le baroque* (Paris: Corti,
1998), 75–186.
33 Francillon, *Jean Rousset*, 137.

6 C.S. Lewis

1 Roger Lancelyn Green and Walter Hooper, *C.S. Lewis: A Biography* (London:
Collins, 1974; rev., expanded ed. London: Collins, 2002); William Griffin,
Clive Staples Lewis: A Dramatic Life (San Francisco: Harper and Row, 1986);
George Sayer, *Jack: C.S. Lewis and His Times* (San Francisco: Harper and Row,
1988); A.N. Wilson, *C.S. Lewis: A Biography* (London: Collins, 1990); and
Humphrey Carpenter, *The Inklings: C.S. Lewis, J.R.R. Tolkien, Charles Williams,
and Their Friends* (London: Allen and Unwin, 1978). Also, Walter Hooper,
Through Joy and Beyond: A Pictorial Biography of C.S. Lewis (New York: Macmillan, 1982).
2 Anne Arnott, *The Secret Country of C.S. Lewis* (London: Hodder and Stoughton, 1974); Beatrice Gormley, *C.S. Lewis: Christian and Storyteller* (Grand Rapids, MI: Eerdmans, 1998); Michael Coren, *The Man Who Created Narnia: The
Story of C.S. Lewis* (Toronto: Lester, 1994).
3 Lyle W. Dorsett, *And God Came In* (New York: Macmillan, 1983); Brian Sibley, *Shadowlands: The Story of C.S. Lewis and Joy Davidman* (London: Hodder and Stoughton,
1985); Douglas H. Gresham, *Lenten Lands* (New York: Macmillan, 1988).
4 William Nicholson, *Shadowlands: A Play* (London: French, 1990) won the
Evening Standard Drama Award for the Best Play of 1990. The motion picture *Shadowlands*, starring Anthony Hopkins and Debra Winger and directed
by Richard Attenborough, was released in 1993 by Spelling Films International and Savoy Pictures.
5 The scholarly journals are *Seven* (ceased publication after 1991), *Mythlore*, and
Inklings Jahrbuch. The semi-scholarly ones are: *CSL: The Bulletin of the New York
C.S. Lewis Society, The Lamp-Post of the Southern California C.S. Lewis Society, The
Canadian C.S. Lewis Journal,* and *The Chronicle of the Portland C.S. Lewis Society.*

6 For full-length studies on Lewis's criticism, see Dabney Adams Hart, *Through the Open Door: A New Look at C.S. Lewis* (Tuscaloosa: University of Alabama Press, 1984), and Bruce L. Edwards, Jr., *A Rhetoric of Reading: C.S. Lewis's Defense of Western Literature* (Provo, UT: Brigham Young University, 1986). For article collections, see Bruce L. Edwards, ed., *The Taste of the Pineapple: Essays on C.S. Lewis as Reader, Critic, and Imaginative Writer* (Bowling Green: Bowling Green State University Popular Press, 1988), and Thomas L. Martin, ed., *Reading the Classics with C.S. Lewis* (Grand Rapids, MI: Baker, 2000). George Watson has reprinted a judicious selection of reviews of Lewis's books as they appeared, *Critical Essays on C.S. Lewis* (Aldershot, Hants: Scolar Press, 1992). I also recommend the appropriate chapters in books by Lionel Adey, *C.S. Lewis: Writer, Dreamer, and Mentor* (Grand Rapids, MI: Eerdmans, 1998) and Peter J. Schakel, *Imagination and the Arts in C.S. Lewis: Journeying to Narnia and Other Worlds* (Columbia: University of Missouri Press, 2002). Still authoritative is J.A.W. Bennett, *The Humane Medievalist: An Inaugural Lecture* (Cambridge: Cambridge University Press, 1965), reprinted in *The Humane Medievalist and Other Essays in English Literature and Learning, from Chaucer to Eliot*, 358–81 (Rome: Edizioni di Storia e Letteratura, 1982).
7 Nevill Coghill, 'The Approach to English,' in *Light on C.S. Lewis*, ed. Jocelyn Gibb, 51–66 (New York: Harcourt, Brace and World, 1965), esp. 60–1.
8 Sayer, *Jack*, 195. Note also, in a letter to A.K. Hamilton Jenkin, 'Did I tell you I have discovered the Renaissance never occurred?' quoted by Brian Barbour, 'Lewis and Cambridge,' *Modern Philology* 96 (1998–9): 439–84, esp. 453.
9 C.S. Lewis, *English Literature in the Sixteenth Century (Excluding Drama)* (Oxford: Oxford University, Clarendon Press, 1954), 55.
10 Lewis, *De Descriptione Temporum: An Inaugural Lecture* (Cambridge: Cambridge University Press, 1955), reprinted in *Selected Literary Essays*, ed. Walter Hooper, 1–14 (Cambridge: Cambridge University Press, 1969).
11 Lewis, *A Preface to 'Paradise Lost'* (London: Oxford University Press, 1942).
12 Lewis, *The Allegory of Love: A Study in Medieval Tradition* (Oxford: Oxford University, Clarendon Press, 1936).
13 On Spenser, *Allegory*, 297–360; *English Literature*, 348–93; the posthumous *Spenser's Images of Life*, ed. Alastair Fowler (Cambridge: Cambridge University Press, 1967); and five articles collected in *Studies in Medieval and Renaissance Literature*, ed. Walter Hooper (Cambridge: Cambridge University Press, 1966), 121–74. On Milton, *Preface*, and 'A Note on *Comus*,' in *Studies*, 175–81.
14 Lewis, *The Discarded Image: An Introduction to Medieval and Renaissance Literature* (Cambridge: Cambridge University Press, 1964).
15 Lewis, 'What Chaucer Really Did to *Il Filostrato*,' *Essays and Studies* 19 (1934): 7–28, reprinted in *Selected Literary Essays*, 27–44.

16 As in T.S. Eliot, 'A Note on the Verse of John Milton,' *Essays and Studies* 21 (1936): 32–40; and F.R. Leavis, *Revaluation: Tradition and Development in English Poetry* (London: Chatto and Windus, 1936), 42–67.

17 Lewis, *Preface*, 33–9.

18 Lewis, *Allegory*, 112–37.

19 Lewis, *English Literature*, 329–42.

20 In articles published in 1939, 1946, 1947, 1948, and 1956. The Shelley, Scott, Morris, and Kipling pieces can be found in *Selected Literary Essays*, 187–250. The articles on MacDonald and Williams have yet to be re-edited in a Lewis collection; for them, see the 'Preface' to *George MacDonald: An Anthology*, ed. C.S. Lewis (London: Bles, 1946), and 'Williams and the Arthuriad,' in Charles Williams and C.S. Lewis, *Arthurian Torso* (London: Oxford University Press, 1948), 91–200.

21 Among others, in alphabetical order, Joan Bennett, 'The Love Poetry of John Donne: A Reply to Mr. C.S. Lewis,' in *Seventeenth Century Studies Presented to Sir Herbert Grierson*, 85–104 (Oxford: Oxford University, Clarendon Press, 1938); S.L. Goldberg, 'C.S. Lewis and the Study of English,' *Melbourne Critical Review* 5 (1962): 119–27; Roger Sherman Loomis, 'Literary History and Literary Criticism: A Critique of C.S. Lewis,' *Modern Language Review* 60 (1965): 508–11; Peter Milward, S.J., 'A Judgment Judged – Lewis on the More-Tyndale Controversy,' *Moreana* 64 (March 1980): 28–36; Paul Piehler, 'Visions and Revisions: C.S. Lewis's Contribution to the Theory of Allegory,' in *The Taste of the Pineapple*, ed. Edwards, 79–91; Roger Sharrock, 'Second Thoughts: C.S. Lewis on Chaucer's *Troilus*,' *Essays in Criticism* 8 (1958): 123–37; Elmer Edgar Stoll, 'Give the Devil His Due: A Reply to Mr. Lewis,' *Review of English Studies* 20 (1944): 108–24; Francis Lee Utley, 'Anglicanism and Anthropology: C.S. Lewis and John Speirs,' *Southern Folklore Quarterly* 31 (1967): 1–11; and Eugene Vinaver, 'On Art and Nature: A Letter to C.S. Lewis,' in *Essays on Malory*, ed. J.A.W. Bennett, 29–40 (Oxford: Oxford University, Clarendon Press, 1963). See also Sam McBride, 'C.S. Lewis's *A Preface to "Paradise Lost,"* the Milton Controversy, and Lewis Scholarship,' *Bulletin of Bibliography* 52 (1995): 317–31.

22 Olaf Tollefsen, 'C.S. Lewis on Evaluative Judgments of Literature,' *Modern Schoolman* 56 (1978–9): 356–63.

23 E.M.W. Tillyard and C.S. Lewis, *The Personal Heresy: A Controversy* (London: Oxford University Press, 1939).

24 Lewis, *An Experiment in Criticism* (Cambridge: Cambridge University Press, 1961).

25 Wolfgang Iser, *The Implied Reader* and *The Act of Reading*; Robert Escarpit, *Sociologie de la littérature* (Paris: Presses Universitaires de France, 1958), and

Le littéraire et le social: Éléments pour une sociologie de la littérature (Paris: Flammarion, 1970); Raymond Williams, *Culture and Society, 1780–1950* (London: Chatto and Windus, 1958), and *The Country and the City* (London: Chatto and Windus, 1973); Hans Robert Jauss, *Toward an Aesthetic of Reception*, trans. Timothy Bahti (Minneapolis: University of Minnesota Press, 1982), and *Ästhetische Erfahrung und literarische Hermeneutik*, vol. 1: *Versuche im Feld der ästhetischen Erfahrung* (Munich: Fink, 1977), trans. Michael Shaw, *Aesthetic Experience and Literary Hermeneutics* (Minneapolis: University of Minnesota Press, 1982).

26   How to 'place' Lewis vis-à-vis current critical practice remains, inevitably, an open question. Edwards, *Rhetoric of Reading*, sets Lewis against New Criticism, deconstruction, and reader response, approaches that Edwards finds antipathetic to Lewis (and himself). David C. Downing, on the contrary, in a most perceptive essay, sees ways in which Lewis resembles postmodern thinkers: 'From Pillar to Postmodernism: C.S. Lewis and Current Critical Discourse,' *Christianity and Literature* 46 (1996–7): 169–78.

27   See three essays published in *Studies in the Literary Imagination* 14:2 (Fall 1981): Alan Jones and Edmund Fuller, 'An Affectionate and Muted Exchange anent Lewis': 7–11; Norman Pittenger, 'C.S. Lewis: Combative in Defense': 13–20; Walter F. Hartt, 'Godly Influences: The Theology of J.R.R. Tolkien and C.S. Lewis': 21–9.

28   For example, Kath Filmer, *The Fiction of C.S. Lewis: Mask and Mirror* (New York: St Martin's Press, 1993), 88–131, devotes three chapters to denouncing Lewis for alleged antifeminism. Candice Fredrick and Sam McBride, *Women among the Inklings: Gender, C.S. Lewis, J.R.R. Tolkien, and Charles Williams* (Westport, CT: Greenwood, 2001), expand the topic – the purported subjection of women – to include the entire Inklings' circle.

29   Helen Gardner, 'Clive Staples Lewis: 1898–1963,' *Proceedings of the British Academy* 51 (1965): 417–28. Gardner, one of the most eminent Donne scholars of the century, may have been angered by the fact that Lewis reserved his greatest praise for 'golden' poets such as Sidney and Spenser. It is true, according to Owen Barfield, quoting Alan Watts, that Lewis manifested 'a certain ill-concealed glee in adopting an old-fashioned and unpopular position' (*Light on C.S. Lewis*, xi). Personally, I consider the glee to be one of Lewis's many positive traits.

30   Robertson, *A Preface to Chaucer*; Huppé, *A Reading of the Canterbury Tales*; Huppé and Robertson, *Fruyt and Chaf*; Fleming, *The 'Roman de la Rose.'*

31   Peter Milward, S.J., *A Challenge to C.S. Lewis* (Madison and Teaneck: Fairleigh Dickinson University Press, 1995).

32   For a recent belated Robertsonian reading, see David Lyle Jeffrey, 'Medieval Literature,' in *Reading the Classics*, 72–86.

33 The four traits are Humility, Courtesy, Adultery, and the Religion of Love (*Allegory*, 2).
34 Also, Piehler, 'Visions and Revisions,' points out the weaknesses in Lewis's theory of allegory.
35 Gardner, 'Clive Staples Lewis,' 427, observes that in *English Literature* Lewis devotes eight pages to magic and only two to education.
36 Kathryn Kerby-Fulton, '"Standing on Lewis's Shoulders": C.S. Lewis as Critic of Medieval Literature,' *Studies in Medievalism* 3 (1990–1): 257–78, alludes several times to Lewis's less "than enthusiastic response to *Piers Plowman.*
37 Lewis, *Experiment*, chapter 9 (88–94) and chapter 11 (104–29). Note that some readers of Lewis are convinced that he only praises books and says the best about them. According to Eugene McGovern, 'Reflections Provoked by *On Stories*,' *CSL: The Bulletin of the New York C.S. Lewis Society* 13:9 (July 1982): 3–6, esp. 4: 'His efforts were in rehabilitation rather than in revaluation … It is hard to find in Lewis's published work an attempt to lower a reputation … Broadly characterized, Lewis's practice was to say all that could be said about an author's strengths, and to say no more than had to be said about his weaknesses.'
38 Is it an example of contradiction? Schakel offers a challenging thesis of evolution in Lewis's aesthetics, from the 1930s to the 1960s: *Reason and Imagination in C.S. Lewis: A Study of 'Till We Have Faces'* (Grand Rapids, MI: Eerdmans, 1984), 111–16, 163–7.
39 Carpenter, *The Inklings*, 230–1.
40 Lewis, *Experiment*, 112, 121, 127.
41 Barbour, 'Lewis and Cambridge.'
42 Tillyard, *The Muse Unchained: An Intimate Account of the Revolution in English Studies at Cambridge* (London: Bowes and Bowes, 1958).
43 Lewis, *De Descriptione Temporum*, 20–1.
44 For two first-rate studies in this kind of medievalism, see Alice Chandler, *A Dream of Order: The Medieval Idea in Nineteenth-Century English Literature* (Lincoln: University of Nebraska Press, 1970), and Kim Moreland, *The Medievalist Impulse in American Literature: Twain, Adams, Fitzgerald, and Hemingway* (Charlottesville: University Press of Virginia, 1996). I have argued that such modernist antimodernity medievalism is not limited to the Right. On the Continent, especially, we find a leftist medievalism. See Calin, 'The Medieval Presence in Modern Literature: A Question of Criticism and Culture,' *Philological Papers* 27 (1981): 1–7, and *Minority Literatures and Modernism: Scots, Breton, and Occitan, 1920–1990* (Toronto: University of Toronto Press, 2000).
45 Statements by Lewis as cited by Terry W. Glaspey, *Not a Tame Lion: The Spiritual Legacy of C.S. Lewis* (Nashville: Cumberland House, 1996), 143 and 144.

46 See Margaret Patterson Hannay, *C.S. Lewis* (New York: Ungar, 1981), 181; and Milward, *Challenge*, 103–8.

47 John Wain, in *Critical Essays on C.S. Lewis*, ed. Watson, 31; Graham Hough, 'Old Western Man,' ibid., 241.

48 The title of one of MacDiarmid's early lyric collections: *Penny Wheep* (Edinburgh: Blackwood, 1926).

49 On a personal note, Lewis and Reto R. Bezzola, *Les origines et la formation de la littérature courtoise en Occident (500–1200)*, 3 vols in 5 (Paris: Champion, 1944–63), gave me the idea of a French/Anglo-Norman/English common culture in the Middle Ages, a founding culture of the modern West. I explore this in *The French Tradition and the Literature of Medieval England* (Toronto: University of Toronto Press, 1994).

50 Curtius, *Essays on European Literature*, 5.

7 F.O. Matthiessen

1 F.O. Matthiessen, *American Renaissance: Art and Expression in the Age of Emerson and Whitman* (London: Oxford University Press, 1941).

2 See the full-length studies by Giles B. Gunn, *F.O. Matthiessen: The Critical Achievement* (Seattle: University of Washington Press, 1975); Frederick C. Stern, *F.O. Matthiessen: Christian Socialist as Critic* (Chapel Hill: University of North Carolina Press, 1981); William E. Cain, *F.O. Matthiessen and the Politics of Criticism* (Madison: University of Wisconsin Press, 1988); and the pioneering extended chapter by Richard Ruland, 'F.O. Matthiessen, Christian Socialist: Literature and the Repossession of Our Cultural Past,' in *The Rediscovery of American Literature: Premises of Critical Taste, 1900–1940*, 209–73 (Cambridge, MA: Harvard University Press, 1967).

3 René Wellek, *A History of Modern Criticism: 1750–1950*, vol. 6, *American Criticism, 1900–1950* (New Haven: Yale University Press, 1986), 74–84, esp. 75.

4 Matthiessen, 'Irving Babbitt,' in *The Responsibilities of the Critic: Essays and Reviews*, ed. John Rackliffe (New York: Oxford University Press, 1952), 165.

5 Wellek, *A History of Modern Criticism*, 6: 74.

6 Matthiessen, *Sarah Orne Jewett* (Boston: Houghton Mifflin, 1929); *Translation: An Elizabethan Art* (Cambridge, MA: Harvard University Press, 1931); *From the Heart of Europe* (New York: Oxford University Press, 1948). Like so many scholars, Matthiessen had his limits. Sentimental antiquarianism, as in the later Van Wyck Brooks, was not his forte; nor was political and intellectual journalism as in Edmund Wilson, Dwight Macdonald, and Susan Sontag.

7 Matthiessen, *The Achievement of T.S. Eliot: An Essay on the Nature of Poetry* (New York: Oxford University Press, 1935); 2nd ed., revised and enlarged, 1947; 3rd ed., with a chapter on Eliot's later work by C.L. Barber, 1958.

8 Matthiessen departed from the topical approach in the second, revised edition, with chapters devoted to the plays and to *Four Quartets*. In 1958 Barber's chapter treated Eliot's later criticism and his two most recent plays.

9 Gunn: '*The Achievement of T.S. Eliot* ... is so dependent upon Eliot's own standards for a critical evaluation of his poetry that it never quite escapes from the shadow cast by its subject or attains a genuine authority of its own' (31); and Cain: '*The Achievement of T.S. Eliot* ... is a book that now appears uncritical. Matthiessen ... never attains a detached relation to Eliot ... He does not hone a language of his own – there is no competitive dialogue between the critic and the author' (55–6). See also Bertrand Bowron, 'The Making of an American Scholar,' in *F.O. Matthiessen (1902–1950): A Collective Portrait*, ed. Paul M. Sweezy and Leo Huberman, 44–54 (New York: Schuman, 1950).

10 Erich Auerbach, *Dante als Dichter der irdischen Welt* (Berlin: de Gruyter, 1929), trans. Ralph Manheim, *Dante, Poet of the Secular World* (Chicago: University of Chicago Press, 1961); John Freccero, *Dante: The Poetics of Conversion* (Cambridge, MA: Harvard University Press, 1986).

11 György Lukács, *Studies in European Realism*, trans. Edith Bone (London: Hillway, 1950); Pierre Barbéris, *Balzac et le mal du siècle*, 2 vols. (Paris: Gallimard, 1970), *Balzac: Une mythologie réaliste* (Paris: Larousse, 1971), and *Mythes balzaciens* (Paris: Colin, 1972). Leo Marx, 'Double Consciousness and the Cultural Politics of F.O. Matthiessen,' *Monthly Review* 34:9 (February 1983): 34–56, observes that Matthiessen is closer to today's Hegelian Marxists than he was to the vulgar Marxism of his time.

12 Matthiessen, *Henry James: The Major Phase* (London: Oxford University Press, 1944).

13 Van Wyck Brooks, *The Pilgrimage of Henry James* (New York: Dutton, 1925); Vernon L. Parrington, *Main Currents in American Thought: An Interpretation of American Literature from the Beginnings to 1920*, 3 vols. (New York: Harcourt, Brace, 1927–30); Granville Hicks, *The Great Tradition: An Interpretation of American Literature since the Civil War* (New York: Macmillan, 1933), 105–24.

14 *The Notebooks of Henry James*, ed. F.O. Matthiessen and Kenneth B. Murdock (New York: Oxford University Press, 1947); F.O. Matthiessen, *The James Family, Including Selections from the Writings of Henry James, Senior, William, Henry, and Alice James.* (New York: Knopf, 1947).

15 Matthiessen, *Theodore Dreiser,* The American Men of Letters Series (William Sloane Associates, 1951), a posthumous publication. At Dreiser's death the manuscript was completed but not yet revised in its entirety.

16 The point is argued by Stern, *Matthiessen,* 175–6. An example would be Gunn, *Matthiessen,* 170–82, and also Stern himself, 181–2.

17 Cain, *Matthiessen,* 91–131.

18 *The Oxford Book of American Verse,* ed. F.O. Matthiessen (New York: Oxford University Press, 1950); 'Poetry,' in *Literary History of the United States,* ed. Robert E. Spiller et al., 2:1335–57 (New York: Macmillan, 1948); *The Responsibilities of the Critic,* ed. John Rackliffe (New York: Oxford University Press, 1952).

19 Cain himself, *Matthiessen,* 180–90, offers the discussion that Matthiessen avoided.

20 In addition to her other publications in the same line, Jane Tompkins, 'The Other American Renaissance,' in *The American Renaissance Reconsidered,* ed. Walter Benn Michaels and Donald Peace, 34–57 (Baltimore: Johns Hopkins University Press, 1983). I discuss the matter further in chapter 9.

21 Some of Cain's observations were preceded by Stern, *Matthiessen,* 43, and by Jonathan Arac, 'F.O. Matthiessen: Authorizing an American Renaissance,' in *The American Renaissance Reconsidered,* 90–112.

22 Cain, *Matthiessen,* 84–90. L. Freitas Caton, 'The Old, the New, the American Canon: Reputation, History, Form,' *Interdisciplinary Literary Studies* 1:1 (Fall 1999): 60–80, points to the distortion of Matthiessen's record by recent practitioners of cultural studies who mistakenly lump Matthiessen together with the New Critics. Reasonably sympathetic to Matthiessen and Hicks, Freitas nonetheless approves of the condemnation, with language such as: 'Narrow, biased, and inequitable, their editorial methodology would never survive today ... as unfair as it was, the inequities related to their methodology ... their decision not to consider equitable social representation as a central tenet of literary criticism' (63).

23 Ruland and Wellek are also of the opinion that Matthiessen overrated Melville and/or that some of the critic's weakest pages are devoted to arguing stylistic analogies between Melville and Shakespeare.

24 Gunn, *Matthiessen,* 183–4.

25 Five articles treating Matthiessen from the perspective of queer theory appeared between 1989 and 1998: Eric Cheyfitz, 'Matthiessen's *American Renaissance*: Circumscribing the Revolution,' *American Quarterly* 41 (1989): 341–61; David Bergman, 'F.O. Matthiessen: The Critic as Homosexual,' *Raritan* 9:4 (Spring 1990): 62–82; Michael Cadden, 'Engendering F.O. Matthiessen: The Private Life of *American Renaissance*,' in *Engendering Men: The Question of Male Feminist Criticism,* ed. Joseph A. Boone and Michael Cadden,

26–35 (New York: Routledge, 1990); Jay Grossman, 'The Canon in the
Closet: Matthiessen's Whitman, Whitman's Matthiessen,' *American Literature*
70 (1998): 799–832; Charles E. Morris III, '"The Responsibility of the Critic":
F.O. Matthiessen's Homosexual Palimpsest,' *Quarterly Journal of Speech* 84
(1998): 261–82.

8 Northrop Frye

1 John Ayre wrote *Northrop Frye: A Biography* (Toronto: Random House, 1989);
see also the short biography by Joseph Adamson, *Northrop Frye: A Visionary Life*
(Toronto: ECW, 1993). Robert D. Denham's path-breaking *Northrop Frye and
Critical Method* (University Park: Pennsylvania State University Press, 1978)
remains invaluable. The same can be said for the powerfully intelligent book
by A.C. Hamilton, *Northrop Frye: Anatomy of His Criticism* (Toronto: University of
Toronto Press, 1990). First-rate insight can be found in Ronald Bates, *Northrop
Frye* (Toronto: McClelland and Stewart, 1971); David Cook, *Northrop Frye: A
Vision of the New World* (Montreal: New World Perspectives, 1985); Ian Balfour,
Northrop Frye (Boston: Twayne, 1988); Marc Manganaro, *Myth, Rhetoric, and the
Voice of Authority: A Critique of Frazer, Eliot, Frye, and Campbell* (New Haven: Yale
University Press, 1992); Jonathan Hart, *Northrop Frye: The Theoretical Imagina-
tion* (London: Routledge, 1994); Lars Ole Sauerberg, *Versions of the Past –
Visions of the Future: The Canonical in the Criticism of T.S. Eliot, F.R. Leavis, Northrop
Frye, and Harold Bloom* (London: Macmillan, 1997); Ford Russell, *Northrop Frye
on Myth: An Introduction* (New York: Garland, 1998); Caterina Nella Cotrupi,
Northrop Frye and the Poetics of Process (Toronto: University of Toronto Press,
2000); János Kenyeres, *Revolving around the Bible: A Study of Northrop Frye*
(Budapest: Anonymus, 2003). There are also quite a few published conference proceedings and special issues of journals.
2 Northrop Frye, *Fearful Symmetry: A Study of William Blake* (Princeton: Princeton University Press, 1947).
3 Frye, *Anatomy of Criticism: Four Essays* (Princeton: Princeton University Press,
1957).
4 In this context Frye defines the archetype as 'a symbol which connects one
poem with another and thereby helps to unify and integrate our literary
experience' (99).
5 Denham, *Northrop Frye and Critical Method*, 31–57.
6 Fredric Jameson, *The Political Unconscious: Narrative as a Socially Symbolic Act*
(Ithaca: Cornell University Press, 1981), 68–74, praises Frye for his remodel-
ing and renewal of medieval typology, a powerful vision of history which
affirms continuity between the past and the present.

7 Hamilton, *Northrop Frye*, 155–84.
8 Frye offers the example of comparing Shakespeare, Milton, and Shelley. Depending on one's criterion of value, any one of the three can be declared superior to the other two (23–4).
9 Frye, *The Well-Tempered Critic* (Bloomington: Indiana University Press, 1963).
10 *The Well-Tempered Critic* also contains Frye's scathing rejection of those who employ the organic analogy to posit a golden age in the past and our present decline from it. He alludes to 'some book with a butterslide theory of Western culture, according to which this or that spiritual or cultural entity was "lost" after Dante or Raphael or Mozart or whatever the author was attaching his pastoral myth to' (126).
11 Frye, *The Secular Scripture: A Study of the Structure of Romance* (Cambridge, MA: Harvard University Press, 1976).
12 Frye, *A Natural Perspective: The Development of Shakespearean Comedy and Romance* (New York: Columbia University Press, 1965). See, among other studies, Keir Elam, 'A Natural Perspectivism: Frye on Shakespearean Comedy,' in *Ritratto di Northrop Frye*, ed. Agostino Lombardo, 181–94 (Rome: Bulzoni, 1989).
13 Frye, 'Literature as Context: Milton's *Lycidas*,' in *Fables of Identity: Studies in Poetic Mythology*, 119–29 (New York: Harcourt, Brace and World, 1963). This collection includes also a fine essay on Spenser, 'The Structure of Imagery in the *Faerie Queene*,' 69–87.
14 Frye, *The Return of Eden: Five Essays on Milton's Epics* (Toronto: University of Toronto Press, 1965).
15 Frye, *A Study of English Romanticism* (New York: Random House, 1968).
16 Frye, *T.S. Eliot* (Edinburgh: Oliver and Boyd, 1963).
17 Frye, *The Modern Century* (Toronto: Oxford University Press, 1967).
18 The Whidden Lectures at McMaster University; the selection of Frye for the year 1967 coincided with Canada's centennial. Except for the occasional visiting professorship or lecture tour, Frye spent his entire career at the University of Toronto.
19 Frye, *The Bush Garden: Essays on the Canadian Imagination* (Toronto: Anansi, 1971); *Divisions on a Ground: Essays on Canadian Culture*, ed. James Polk (Toronto: Anansi, 1982). The articles in these collections plus a number of other pieces are published in *Northrop Frye on Canada*, vol. 12 of *The Collected Works of Northrop Frye*, ed. Jean O'Grady and David Staines (Toronto: University of Toronto Press, 2003).
20 Frye, *Bush Garden*, 1–127; *Collected Works* 12: 91–229.
21 Frye, 'Canada and Its Poetry,' *Bush Garden*, 129–43; *Collected Works* 12: 26–38.
22 *Bush Garden*, 213–51; *Collected Works* 12: 339–72. The two-volume *Literary History of Canada*, ed. Carl F. Klinck (Toronto: University of Toronto Press,

1965) was shaped in large measure by Frye according to his own understanding of the topic. This work played a crucial role in making Canadian literature a field of academic study and in drawing forth public appreciation for it. See Sandra Djwa, '"Canadian Angles of Vision": Northop Frye, Carl Klinck, and the *Literary History of Canada*,' in *Northrop Frye: Eastern and Western Perspectives*, ed. Jean O'Grady and Wang Ning, 95–109 (Toronto: University of Toronto Press, 2003).

23 David Staines, 'Northrop Frye in a Canadian Context,' in *Visionary Poetics: Essays on Northrop Frye's Criticism*, ed. Robert D. Denham and Thomas Willard, 47–56 (New York: Lang, 1991), and 'Frye: Canadian Critic/Writer,' in *The Legacy of Northrop Frye*, ed. Alvin A. Lee and Robert D. Denham, 155–63 (Toronto: University of Toronto Press, 1994); Eli Mandel, 'Northrop Frye and the Canadian Literary Imagination,' in *Centre and Labyrinth: Essays in Honour of Northrop Frye*, ed. Eleanor Cook et al., 284–97 (Toronto: University of Toronto Press, 1983); Thomas Willard, 'Gone Primitive: The Critic in Canada,' in *Northrop Frye*, ed. O'Grady and Ning, 110–20; and Alessandro Gebbia, 'L'idea di letteratura canadese in Frye,' in *Ritratto di Northrop Frye*, ed. Lombardo, 313–19.

24 The seminal volumes are D.G. Jones, *Butterfly on Rock: A Study of Themes and Images in Canadian Literature* (Toronto: University of Toronto Press, 1970); Margaret Atwood, *Survival: A Thematic Guide to Canadian Literature* (Toronto: Anansi, 1972); and John Moss, *Patterns of Isolation in English Canadian Fiction* (Toronto: McClelland and Stewart, 1974).

25 See Henry Nash Smith, *Virgin Land: The American West as Symbol and Myth* (Cambridge, MA: Harvard University Press, 1950); Charles Feidelson, *Symbolism and American Literature* (Chicago: University of Chicago Press, 1953); R.W.B. Lewis, *The American Adam: Innocence, Tragedy, and Tradition in the Nineteenth Century* (Chicago: University of Chicago Press, 1955); Richard Chase, *The American Novel and Its Tradition* (New York: Doubleday, 1957); Leslie A. Fiedler, *Love and Death in the American Novel* (New York: Criterion, 1960); Daniel Hoffman, *Form and Fable in American Fiction* (New York: Oxford University Press, 1961); Leo Marx, *The Machine in the Garden: Technology and the Pastoral Ideal in America* (New York: Oxford University Press, 1964).

26 Under social and cultural critique we can place *The Stubborn Structure: Essays on Criticism and Society* (Ithaca: Cornell University Press, 1970), and *The Critical Path: An Essay on the Social Context of Literary Criticism* (Bloomington: Indiana University Press, 1971), as well as *The Modern Century*. See also *Northrop Frye on Literature and Society, 1936–1989: Unpublished Papers*, vol. 10 of *The Collected Works of Northrop Fry*, ed. Robert D. Denham (Toronto: University of Toronto Press, 2002), and *Northrop Frye on Modern Culture*, vol. 11 of *The*

Collected Works of Northrop Frye, ed. Jan Gorak (Toronto: University of Toronto Press, 2003). For articles, papers, and talks on the topic of education, see *On Education* (Markham, ON: Fitzhenry and Whiteside, 1990), and *Northrop Frye's Writings on Education,* vol. 7 of *The Collected Works of Northrop Frye,* ed. Goldwin French and Jean O'Grady (Toronto: University of Toronto Press, 2000).

27 Frye, *The Great Code: The Bible and Literature* (New York: Harcourt, Brace, Jovanovich, 1982), and *Words with Power: Being a Second Study of 'The Bible and Literature'* (New York: Harcourt, Brace, Jovanovich, 1990). See also *Creation and Recreation* (Toronto: University of Toronto Press, 1980), and *The Double Vision: Language and Meaning in Religion* (Toronto: University of Toronto Press, 1991), both of which are included in *Northrop Frye on Religion,* vol. 4 of *The Collected Works of Northrop Frye,* ed. Alvin A. Lee and Jean O'Grady (Toronto: University of Toronto Press, 2000).

28 A.C. Hamilton, 'Northrop Frye on the Bible and Literature,' *Christianity and Literature* 41 (1991–2): 255–76.

29 Two collections of selected proceedings from the 2000 McMaster University conference: James M. Kee, ed., *Northrop Frye and the Afterlife of the Word,* Semeia 89 (Atlanta: Society of Biblical Literature, 2002); and Jeffery Donaldson and Alan Mendelson, eds., *Frye and the Word: Religious Contexts in the Writings of Northrop Frye* (Toronto: University of Toronto Press, 2004). In the latter collection I profited especially from Alvin A. Lee, 'Sacred and Secular Scripture(s) in the Thought of Northrop Frye,' 23–42; and Imre Salusinszky, '"In the Climates of the Mind": Frye's Career as a Spiral Curriculum,' 43–56. See also Frank Kermode, 'Northrop Frye and the Bible,' in *Ritratto di Northrop Frye,* ed. Lombardo, 105–20; and Kenyeres, *Revolving around the Bible.*

30 A few classic examples: three articles in Murray Krieger, ed., *Northrop Frye in Modern Criticism: Selected Papers from the English Institute* (New York: Columbia University Press, 1966): Geoffrey H. Hartman, 'Ghostlier Demarcations,' 109–31; Murray Krieger, 'Northrop Frye and Contemporary Criticism: Ariel and the Spirit of Gravity,' 1–26; and W.K. Wimsatt, 'Northrop Frye: Criticism as Myth,' 75–107. See also the very acute analysis by Frank Lentricchia, 'The Place of Northrop Frye's *Anatomy of Criticism,*' in *After the New Criticism,* 2–26 (Chicago: University of Chicago Press, 1980). On Canada, see Frank Davey, 'Surviving the Paraphrase,' in *Surviving the Paraphrase: Eleven Essays on Canadian Literature,* 1–12 (Winnipeg: Turnstone, 1983). On the Bible, see Robert Alter, 'Northrop Frye between Archetype and Typology,' in *Northrop Frye and the Afterlife of the Word,* ed. Kee, 9–21, and in *Frye and the Word,* ed. Donaldson and Mendelson, 137–50.

31 Frye, 'Letter to the English Institute, 1965,' in *Northrop Frye in Modern Criticism*, ed. Krieger, 27–30, esp. 28.
32 See Helen Vendler, 'Frye's *Endymion*: Myth, Ethics, and Literary Description,' in *The Legacy of Northrop Frye*, ed. Lee and Denham, 201–12; and Davey, 'Surviving the Paraphrase.'
33 Pauline Kogan, *Northrop Frye: The High Priest of Clerical Obscurantism* (Montreal: Progressive Books and Periodicals, 1969).
34 John Fekete, *The Critical Twilight: Explorations in the Ideology of Anglo-American Literary Theory from Eliot to McLuhan* (London: Routledge and Kegan Paul, 1977), 105–31.
35 Angus Fletcher, 'Utopian History and the *Anatomy of Criticism*,' in *Northrop Frye in Modern Criticism*, ed. Krieger, 31–73.
36 In addition to the books by Balfour, Denham, and Hamilton, see, for example, Salusinszky, 'Frye and Ideology,' in *Legacy of Northrop Frye*, ed. Lee and Denham, 76–83; Adamson, 'The Treason of the Clerks: Frye, Ideology, and the Authority of Imaginative Culture,' in *Rereading Frye: The Published and Unpublished Works*, ed. David Boyd and Imre Salusinszky, 72–102 (Toronto: University of Toronto Press, 1999); Hamilton, 'Northrop Frye as a Cultural Theorist,' ibid., 103–21; Gary Kuchar, 'Typology and the Language of Concern in the Work of Northrop Frye,' *Canadian Review of Comparative Literature* 27 (2000): 159–80; and Jean O'Grady, 'Northrop Frye on Liberal Education,' in *Northrop Frye*, ed. O'Grady and Ning, 29–41.
37 Linda Hutcheon, 'Eruptions of Postmodernity: The Postcolonial and the Ecological,' *Essays on Canadian Writing* 51–2 (Winter 1993-Spring 1994): 146–63; John Willinsky, 'Frye among (Postcolonial) Schoolchildren: The Educated Imagination,' *Canadian Children's Literature* 79 (Fall 1995): 6–24; Eva Mackey, 'Death by Landscape: Race, Nature, and Gender in Canadian Nationalist Mythology,' *Canadian Woman Studies* 20:2 (Summer 2000): 125–30; L.M. Findlay, 'Frye's Shakespeare, Frye's Canada,' in *Shakespeare in Canada: 'A World Elsewhere'?*, ed. Diana Brydon and Irena R. Makaryk, 292–308 (Toronto: University of Toronto Press, 2002).
38 Alter, 'Northrop Frye between Archetype and Typology'; Harold Bloom, '"Before Moses Was, I am": The Original and Belated New Testaments,' in *Poetics of Influence*, ed. John Hollander (New Haven: Schwab, 1988).
39 Frye, *Well-Tempered Critic*, 114–31.
40 Frye, *Anatomy*, 3.
41 Adamson, 'Treason of the Clerks'; Salusinszky, 'Frye and Ideology.'
42 Indeed, a number of the pieces in *Northrop Frye's Writings on Education* express his disapproval of some of the developments from the student rebellion of the 1960s.

9 Discussion

1 Hans Baron, *The Crisis of the Early Italian Renaissance: Civic Humanism and Republican Liberty in an Age of Classicism and Tyranny*, 2 vols. (Princeton: Princeton University Press, 1955), *Humanistic and Political Literature in Florence and Venice at the Beginning of the Quattrocento: Studies in Criticism and Chronology* (Cambridge, MA: Harvard University Press, 1955), and *From Petrarch to Leonardo Bruni: Studies in Humanistic and Political Literature* (Chicago: University of Chicago Press, 1968); Paul Oskar Kristeller, *The Classics and Renaissance Thought* (Cambridge, MA: Harvard University Press, 1955), *Studies in Renaissance Thought and Letters* (Rome: Edizioni di Storia e Letteratura, 1956), *Renaissance Thought: The Classic, Scholastic, and Humanist Strains* (New York: Harper and Row, 1961), and *Eight Philosophers of the Italian Renaissance* (Stanford: Stanford University Press, 1964); Williams J. Bouwsma, *The Interpretation of Renaissance Humanism* (Washington, DC: American Historical Association, 1959), and *The Culture of Renaissance Humanism* (Washington, DC: American Historical Association, 1973). See also Tony Davies, *Humanism* (London: Routledge, 1997); Kenneth Gouwens, 'Perceiving the Past: Renaissance Humanism after the "Cognitive Turn,"' *American Historical Review* 103 (1998): 55–82; and Jill Kraye, ed., *The Cambridge Companion to Renaissance Humanism* (Cambridge: Cambridge University Press, 1996).
2 Corliss Lamont, *The Philosophy of Humanism*, 7th ed., revised and enlarged (New York: Continuum, 1993); Paul Kurtz, *Humanist Manifesto II* (Buffalo: Prometheus, 1973), *A Secular Humanist Declaration* (Buffalo: Prometheus, 1980), and *In Defense of Secular Humanism* (Buffalo: Prometheus, 1984).
3 James Hankins, 'Two Twentieth-Century Interpreters of Renaissance Humanism: Eugenio Garin and Paul Oskar Kristeller,' *Comparative Criticism* 23 (2001): 3–19.
4 Jean-Paul Sartre, *L'existentialisme est un humanisme* (Paris: Nagel, 1946), trans. Bernard Frechtman, *Existentialism* (New York: Philosophical Library, 1947).
5 Jacques Maritain, *Humanisme intégral: Problèmes temporels et spirituels d'une nouvelle chrétienté* (Paris: Aubier, 1936), trans. Margot Adamson, *True Humanism* (New York: Scribner, 1938).
6 Martin Heidegger, *Brief über den Humanismus*, in *Gesamtausgabe*, vol. 9 (Frankfurt: Klostermann, 1976), trans. in *Basic Writings*, ed. David Farrell Krell, 189–242 (New York: Harper and Row, 1977).
7 Among many authorities, see the American Trotskyite George Novack, *Humanism and Socialism* (New York: Pathfinder, 1973); and the one-time French Communist Roger Garaudy, *Le communisme et la morale* (Paris: Éditions Sociales, 1947), *Humanisme marxiste: Cinq essais polémiques* (Paris: Éditions

Sociales, 1957), and *Perspectives de l'homme: Existentialisme, pensée catholique, marxisme* (Paris: Presses Universitaires de France, 1959).

8 Among other examples, Daniel R. Schwarz, *The Case for a Humanist Poetics* (London: Macmillan, 1990); Stephen R. Yarbrough, *Deliberate Criticism: Toward a Postmodern Humanism* (Athens, GA: University of Georgia Press, 1992); Richard A. Etlin, *In Defense of Humanism: Value in the Arts and Letters* (Cambridge: Cambridge University Press, 1996); Iain Chambers, *Culture after Humanism: History, Culture, Subjectivity* (London: Routledge, 2001); Lorenzo C. Simpson, *The Unfinished Project: Toward a Postmetaphysical Humanism* (New York: Routledge, 2001); Martin Halliwell and Andy Mousley, *Critical Humanisms: Humanist/Anti-Humanist Dialogues* (Edinburgh: Edinburgh University Press, 2003); Jeffrey Noonan, *Critical Humanism and the Politics of Difference* (Montreal: McGill-Queen's University Press, 2003). See also, by Tzvetan Todorov, *Le jardin imparfait: La pensée humaniste en France* (Paris: Grasset, 1998), trans. Carol Cosman, *Imperfect Garden: The Legacy of Humanism* (Princeton: Princeton University Press, 2002).

9 Edward W. Said, *Humanism and Democratic Criticism* (New York: Columbia University Press, 2004).

10 Hugo Friedrich, *Die Struktur der modernen Lyrik: Von Baudelaire bis zur Gegenwart* (Hamburg: Rowohlt, 1956), trans. Joachim Neugroschel, *The Structure of Modern Poetry, from the Mid-nineteenth to the Mid-twentieth Century* (Evanston: Northwestern University Press, 1974); Frye, *The Modern Century*.

11 Especially pertinent in demystifying this weakness are Astradur Eysteinsson, *The Concept of Modernism* (Ithaca: Cornell University Press, 1990), and Joseph Frank, 'Spatial Form in Modern Literature,' in *The Idea of Spatial Form*, 3–66 (New Brunswick, NJ: Rutgers University Press, 1991).

12 Edmund Wilson, *Axel's Castle: A Study in the Imaginative Literature of 1870–1930* (New York: Scribner, 1931); György Lukács, *Die Gegenwartsbedeutung des kritischen Realismus/Wider den missverstandenen Realismus* (Hamburg: Claassen, 1958), trans., John and Necke Mander, *The Meaning of Contemporary Realism* (London: Merlin Press, 1963).

13 Renato Poggioli, *Teoria dell'arte d'avanguardia* (Milan: Il Mulino, 1962), trans. Gerald Fitzgerald, *The Theory of the Avant-Garde* (Cambridge, MA: Harvard University, Belknap Press, 1968).

14 In addition to the works cited above, I benefited from the following studies on modernism:

  1 early classics in the field: Harry Levin, 'What Was Modernism?' in *Refractions: Essays in Comparative Literature*, 271–95 (New York: Oxford University Press, 1966); Irving Howe, 'The Culture of Modernism,' in *Decline of the New*, 3–33 (New York: Harcourt, Brace and World, 1970); Peter

Bürger, *Theorie der Avantgarde* (Frankfurt: Suhrkamp, 1974), trans. Michael
Shaw, *Theory of the Avant-Garde* (Manchester: Manchester University Press,
1984); Gabriel Josipovici, *The Lessons of Modernism and Other Essays*
(Totowa, NJ: Rowman and Littlefield, 1977); Matei Calinescu, *Faces of
Modernity: Avant-Garde, Decadence, Kitsch* (Bloomington: Indiana University
Press, 1977).

2 Full-length studies since 1990: Néstor García Canclini, *Culturas híbridas:
Estrategías para entrar y salir de la modernidad* (Mexico City: Editorial Gri-
jalbo, 1990), trans. Christopher L. Chiappari and Silvia L. López, *Hybrid
Cultures: Strategies for Entering and Leaving Modernity* (Minneapolis: Univer-
sity of Minnesota Press, 1995); Peter Nicholls, *Modernisms: A Literary Guide*
(London: Macmillan, 1995); John Jervis, *Exploring the Modern: Patterns of
Western Culture and Civilization* (Oxford: Blackwell, 1998); Charles Ferrall,
Modernist Writing and Reactionary Politics (Cambridge: Cambridge Univer-
sity Press, 2001); Paul Sheehan, *Modernism, Narrative, and Humanism*
(Cambridge: Cambridge University Press, 2002); Louise Blakeney Wil-
liams, *Modernism and the Ideology of History: Literature, Politics, and the Past*
(Cambridge: Cambridge University Press, 2002).

15 Jean-François Lyotard, *La condition postmoderne: Rapport sur le savoir* (Paris:
Minuit, 1979), trans. Geoff Bennington and Brian Massumi, *The Postmodern
Condition: A Report on Knowledge* (Manchester: Manchester University Press,
1984); *Le postmodernisme expliqué aux enfants: Correspondance 1982–1985* (Paris:
Galilée, 1986), trans. Don Barry et al., *The Postmodern Explained: Correspon-
dence, 1982–1985* (Minneapolis: University of Minnesota Press, 1993); Jean
Baudrillard, *Simulacres et simulation* (Paris: Galilée, 1981), trans. Sheila Faria
Glaser, *Simulacra and Simulation* (Ann Arbor: University of Michigan Press,
1994); Fredric Jameson, *Postmodernism, or, The Cultural Logic of Late Capitalism*
(Durham, NC: Duke University Press, 1991); *The Cultural Turn: Selected Writ-
ings on the Postmodern, 1983–1998* (London: Verso, 1998).

16 Perry Anderson, *The Origins of Postmodernity* (London: Verso, 1998), 3–6,
observes that the term *postmodernismo* surfaced in the 1930s in a circumscribed, particular sense, to designate a conservative strain in modern Hispanic poetry, and that the 'post-modern age' was used by Arnold Toynbee to
designate the epoch from 1870 to the present, what most of us call
modernity.

17 Linda Hutcheon, *A Poetics of Postmodernism: History, Theory, Fiction* (London:
Routledge, 1988).

18 For example, Christopher Norris, *What's Wrong with Postmodernism: Critical
Theory and the Ends of Philosophy* (Baltimore: Johns Hopkins University Press,
1990), and *The Truth about Postmodernism* (Oxford: Blackwell, 1993); Terry

Eagleton, *The Illusions of Postmodernism* (Oxford: Blackwell, 1996), and *The Idea of Culture* (Oxford: Blackwell, 2000). As philosophers, Norris and Eagleton critique postmodernism on a number of points from a number of intellectual vantage points.

19 Calinescu, *Five Faces of Modernity: Modernism, Avant-Garde, Decadence, Kitsch, Postmodernism* (Durham, NC: Duke University Press, 1987).

20 Richard Murphy, *Theorizing the Avant-Garde: Modernism, Expressionism, and the Problem of Postmodernity* (Cambridge: Cambridge University Press, 1999).

21 Ihab Hassan, *The Dismemberment of Orpheus: Toward a Postmodern Literature* (New York: Oxford University Press, 1971), and *Paracriticisms: Seven Speculations of the Times* (Urbana: University of Illinois Press, 1975); William V. Spanos, 'The Detective and the Boundary: Some Notes on the Postmodern Literary Imagination,' *Boundary 2* 1 (1972–3): 147–68.

22 In addition to the works cited above, I benefited from Hutcheon, *The Politics of Postmodernism* (London: Routledge, 1989); Steven Connor, *Postmodernist Culture: An Introduction to Theories of the Contemporary* (Oxford: Blackwell, 1989); David Harvey, *The Condition of Postmodernity: An Enquiry into the Origins of Cultural Change* (Oxford: Blackwell, 1990); John McGowan, *Postmodernism and Its Critics* (Ithaca: Cornell University Press, 1991); Horace L. Fairlamb, *Critical Conditions: Postmodernity and the Question of Foundations* (Cambridge: Cambridge University Press, 1994); Vincent B. Leitch, *Postmodernism: Local Effects, Global Flows* (Albany: State University of New York Press, 1996); James Longenbach, *Modern Poetry after Modernism* (New York: Oxford University Press, 1997); Ian Gregson, *Postmodern Literature* (London: Arnold, 2004).

23 C.S. Lewis, *Studies in Words* (Cambridge: Cambridge University Press, 1960, 2nd expanded edition, 1967).

24 Holquist, 'The Last European'; Green, 'Erich Auerbach and the "Inner Dream"'; White, 'Auerbach's Literary History.'

25 Similarly, Wesley Morris, *Toward a New Historicism* (Princeton: Princeton University Press, 1972), argues pertinently that all good critics will avoid the two extremes: relativism, that the work of art is to be understood only in terms of its moment of creation; and subjectivism, that it is to be understood only in terms of the interpreter's time.

26 Calin, in *A Muse for Heroes* against the dictates of classical Frenchness, and in *In Defense of French Poetry* against romantic and symbolist strictures on the nature of poetry.

27 For the American tradition, Gerald Graff, *Professing Literature: An Institutional History* (Chicago: University of Chicago Press, 1987), remains one of the most acute studies.

28 Roland Barthes, 'Réflexions sur un manuel,' in *Essais critiques IV: Le bruissement de la langue*, 49–56 (Paris: Seuil, 1984), trans. Richard Howard, 'Reflections on a Manual,' in *The Rustle of Language*, 22–8 (New York: Hill and
Wang, 1986).

29 As in Ferdinand Brunetière, *L'évolution des genres dans l'histoire de la littérature:
Leçons professées à l'École Normale Supérieure* (Paris: Hachette, 1890).

30 Harold Bloom, *The Anxiety of Influence: A Theory of Poetry* (New York: Oxford
University Press, 1973); see also other volumes of practical criticism by
Bloom, and W. Jackson Bate, *The Burden of the Past and the English Poet* (Cam-
bridge, MA: Harvard University, Belknap Press, 1970).

31 Henri Peyre, *Qu'est-ce que le classicisme?* (Paris: Nizet, 1965).

32 We find a comparable enlarged scholarly canon for all the major periods of
all the major European literatures.

33 See, among others, Jeffrey L. Sammons, 'The Land Where the Canon
B(l)ooms: Observations on the German Canon and Its Opponents, There
and Here,' in *Canon vs. Culture: Reflections on the Current Debate*, ed. Jan
Gorak, 117-33 (New York: Garland, 2001).

34 See Barthes, *Le degré zéro de l'écriture* (Paris: Seuil, 1953), trans. Annette
Levers and Colin Smith, *Writing Degree Zero* (New York: Hill and Wang, 1968);
Sartre, *Qu'est-ce que la littérature?* (Paris: Gallimard, 1948), trans. Bernard
Frechtman, *What Is Literature?* (New York: Philosophical Library, 1949), and
the various volumes of *L'idiot de la famille: Gustave Flaubert de 1821 à 1857*
(Paris: Gallimard, 1971–88), trans. Carol Cosman, *The Family Idiot: Gustave
Flaubert 1821–1857* (Chicago: University of Chicago Press, 1981–91).

35 Said, 'Jane Austen and Empire,' in *Culture and Imperialism*, 95–116 (New
York: Knopf, 1993); Gayatri Chakravorty Spivak, 'Three Women's Texts and
a Critique of Imperialism,' *Critical Inquiry* 12 (1985–6): 243–61, repr. in *A
Critique of Postcolonial Reason: Toward a History of the Vanishing Present*, 112–40
(Cambridge, MA: Harvard University Press, 1999).

36 Calin, *Minority Literatures and Modernism: Scots, Breton, and Occitan, 1920–1990*
(Toronto: University of Toronto Press, 2000).

37 Jeffrey Wallen, *Closed Encounters: Literary Politics and Public Culture* (Minneapolis: University of Minnesota Press, 1998).

38 Peter Demetz, *Marx, Engels und die Dichter: Zur Grundlagenforschung des Marxismus* (Stuttgart: Deutsche Verlags-Anstalt, 1959), trans. Jeffrey L. Sammons,
Marx, Engels, and the Poets: Origins of Marxist Literary Criticism (Chicago: University of Chicago Press, 1967).

39 Alain Finkielkraut, *La défaite de la pensée* (Paris: Gallimard, 1987), trans.
Judith Friedlander, *The Defeat of the Mind* (New York: Columbia University
Press, 1995). See also David A. Hollinger, *Postethnic America: Beyond*

Multiculturalism (New York: Basic Books, 1995) and the luminous defense of high culture by Geoffrey H. Hartman, *The Fateful Question of Culture* (New York: Columbia University Press, 1997).

40 Cain, 'Opening the American Mind: Reflections on the "Canon" Controversy,' in *Canon vs. Culture*, 3–16.

41 Nina Baym, *Woman's Fiction: A Guide to Novels by and about Women in America, 1820–1870* (Ithaca: Cornell University Press, 1978), and *Feminism and American Literary History: Essays* (New Brunswick, NJ: Rutgers University Press, 1992); Jane Tompkins, *Sensational Designs: The Cultural Work of American Fiction 1790–1860* (New York: Oxford University Press, 1985).

42 John Guillory, *Cultural Capital: The Problem of Literary Canon Formation* (Chicago: University of Chicago Press, 1993).

Bibliography

Theory and General Criticism

Anderson, Perry. *The Origins of Postmodernity.* London: Verso, 1998.

Barbéris, Pierre. *Balzac et le mal du siècle.* 2 vols. Paris: Gallimard, 1970.

– *Balzac: Une mythologie réaliste.* Paris: Larousse, 1971.

– *Mythes balzaciens.* Paris: Colin, 1972.

Baron, Hans. *The Crisis of the Early Italian Renaissance: Civic Humanism and Republican Liberty in an Age of Classicism and Tyranny.* 2 vols. Princeton: Princeton University Press, 1955.

– *From Petrarch to Leonardo Bruni: Studies in Humanistic and Political Literature.* Chicago: University of Chicago Press, 1968.

– *Humanistic and Political Literature in Florence and Venice at the Beginning of the Quattrocento: Studies in Criticism and Chronology.* Cambridge, MA: Harvard University Press, 1955.

Barthes, Roland. *Le degré zéro de l'écriture.* Paris: Seuil, 1953. Trans. Annette Levers and Colin Smith. *Writing Degree Zero.* New York: Hill and Wang, 1968.

– 'Réflexions sur un manuel.' In *Essais critiques IV: Le bruissement de la langue,* 49–56. Paris: Seuil, 1984. Trans. Richard Howard. 'Reflections on a Manual.' In *The Rustle of Language,* 22–8. New York: Hill and Wang, 1986.

– *S/Z.* Paris: Seuil, 1970. Trans. Richard Miller. *S/Z.* New York: Hill and Wang, 1974.

Bate, W. Jackson. *The Burden of the Past and the English Poet.* Cambridge, MA: Harvard University, Belknap Press, 1970.

Baudrillard, Jean. *Simulacres et simulation.* Paris: Galilée, 1981. Trans. Sheila Faria Glaser. *Simulacra and Simulation.* Ann Arbor: University of Michigan Press, 1994.

Baym, Nina. *Feminism and American Literary History: Essays.* New Brunswick, NJ: Rutgers University Press, 1992.

- *Woman's Fiction: A Guide to Novels by and about Women in America, 1820–1870.* Ithaca: Cornell University Press, 1978.

Bezzola, Reto R. *Les origines et la formation de la littérature courtoise en Occident (500–1200).* 3 vols. in 5. Paris: Champion, 1944–63.

Bloom, Harold. *The Anxiety of Influence: A Theory of Poetry.* New York: Oxford University Press, 1973.

Booth, Wayne C. *The Rhetoric of Fiction.* Chicago: University of Chicago Press, 1961.

Bouwsma, William J. *The Culture of Renaissance Humanism.* Washington, DC: American Historical Association, 1973.

- *The Interpretation of Renaissance Humanism.* Washington, DC: American Historical Association, 1959.

Brémond, Claude. *Logique du récit.* Paris: Seuil, 1973.

Brunetière, Ferdinand. *L'évolution des genres dans l'histoire de la littérature: Leçons professées à l'École Normale Supérieure.* Paris: Hachette, 1890.

Bürger, Peter. *Theorie der Avantgarde.* Frankfurt: Suhrkamp, 1974. Trans. Michael Shaw. *Theory of the Avant-Garde.* Manchester: Manchester University Press, 1984.

Cain, William E. 'Opening the American Mind: Reflections on the "Canon" Controversy.' In *Canon vs. Culture: Reflections on the Current Debate,* ed. Jan Gorak, 3–16. New York: Garland, 2001.

Calin, William. 'Aubanel's *Mióugrano* and the Romantic Persona: A Modern Reading.' *Tenso* 3 (1987–8): 43–57.

- *Crown, Cross, and 'Fleur-de-lis': An Essay on Pierre Le Moyne's Baroque Epic 'Saint Louis.'* Stanford French and Italian Studies: 1977.

- 'Dante on the Edwardian Stage: Stephen Phillips's *Paolo and Francesca.*' In *Medievalism in the Modern World,* ed. Richard Utz and Tom Shippey, 255–61. Turnhout: Brepols, 1998.

- *The French Tradition and the Literature of Medieval England.* Toronto: University of Toronto Press, 1994.

- *In Defense of French Poetry: An Essay in Revaluation.* University Park: Pennsylvania State University Press, 1987.

- 'The Medieval Presence in Modern Literature: A Question of Criticism and Culture.' *Philological Papers* 27 (1981): 1–7.

- *Minority Literatures and Modernism: Scots, Breton, and Occitan, 1920–1990.* Toronto: University of Toronto Press, 2000.

- *A Muse for Heroes: Nine Centuries of the Epic in France.* Toronto: University of Toronto Press, 1983.

- 'What *Tales from a Wayside Inn* Tells Us about Longfellow and about Chaucer.' *Studies in Medievalism* 12 (2002): 197–213.

Calinescu, Matei. *Faces of Modernity: Avant-Garde, Decadence, Kitsch.* Bloomington: Indiana University Press, 1977.

 – *Five Faces of Modernity: Modernism, Avant-Garde, Decadence, Kitsch, Postmodernism.* Durham, NC: Duke University Press, 1987.

Cerquiglini, Bernard. *Éloge de la variante: Histoire critique de la philologie.* Paris: Seuil, 1989.

Chambers, Iain. *Culture after Humanism: History, Culture, Subjectivity.* London: Routledge, 2001.

Chandler, Alice. *A Dream of Order: The Medieval Idea in Nineteenth-Century English Literature.* Lincoln: University of Nebraska Press, 1970.

Chase, Richard. *The American Novel and Its Tradition.* New York: Doubleday, 1957.

Connor, Steven. *Postmodernist Culture: An Introduction to Theories of the Contemporary.* Oxford: Blackwell, 1989.

Davies, Tony. *Humanism.* London: Routledge, 1997.

Demetz, Peter. *Marx, Engels und die Dichter: Zur Grundlagenforschung des Marxismus.* Stuttgart: Deutsche Verlags-Anstalt, 1959. Trans. Jeffrey L. Sammons. *Marx, Engels, and the Poets: Origins of Marxist Literary Criticism.* Chicago: University of Chicago Press, 1967.

Eagleton, Terry. *The Idea of Culture.* Oxford: Blackwell, 2000.

 – *The Illusions of Postmodernism.* Oxford: Blackwell, 1996.

Escarpit, Robert. *Le littéraire et le social: Éléments pour une sociologie de la littérature.* Paris: Flammarion, 1970.

 – *Sociologie de la littérature.* Paris: Presses Universitaires de France, 1958.

Etlin, Richard A. *In Defense of Humanism: Value in the Arts and Letters.* Cambridge: Cambridge University Press, 1996.

Eysteinsson, Astradur. *The Concept of Modernism.* Ithaca: Cornell University Press, 1990.

Fairlamb, Horace L. *Critical Conditions: Postmodernity and the Question of Foundations.* Cambridge: Cambridge University Press, 1994.

Feidelson, Charles. *Symbolism and American Literature.* Chicago: University of Chicago Press, 1953.

Ferrall, Charles. *Modernist Writing and Reactionary Politics.* Cambridge: Cambridge University Press, 2001.

Fiedler, Leslie A. *Love and Death in the American Novel.* New York: Criterion, 1960.

Finkielkraut, Alain. *La défaite de la pensée.* Paris: Gallimard, 1987. Trans. Judith Friedlander. *The Defeat of the Mind.* New York: Columbia University Press, 1995.

Fleming, John V. *The 'Roman de la Rose': A Study in Allegory and Iconography.* Princeton: Princeton University Press, 1969.

Frank, Joseph. *The Idea of Spatial Form.* New Brunswick, NJ: Rutgers University Press, 1991.

Freccero, John. *Dante: The Poetics of Conversion.* Cambridge, MA: Harvard University Press, 1986.

Friedrich, Hugo. *Die Struktur der modernen Lyrik: Von Baudelaire bis zur Gegenwart*. Hamburg: Rowohlt, 1956. Trans. Joachim Neugroschel. *The Structure of Modern Poetry, from the Mid-nineteenth to the Mid-twentieth Century*. Evanston: Northwestern University Press, 1974.

Garaudy, Roger. *Le communisme et la morale*. Paris: Éditions Sociales, 1947.

– *Humanisme marxiste: Cinq essais polémiques*. Paris: Éditions Sociales, 1957.

– *Perpectives de l'homme: Existentialisme, pensée catholique, marxisme*. Paris: Presses Universitaires de France, 1959.

García Canclini, Néstor. *Culturas híbridas: Estrategías para entrar y salir de la modernidad*. Mexico City: Editorial Grijalbo, 1990. Trans. Christopher L. Chiappari and Silvia L. López. *Hybrid Cultures: Strategies for Entering and Leaving Modernity*. Minneapolis: University of Minnesota Press, 1995.

Genette, Gérard. *Figures III*. Paris: Seuil, 1972. Trans. Alan Sheridan. *Figures of Literary Discourse*. New York: Columbia University Press, 1982.

Gouwens, Kenneth. 'Perceiving the Past: Renaissance Humanism after the "Cognitive Turn."' *American Historical Review* 103 (1998): 55–82.

Graff, Gerald. *Professing Literature: An Institutional History*. Chicago: University of Chicago Press, 1987.

Gregson, Ian. *Postmodern Literature*. London: Arnold, 2004.

Greimas, A.-J. *Sémantique structurale: Recherche de méthode*. Paris: Larousse, 1966. Trans. Danièle McDowell et al. *Structural Semantics: An Attempt at a Method*. Lincoln: University of Nebraska Press, 1983.

Guillory, John. *Cultural Capital: The Problem of Literary Canon Formation*. Chicago: University of Chicago Press, 1993.

Halliwell, Martin, and Andy Mousley. *Critical Humanisms: Humanist/Anti-Humanist Dialogues*. Edinburgh: Edinburgh University Press, 2003.

Hankins, James. 'Two Twentieth-Century Interpreters of Renaissance Humanism: Eugenio Garin and Paul Oskar Kristeller.' *Comparative Criticism* 23 (2001): 3–19.

Hartman, Geoffrey H. *The Fateful Question of Culture*. New York: Columbia University Press, 1997.

Harvey, David. *The Condition of Postmodernity: An Enquiry into the Origins of Cultural Change*. Oxford: Blackwell, 1990.

Hassan, Ihab. *The Dismemberment of Orpheus: Toward a Postmodern Literature*. New York: Oxford University Press, 1971.

– *Paracriticisms: Seven Speculations of the Times*. Urbana: University of Illinois Press, 1975.

Heidegger, Martin. *Brief über den Humanismus*. In *Gesamtausgabe*. Vol. 9. Frankfurt: Klostermann, 1976. Trans. in *Basic Writings*, ed. David Farrell Krell, 189–242. New York: Harper and Row, 1977.

Hoffman, Daniel. *Form and Fable in American Fiction.* New York: Oxford University Press, 1961.

Hollinger, David A. *Postethnic America: Beyond Multiculturalism.* New York: Basic Books, 1995.

Howe, Irving. 'The Culture of Modernism.' In *Decline of the New,* 3–33. New York: Harcourt, Brace and World, 1970.

Huppé, Bernard F. *A Reading of the Canterbury Tales.* Albany: State University of New York Press, 1964.

Huppé, Bernard F., and D.W. Robertson, Jr. *Fruyt and Chaf: Studies in Chaucer's Allegories.* Princeton: Princeton University Press, 1963.

Hutcheon, Linda. *A Poetics of Postmodernism: History, Theory, Fiction.* London: Routledge, 1988.

– *The Politics of Postmodernism.* London: Routledge, 1989.

Iser, Wolfgang. *Der Akt des Lesens: Theorie ästhetischer Wirkung.* Munich: Fink, 1976. Trans. *The Act of Reading: A Theory of Aesthetic Response.* Baltimore: Johns Hopkins University Press, 1978.

– *Der implizite Leser: Kommunikationsformen des Romans von Bunyan bis Beckett.* Munich: Fink, 1972. Trans. *The Implied Reader: Patterns of Communication in Prose Fiction from Bunyan to Beckett.* Baltimore: Johns Hopkins University Press, 1974.

Jakobson, Roman. *Questions de poétique.* Paris: Seuil, 1973.

Jameson, Fredric. *The Cultural Turn: Selected Writings on the Postmodern, 1983–1998.* London: Verso, 1998.

– *The Political Unconscious: Narrative as a Socially Symbolic Act.* Ithaca: Cornell University Press, 1981.

– *Postmodernism, or, the Cultural Logic of Late Capitalism.* Durham, NC: Duke University Press, 1991.

Jauss, Hans Robert. *Ästhetische Erfahrung und literarische Hermeneutik.* Vol. 1. *Versuche im Feld der ästhetischen Erfahrung.* Munich: Fink, 1977. Trans. Michael Shaw. *Aesthetic Experience and Literary Hermeneutics.* Minneapolis: University of Minnesota Press, 1982.

– *Toward an Aesthetic of Reception.* Trans. Timothy Bahti. Minneapolis: University of Minnesota Press, 1982.

Jervis, John. *Exploring the Modern: Patterns of Western Culture and Civilization.* Oxford: Blackwell, 1998.

Josipovici, Gabriel. *The Lessons of Modernism and Other Essays.* Totowa, NJ: Rowman and Littlefield, 1977.

Kazin, Alfred. *Writing Was Everything.* Cambridge, MA: Harvard University Press, 1995.

Kraye, Jill, ed. *The Cambridge Companion to Renaissance Humanism.* Cambridge: Cambridge University Press, 1996.

Kristeller, Paul Oskar. *The Classics and Renaissance Thought.* Cambridge, MA: Harvard University Press, 1955.
– *Eight Philosophers of the Italian Renaissance.* Stanford: Stanford University Press, 1964.
– *Renaissance Thought: The Classic, Scholastic, and Humanist Strains.* New York: Harper and Row, 1961.
– *Studies in Renaissance Thought and Letters.* Rome: Edizioni di Storia e Letteratura, 1956.
Kurtz, Paul. *Humanist Manifesto II.* Buffalo: Prometheus, 1973.
– *In Defense of Secular Humanism.* Buffalo: Prometheus, 1984.
– *A Secular Humanist Declaration.* Buffalo: Prometheus, 1980.
Lamont, Corliss. *The Philosophy of Humanism.* 7th ed., revised and enlarged. New York: Continuum, 1993.
Lanson, Gustave. *Histoire de la littérature française.* Paris: Hachette, 1895.
Leavis, F.R. *Revaluation: Tradition and Development in English Poetry.* London: Chatto and Windus, 1936.
Leitch, Vincent B. *Postmodernism: Local Effects, Global Flows.* Albany: State University of New York Press, 1996.
Levin, Harry. 'What Was Modernism?' In *Refractions: Essays in Comparative Literature,* 271–95. New York: Oxford University Press, 1966.
Lewis, R.W.B. *The American Adam: Innocence, Tragedy, and Tradition in the Nineteenth Century.* Chicago: University of Chicago Press, 1955.
Longenbach, James. *Modern Poetry after Modernism.* New York: Oxford University Press, 1997.
Lukács, György. *Die Gegenwartsbedeutung des kritischen Realismus / Wider den missverstandenen Realismus.* Hamburg: Claassen, 1958. Trans. John and Necke Mander. *The Meaning of Contemporary Realism.* London: Merlin Press, 1963.
– *Studies in European Realism.* Trans. Edith Bone. London: Hillway, 1950.
Lyotard, Jean-François. *La condition postmoderne: Rapport sur le savoir.* Paris: Minuit, 1979. Trans. Geoff Bennington and Brian Massumi. *The Postmodern Condition: A Report on Knowledge.* Manchester: Manchester University Press, 1984.
– *Le postmodernisme expliqué aux enfants: Correspondance 1982–1985.* Paris: Galilée, 1986. Trans. Don Barry et al. *The Postmodern Explained: Correspondence, 1982–1985.* Minneapolis: University of Minnesota Press, 1993.
Maritain, Jacques. *Humanisme intégral: Problèmes temporels et spirituels d'une nouvelle chrétienté.* Paris: Aubier, 1936. Trans. Margot Adamson. *True Humanism.* New York: Scribner, 1938.
Marx, Leo. *The Machine in the Garden: Technology and the Pastoral Ideal in America.* New York: Oxford University Press, 1964.

McGowan, John. *Postmodernism and Its Critics.* Ithaca: Cornell University Press, 1991.

Moreland, Kim. *The Medievalist Impulse in American Literature: Twain, Adams, Fitzgerald, and Hemingway.* Charlottesville: University Press of Virginia, 1996.

Morris, Wesley. *Toward a New Historicism.* Princeton: Princeton University Press, 1972.

Murphy, Richard. *Theorizing the Avant-Garde: Modernism, Expressionism, and the Problem of Postmodernity.* Cambridge: Cambridge University Press, 1999.

Nicholls, Peter. *Modernisms: A Literary Guide.* London: Macmillan, 1995.

Noonan, Jeffrey. *Critical Humanism and the Politics of Difference.* Montreal: McGill-Queen's University Press, 2003.

Norris, Christopher. *The Truth about Postmodernism.* Oxford: Blackwell, 1993.

– *What's Wrong with Postmodernism: Critical Theory and the Ends of Philosophy.* Baltimore: Johns Hopkins University Press, 1990.

Novack, George. *Humanism and Socialism.* New York: Pathfinder, 1973.

Patterson, Lee. *Negotiating the Past: The Historical Understanding of Medieval Literature.* Madison: University of Wisconsin Press, 1987.

Perkins, David. *A History of Modern Poetry.* 2 vols. Cambridge, MA: Harvard University Press, 1976–87.

– *Is Literary History Possible?* Baltimore: Johns Hopkins University Press, 1992.

Peyre, Henri. *Qu'est-ce que le classicisme?* Paris: Nizet, 1965.

Poggioli, Renato. *Teoria dell'arte d'avanguardia.* Milan: Il Mulino, 1962. Trans. Gerald Fitzgerald. *The Theory of the Avant-Garde.* Cambridge, MA: Harvard University, Belknap Press, 1968.

Prince, Gerald. *Narratology: The Form and Functioning of Narrative.* Berlin: Mouton, 1982.

Robertson, Durant Waite, Jr. *A Preface to Chaucer: Studies in Medieval Perspectives.* Princeton: Princeton University Press, 1962.

Rychner, Jean. *La chanson de geste: Essai sur l'art épique des jongleurs.* Geneva: Droz, 1955.

Said, Edward W. *Humanism and Democratic Criticism.* New York: Columbia University Press, 2004.

– 'Jane Austen and Empire.' In *Culture and Imperialism,* 95–116. New York: Knopf, 1993.

Sammons, Jeffrey L. 'The Land Where the Canon B(l)ooms: Observations on the German Canon and Its Opponents, There and Here.' In *Canon vs. Culture: Reflections on the Current Debate,* ed. Jan Gorak, 117–33. New York: Garland, 2001.

Sartre, Jean-Paul. *L'existentialisme est un humanisme.* Paris: Nagel, 1946. Trans. Bernard Frechtman. *Existentialism.* New York: Philosophical Library, 1947.

– *L'idiot de la famille: Gustave Flaubert de 1821 à 1857.* Paris: Gallimard, 1971–88. Trans. Carol Cosman. *The Family Idiot: Gustave Flaubert 1821–1857.* Chicago: University of Chicago Press, 1981–91.

– *Qu'est-ce que la littérature?* Paris: Gallimard, 1948. Trans. Bernard Frechtman. *What Is Literature?* New York: Philosophical Library, 1949.

Schwarz, Daniel R. *The Case for a Humanist Poetics.* London: Macmillan, 1990.

Sheehan, Paul. *Modernism, Narrative, and Humanism.* Cambridge: Cambridge University Press, 2002.

Simpson, Lorenzo C. *The Unfinished Project: Toward a Postmetaphysical Humanism.* New York: Routledge, 2001.

Smith, Henry Nash. *Virgin Land: The American West as Symbol and Myth.* Cambridge, MA: Harvard University Press, 1950.

Spanos, William V. 'The Detective and the Boundary: Some Notes on the Postmodern Literary Imagination.' *Boundary 2* 1 (1972–3): 147–68.

Spivak, Gayatri Chakravorty. 'Three Women's Texts and a Critique of Imperialism.' *Critical Inquiry* 12 (1985–6): 243–61. Repr. in *A Critique of Postcolonial Reason: Toward a History of the Vanishing Present,* 112–40. Cambridge, MA: Harvard University Press, 1999.

Stanzel, Franz. *Die typischen Erzählsituationen im Roman.* Vienna: Braumüller, 1955. Trans. James P. Pusack. *Narrative Situations in the Novel.* Bloomington: Indiana University Press, 1971.

Thibaudet, Albert. *Le liseur de romans.* Paris: Crès, 1925.

Todorov, Tzvetan. *Grammaire du Décaméron.* The Hague: Mouton, 1969.

– *Le jardin imparfait: La pensée humaniste en France.* Paris: Grasset, 1998. Trans. Carol Cosman. *Imperfect Garden: The Legacy of Humanism.* Princeton: Princeton University Press, 2002.

Tompkins, Jane. *Sensational Designs: The Cultural Work of American Fiction 1790–1860.* New York: Oxford University Press, 1985.

Vossler, Karl. *Die göttliche Komödie.* 2 vols. Heidelberg: Winter, 1907–10. Trans. William Cranston Lawton. *Medieval Culture: An Introduction to Dante and His Times.* New York: Harcourt, Brace, 1929.

Wallen, Jeffrey. *Closed Encounters: Literary Politics and Public Culture.* Minneapolis: University of Minnesota Press, 1998.

Wellek, René. *A History of Modern Criticism: 1750–1950.* Vols. 6–8. New Haven: Yale University Press, 1986–92.

Williams, Louise Blakeney. *Modernism and the Ideology of History: Literature, Politics, and the Past.* Cambridge: Cambridge University Press, 2002.

Williams, Raymond. *The Country and the City.* London: Chatto and Windus, 1973.

– *Culture and Society, 1780–1950.* London: Chatto and Windus, 1958.

Wilson, Edmund. *Axel's Castle: A Study in the Imaginative Literature of 1870–1930.*
New York: Scribner, 1931.
Yarbrough, Stephen R. *Deliberate Criticism: Toward a Postmodern Humanism.*
Athens, GA: University of Georgia Press, 1992.
Zumthor, Paul. *Essai de poétique médiévale.* Paris: Seuil, 1972.

Leo Spitzer

Andrews, J. Richard, and Joseph H. Silverman. 'On "Destructive Criticism": A
Rejoinder to Mr. Leo Spitzer.' *Modern Language Forum* 42 (1957): 3–24.
Apter, Emily. 'CNN Creole: Trademark Literacy and Global Language Travel.'
Sites 5 (2001): 27–46.
– 'The Human in the Humanities.' *October* 96 (Spring 2001): 71–85.
Baer, E. Kristina. 'Leo Spitzer on Philology: An Introduction.' In *Leo Spitzer on
Language and Literature*, ed. Baer and Shenholm, 1–12.
Baer, E. Kristina, and Daisy E. Shenholm. *Leo Spitzer on Language and Literature: A
Descriptive Bibliography.* New York: Modern Language Association, 1991.
Bellos, David. 'Leo Spitzer: An Introduction.' In *Leo Spitzer: Essays on Seventeenth-
Century French Literature*, ed. David Bellos, xi–xxix. Cambridge: Cambridge
University Press, 1983.
Bennett, Benjamin. 'The Politics of the Mörike-Debate and Its Object.' *Germanic
Review* 68 (1993): 60–8.
Brody, Jules. 'Lire La Fontaine: la méthode de Leo Spitzer.' *Papers on French
Seventeenth Century Literature* 23 (1996): 15–21.
Catano, James V. *Language, History, Style: Leo Spitzer and the Critical Tradition.*
Urbana: University of Illinois Press, 1988.
Gilman, Stephen. 'A Rejoinder to Leo Spitzer.' *Hispanic Review* 25 (1957): 112–21.
Green, Geoffrey. *Literary Criticism and the Structures of History: Erich Auerbach and
Leo Spitzer.* Lincoln: University of Nebraska Press, 1982.
Gumbrecht, Hans Ulrich. *Vom Leben und Sterben der grossen Romanisten*, 72–151.
Munich: Hanser, 2002.
Hook, Donald H. 'Spitzer and Key Revisited: The Artfulness of Advertising.'
Language and Style 19 (1986): 184–95.
Hytier, Jean. 'La méthode de M. Leo Spitzer.' *Romanic Review* 41 (1950): 42–59.
Klein, Richard. 'The Object of French Studies: *Gebrauchkunst.*' *Forum for Modern
Language Studies* 37 (2001): 405–15.
Levin, Harry. 'Two *Romanisten* in America: Spitzer and Auerbach.' In *The Intellec-
tual Migration: Europe and America, 1930–1960*, ed. Donald Fleming and
Bernard Bailyn, 463–84. Cambridge, MA: Harvard University Press, 1969.

Lovejoy, Arthur O. 'The Meaning of Romanticism for the Historian of Ideas.'
    Journal of the History of Ideas 2 (1941): 257–78.
Malkiel, Yakov. 'Necrology: Leo Spitzer.' *Romance Philology* 14 (1960–1): 362–4.
Pensom, Roger. 'Form and Meaning in *Aucassin et Nicolette*.' In *Littera et Sensus:
    Essays on Form and Meaning in Medieval French Literature Presented to John Fox*, ed.
    D.A. Trotter, 63–72. Exeter, UK: University of Exeter, 1989.
Spitzer, Leo. 'The Addresses to the Reader in the *Commedia*.' *Italica* 32 (1955):
    143–65.
– 'American Advertising Explained as Popular Art.' In *A Method of Interpreting
    Literature*, 102–49. Northampton: Smith College, 1949.
– *L'amour lointain de Jaufré Rudel et le sens de la poésie des troubadours*. University of
    North Carolina Studies in the Romance Languages and Literature. Chapel
    Hill: University of North Carolina Press, 1944.
– 'El barroco español.' *Boletín del Instituto de Investigaciones Históricas* 28 (1943–4):
    12–30.
– *Betrachtungen eines Linguisten über Houston Stewart Chamberlains Kriegsaufsätze
    und die Sprachbewertung im allgemein*. Leipzig: n.p., 1918.
– *Classical and Christian Ideas of World Harmony*. Ed. Anna Granville Hatcher.
    Baltimore: Johns Hopkins University Press, 1963.
– 'Étude ahistorique d'un texte: "Ballade des dames du temps jadis."' *Modern
    Language Quarterly* 1 (1940): 7–22.
– '*Explication de texte* Applied to Three Great Middle English Poems.' *Archivum
    Linguisticum* 3 (1951): 1–22, 157–65.
– 'The Farcical Elements in *Inferno* XXI–XXIII.' *Modern Language Notes* 59
    (1944): 83–8.
– *Fremdwörterhatz und Fremdvölkerhass: Eine Streitschrift gegen die Sprachreinigung*.
    Vienna: Manzsche, 1918.
– '*Geistesgeschichte* vs. History of Ideas as Applied to Hitlerism.' *Journal of the His-
    tory of Ideas* 5 (1944): 191–203.
– *Leo Spitzer: Representative Essays*. Ed. Alban K. Forcione, Herbert Lindenberger,
    and Madeline Sutherland. Stanford: Stanford University Press, 1988.
– 'La "lettre sur la baguette du coudrier" dans le lai du *Chievrefueil*.' *Romania* 69
    (1947): 80–90.
– 'Linguistics and Literary History.' In *Linguistics and Literary History*, 1–39.
– *Linguistics and Literary History: Essays in Stylistics*. Princeton: Princeton Univer-
    sity Press, 1948. Repr. New York: Russell, 1962.
– 'Marie de France –Dichterin von Problem-Märchen.' *Zeitschrift für Romanische
    Philologie* 50 (1930): 29–67.
– 'A New Book on the Art of *The Celestina*.' *Hispanic Review* 25 (1957): 1–25.

- 'Note on the Poetical and Empirical "I" in Medieval Authors.' *Traditio* 4 (1947): 414–22.
- 'The Prologue to the *Lais* of Marie de France.' *Modern Philology* 40 (1943–4): 96–102.
- 'Pseudo-objektive Motivierung (Eine stilistisch-literaturpsychologische Studie).' *Zeitschrift für Französische Sprache und Literatur* 46 (1923): 359–85.
- *Romanische Literaturstudien, 1936–1956.* Tübingen: Niemeyer, 1959.
- *Romanische Stil- und Literaturstudien.* 2 vols. Marburg: Elwert, 1931.
- 'Sobre el carácter histórico del *Cantar de myo Cid.*' *Nueva Revista de Filología Hispánica* 2 (1948): 105–17.
- 'Speech and Language in *Inferno* XIII.' *Italica* 19 (1942): 81–104.
- *Stilstudien.* 2 vols. Munich: Hueber, 1928.
- *Studien zu Henri Barbusse.* Bonn: Cohen, 1920.
- 'Le style "circulaire."' *Modern Language Notes* 55 (1940): 495–9.
- 'Sviluppo di un metodo.' *Cultura Neolatina* 20 (1960): 109–28. Trans. 'Development of a Method.' In *Leo Spitzer: Representative Essays*, 421–48.
- 'Der Unanismus Jules Romains' im Spiegel seiner Sprache.' *Archivum Romanicum* 8 (1924): 59–122.
- *Die Wortbildung als stilistisches Mittel exemplifiziert an Rabelais, nebst einem Anhang über die Wortbildung bei Balzac in seinen 'Contes drôlatiques.'* Halle: Niemeyer, 1910.
- 'Zum Stil Marcel Prousts.' In *Stilstudien.* Vol. 2, 365–497.
- 'Zur Literaturgeschichte: Zur Auffassung der Kunst des Arcipreste de Hita.' *Zeitschrift für Romanische Philologie* 54 (1934): 237–70.
- 'Zur sprachlichen Interpretation von Wortkunstwerken.' *Neue Jahrbücher für Wissenschaft und Jugendbildung, Leipzig* 6 (1930): 632–50.
Wang, Orrin N.C. 'Allegories of Praxis: The Reading of Romanticism and Fascism in A.O. Lovejoy and Leo Spitzer.' *CLIO* 20 (1990–1): 39–51.
Wellek, René. *A History of Modern Criticism, 1750–1950.* Vol. 7. *German, Russian, and Eastern European Criticism, 1900–1950*, 134–53. New Haven: Yale University Press, 1991.
Wygant, Amy. 'Leo Spitzer's Racine.' *MLN* 109 (1994): 632–49.

Ernst Robert Curtius

Anderson, Mark. 'La restauration de la décadence: Curtius et T.S. Eliot.' In *Ernst Robert Curtius et l'idée d'Europe*, ed. Bem and Guyaux, 167–81.
Baeumer, Max L., ed. *Toposforschung.* Wege der Forschung 195. Darmstadt: Wissenschaftliche Buchgesellschaft, 1973.

Bem, Jeanne, and André Guyaux, eds. *Ernst Robert Curtius et l'idée d'Europe: Actes du Colloque de Mulhouse et Thann*. Paris: Champion, 1995.

Berschin, Walter, and Arnold Rothe, eds. *Ernst Robert Curtius: Werk, Wirkung, Zukunftsperspektiven, Heidelberger Symposion zum hundertsten Geburtstag 1986*. Heidelberg: Winter, 1989.

Bloch, Peter André. 'Curtius visionnaire idéaliste de la littérature contemporaine.' In *Ernst Robert Curtius et l'idée d'Europe*, ed. Bem and Guyaux, 107–18.

Bock, Hans Manfred. 'Die Politik des "Unpolitischen": Zu Ernst Robert Curtius' Ort im politisch-intellektuellen Leben der Weimarer Republik.' *Lendemains* 59 (1990): 16–61.

Christmann, Hans Helmut. 'Ernst Robert Curtius und die deutschen Romanisten.' In *'In Ihnen begegnet sich das Abendland*,' ed. Lange, 65–84.

Curtius, Ernst Robert. *Balzac*. Bonn: Cohen, 1923.

– *Deutsch-französische Gespräche 1920–1950: La correspondance de Ernst Robert Curtius avec André Gide, Charles Du Bos et Valery Larbaud*. Ed. Herbert Dieckmann and Jane M. Dieckmann. Frankfurt: Klostermann, 1980.

– *Deutscher Geist in Gefahr*. Stuttgart: Deutsche Verlags-Anstalt, 1932.

– *Europäische Literatur und lateinisches Mittelalter*. Berne: Francke, 1948. Trans. Willard R. Trask. *European Literature and the Latin Middle Ages*. New York: Pantheon Books, 1953.

– *Ferdinand Brunetière: Beitrag zur Geschichte der französischen Kritik*. Strasbourg: Trübner, 1914.

– *Die französische Kultur: Eine Einführung*. Stuttgart: Deutsche Verlags-Anstalt, 1930. Vol. 1 of *Frankreich*. By Ernst Robert Curtius and Arnold Bergsträsser. Trans. Olive Wyon. *The Civilization of France: An Introduction*. New York: Macmillan, 1932.

– *Französischer Geist im neuen Europa*. Stuttgart: Deutsche Verlags-Anstalt, 1925.

– *Französischer Geist im zwanzigsten Jahrhundert*. Berne: Francke, 1952.

– *Gesammelte Aufsätze zur romanischen Philologie*. Berne: Francke, 1960.

– 'Henri Bremond und die französische Mystik.' In *Französischer Geist im zwanzigsten Jahrhundert*, 437–512.

– *James Joyce und sein 'Ulysses.'* Zürich: Verlag der *Neuen Schweizer Rundschau*, 1929.

– *Kritische Essays zur europäischen Literatur*. Berne: Francke, 1950. Rev. ed. 1954. Trans. Michael Kowal. *Essays on European Literature*. Princeton: Princeton University Press, 1973.

– *Die literarischen Wegbereiter des neuen Frankreich*. Potsdam: Kiepenheuer, 1918.

– *Marcel Proust*. Berlin: Suhrkamp, 1952.

– *Maurice Barrès und die geistigen Grundlagen des französischen Nationalismus*. Bonn: Cohen, 1921.

– *Li quatre livre des Reis: Die Bücher Samuelis und der Könige in einer französischen Bearbeitung des 12. Jahrhunderts.* Dresden: Gesellschaft für Romanische Literatur; Halle: Niemeyer, 1911.

– 'T.S. Eliot.' *Neue Schweizer Rundschau* (Apr. 1927): 348ff.

– 'Vorwort zu einem Buche über das lateinische Mittelalter und die europäischen Literaturen.' *Die Wandlung* 1:11 (November 1946): 969–74.

Dröge, Christoph. 'Avec Goethe, contre Berlin: l'image de l'Allemagne chez Curtius et Gide.' In *Ernst Robert Curtius et l'idée d'Europe*, ed. Bem and Guyaux, 199–215.

Du Bos, Charles. 'Ernst Robert Curtius.' In *Approximations, cinquième série*, 107–39. Paris: Corrêa, 1930.

Evans, Arthur R., Jr. 'Ernst Robert Curtius.' In *On Four Modern Humanists: Hofmannsthal, Gundolf, Curtius, Kantorowicz*, ed. Arthur R. Evans, Jr, 85–145. Princeton: Princeton University Press, 1970.

Fischer, Manfred S. *'Europa' und 'das Nationale' bei Ernst Robert Curtius.* Aachen: Fischer, 2000.

Gross, Stefan. *Ernst Robert Curtius und die deutsche Romanistik der zwanziger Jahre: Zum Problem nationaler Images in der Literaturwissenschaft.* Bonn: Bouvier, 1980.

Gumbrecht, Hans Ulrich. '"Zeitlosigkeit, die durchscheint in der Zeit": Über E.R. Curtius' unhistorisches Verhältnis zur Geschichte.' In *Ernst Robert Curtius: Werk, Wirkung, Zukunftsperspektiven*, ed. Berschin and Rothe, 227–41. Repr. in *Vom Leben und Sterben der grossen Romanisten*, 49–71. Munich: Hanser, 2002.

Hillen, Ursula. *Wegbereiter der romanischen Philologie: Ph.A. Becker im Gespräch mit G. Gröber, J. Bédier und E.R. Curtius.* Frankfurt: Lang, 1993.

Jacquemard-de Gemaux, Christine. *Ernst Robert Curtius (1889–1956): Origines et cheminements d'un esprit européen.* Berne: Lang, 1998.

Jehn, Peter. 'Ernst Robert Curtius: Toposforschung als Restauration.' In *Toposforschung: Eine Dokumentation*, ed. Jehn. vii–lxiv.

Jehn, Peter, ed. *Toposforschung: Eine Dokumentation.* Frankfurt: Athenäum, 1972.

Jurt, Joseph. 'Curtius et la position de l'intellectuel dans la société allemande.' In *Ernst Robert Curtius et l'idée d'Europe*, ed. Bem and Guyaux, 239–55.

Lange, Wolf-Dieter. 'Antiromantische Philologie in Deutschland: E.R. Curtius im Gespräch mit Philipp August Becker (1935–1947).' In *Ernst Robert Curtius: Werk, Wirkung, Zukunftsperspektiven*, ed. Berschin and Rothe, 37–48.

Lange, Wolf-Dieter, ed. *'In Ihnen begegnet sich das Abendland': Bonner Vorträge zur Erinnerung an Ernst Robert Curtius.* Bonn: Bouvier, 1990.

Nerlich, Michael. 'Curtius trahi par les siens: Annotations aux actes d'un colloque sur "le grand Européen cosmopolite."' *Romanische Forschungen* 109 (1997): 436–74.

– 'Romanistik und Anti-Kommunismus.' *Das Argument* 14:1 (1972): 276–313.

- 'Sur les différences nationales dans la capacité de deuil: à propos de Ernst Robert Curtius et Paul de Man.' *Lendemains* 59 (1990): 5–15.
- 'Réponses à Michael Nerlich: 'Curtius trahi par les siens." *Romanische Forschungen* 110 (1998): 478–90.

Richards, Earl Jeffrey. 'La conscience européenne chez Curtius et chez ses détracteurs.' In *Ernst Robert Curtius et l'idée d'Europe*, ed. Bem and Guyaux, 257–86.
- *Modernism, Medievalism, and Humanism: A Research Bibliography on the Reception of the Works of Ernst Robert Curtius*. Tübingen: Niemeyer, 1983.

Sauter, Hermann. Review of *Deutscher Geist in Gefahr*. *Völkischer Beobachter* 83 (24 March 1933).

Theis, Raimund. *Auf der Suche nach dem besten Frankreich: Zum Briefwechsel von Ernst Robert Curtius mit André Gide und Charles Du Bos*. Frankfurt: Klostermann, 1984.

Thönnissen, Karl. *Ethos und Methode: Zur Bestimmung der Metaliteratur nach Ernst Robert Curtius*. Aachen: Aquamarine, 2001.

Westra, Haijo J. Review of *Ernst Robert Curtius: Werk, Wirkung, Zukunftsperspektiven*, edited by Walter Berschin and Arnold Rothe. *Canadian Review of Comparative Literature* 19 (1992): 642–5.

Wuttke, Dieter, ed. *Kosmopolis der Wissenschaft: E.R. Curtius und das Warburg Institute, Briefe 1928 bis 1953 und andere Dokumente*. Berlin: Koerner, 1989.

Erich Auerbach

Auerbach, Erich. *Dante als Dichter der irdischen Welt*. Berlin: de Gruyter, 1929. Trans. Ralph Manheim. *Dante, Poet of the Secular World*. Chicago: University of Chicago Press, 1961.
- 'Epilegomena zu *Mimesis*.' *Romanische Forschungen* 65 (1954): 1–18.
- *Gesammelte Aufsätze zur romanischen Philologie*. Berne: Francke, 1967.
- *Introduction aux études de philologie romane*. Frankfurt: Klostermann, 1949. Trans. Guy Daniels. *Introduction to Romance Languages and Literature*. New York: Capricorn, 1961.
- *Literatursprache und Publikum in der lateinischen Spätantike und im Mittelalter*. Berne: Francke, 1958. Trans. Ralph Manheim. *Literary Language and Its Public in Late Latin Antiquity and in the Middle Ages*. New York: Bollingen Foundation, 1965.
- *Mimesis: dargestellte Wirklichkeit in der abendländischen Literatur*. Berne: Francke, 1946. Trans. Willard R. Trask. *Mimesis: The Representation of Reality in Western Literature*. Princeton: Princeton University Press, 1953.
- *Neue Dantestudien*. Istanbul: Horoz, 1944.

– *Die neue Wissenschaft über die gemeinschaftliche Natur der Völker.* By Giambattista Vico. Trans. Erich Auerbach. Munich: Allgemeine Verlags-Anstalt, 1924.
– 'Philology and Weltliteratur.' *Centennial Review* 13 (1969): 1–17.
– *Scenes from the Drama of European Literature.* Minneapolis: University of Minnesota Press, 1984. First published 1959.
– *Studi su Dante.* Milan: Faltrinelli, 1963.
– 'Vico and Aesthetic Historism.' In *Scenes from the Drama of European Literature,* 181–98.
– *Vier Untersuchungen zur Geschichte der französischen Bildung.* Berne: Francke, 1951.
– *Zur Technik der Frührenaissancenovelle in Italien und Frankreich.* Heidelberg: Winter, 1921.
Barck, Karlheinz. 'Walter Benjamin and Erich Auerbach: Fragments of a Correspondence.' *Diacritics* 22: 3–4 (Fall–Winter 1992): 81–3.
Bové, Paul A. *Intellectuals in Power: A Genealogy of Critical Humanism.* New York: Columbia University Press, 1986.
Busch, Walter, and Gerhart Pickerodt, eds. *Wahrnehmen, Lesen, Deuten: Erich Auerbachs Lektüre der Moderne.* Frankfurt: Klostermann, 1998.
Davis, Robert Gorham. 'The Imitation of Life.' *Partisan Review* 21 (1954): 321–6.
Docherty, Thomas. 'Anti-Mimesis: The Historicity of Representation.' *Forum for Modern Language Studies* 26 (1990): 272–81.
Drabble, Margaret. 'Mimesis: The Representation of Reality in the Post-War British Novel.' *Mosaic* 20:1 (Winter 1987): 1–14.
Eagleton, Terry. Review of *Literary Criticism and the Structures of History* by Geoffrey Green. *Modern Language Review* 79 (1984): 385–6.
Elsky, Martin. 'Erich Auerbach's *Seltsamkeit*: The Seventeenth Century and the History of Feelings.' In *Reading the Renaissance: Ideas and Idioms from Shakespeare to Milton,* ed. Marc Berley, 176–204. Pittsburgh: Duquesne University Press, 2003.
Escola, Marc. 'Vrai caractère du faux dévot: Molière, La Bruyère et Auerbach.' *Poétique* 98 (avril 1994): 181–98.
Evans, Arthur R., Jr. 'Erich Auerbach as European Critic.' *Romance Philology* 25 (1971–2): 193–215.
'Fifty Years after Auerbach's *Mimesis*: The Representation of Reality in Literature.' Selected papers in *Poetics Today* 20:1 (Spring 1999): 1–91.
Gellrich, Jesse M. '*Figura*, Allegory, and the Question of History.' In *Literary History and the Challenge of Philology,* ed. Lerer, 107–23.
Green, Geoffrey. 'Erich Auerbach and the "Inner Dream" of Transcendence.' In *Literary History and the Challenge of Philology,* ed. Lerer, 214–26.
– *Literary Criticism and the Structures of History: Erich Auerbach and Leo Spitzer.* Lincoln: University of Nebraska Press, 1982.

Gronau, Klaus. *Literarische Form und gesellschaftliche Entwicklung: Erich Auerbachs Beitrag zur Theorie und Methodologie der Literaturgeschichte.* Königstein: Forum Academicum, 1979.

Gumbrecht, Hans Ulrich. '"Pathos of the Earthly Progress": Erich Auerbach's Everydays.' In *Literary History and the Challenge of Philology*, ed. Lerer, 13–35.

Hatzfeld, Helmut A. Review of *Mimesis. Romance Philology* 2 (1948–9): 333–8.

Holdheim, W. Wolfgang. 'Auerbach's *Mimesis*: Aesthetics as Historical Understanding.' *CLIO* 10 (1980–1): 143–54.

– 'The Hermeneutic Significance of Auerbach's *Ansatz*.' *New Literary History* 16 (1984–5): 627–31.

Holquist, Michael. 'Erich Auerbach and the Fate of Philology Today.' *Poetics Today* 20:1 (Spring 1999): 77–91.

– 'The Last European: Erich Auerbach as Precursor in the History of Cultural Criticism.' *Modern Language Quarterly* 54 (1993): 371–91.

Landauer, Carl. 'Auerbach's Performance and the American Academy, or How New Haven Stole the Idea of *Mimesis*.' In *Literary History and the Challenge of Philology*, ed. Lerer, 179–94.

Lerer, Seth, ed. *Literary History and the Challenge of Philology: The Legacy of Erich Auerbach.* Stanford: Stanford University Press, 1996.

Lindenberger, Herbert. 'On the Reception of *Mimesis*.' In *Literary History and the Challenge of Philology*, ed. Lerer, 195–213.

Mattenklott, Gert. 'Erich Auerbach in den deutsch-jüdischen Verhältnissen.' In *Wahrnehmen, Lesen, Deuten*, ed. Busch and Pickerodt, 15–30.

Mufti, Aamir R. 'Auerbach in Istanbul: Edward Said, Secular Criticism, and the Question of Minority Culture.' *Critical Inquiry* 25 (1998–9): 95–125.

Muscatine, Charles. Review of *Mimesis. Romance Philology* 9 (1955–6): 448–57.

Paden, William D. 'Tenebrism in the *Song of Roland*.' *Modern Philology* 86 (1988–9): 339–56.

Said, Edward W. 'Introduction to Erich Auerbach's *Mimesis*.' In *Humanism and Democratic Criticism*, 85–118. New York: Columbia University Press, 2004.

Wellek, René. *A History of Modern Criticism: 1750–1950.* Vol. 7. *German, Russian, and Eastern European Criticism, 1900–1950.* New Haven: Yale University Press, 1991.

White, Hayden. 'Auerbach's Literary History: Figural Causation and Modernist Historicism.' In *Literary History and the Challenge of Philology*, ed. Lerer, 124–39.

Ziolkowski, Jan M. 'Forward to Auerbach, *Literary Language and Its Public*, ix–xxxix.

Zumthor, Paul. 'Erich Auerbach ou l'éloge de la philologie.' *Littérature* 5 (février 1972): 107–16.

Albert Béguin

Béguin, Albert. *L'âme romantique et le rêve: Essai sur le romantisme allemand et la poésie française.* 2 vols. Marseille: Éditions des Cahiers du Sud, 1937. Repr. Geneva: Slatkine, 1993.
– *Balzac lu et relu.* Paris: Seuil, 1965.
– *Balzac visionnaire: Propositions.* Geneva: Skira, 1946.
– *Bernanos par lui-même.* Paris: Seuil, 1954.
– *Création et destinée: Essais de critique littéraire.* Paris: Seuil, 1973.
– *Création et destinée II: La réalité du rêve.* Paris: Seuil, 1974.
– *L' 'Ève' de Péguy: Essai de lecture commentée.* Paris: Labergerie, 1948.
– *Gérard de Nerval.* Paris: Corti, 1945.
– *Gérard de Nerval,* suivi de *Poésie et mystique.* Paris: Stock, 1937.
– *Léon Bloy, l'impatient.* Fribourg: Egloff, 1944.
– *Léon Bloy, mystique de la douleur.* Paris: Labergerie, 1948.
– *Pascal par lui-même.* Paris: Seuil, 1952.
– *Poésie de la présence, de Chrétien de Troyes à Pierre Emmanuel.* Neuchâtel: Baconnière, 1957.
– *La prière de Péguy.* Neuchâtel: Baconnière, 1942.
Béguin, Albert, ed. *Le mystère de la charité de Jeanne d'Arc.* By Charles Péguy. Paris: Club du meilleur livre, 1956.
Böschenstein, Bernard. 'Albert Béguin face aux poètes du romantisme allemand.' In *Albert Béguin et Marcel Raymond,* ed. Grotzer, 85–93.
Cahiers du Sud 360 (avril–mai 1961). On Albert Béguin.
Chudak, Henryk, and Alain Grosrichard, eds. *Bilan de l'École de Genève: Actes du colloque polono-suisse … Varsovie, mai 1992.* Warsaw: Éditions de l'Université de Varsovie, 1995.
Civitas 11 (juillet 1973). On Albert Béguin.
'La critique littéraire suisse: Autour de l'Ecole de Genève.' Topic of *Œuvres et Critiques* 27:2 (2002).
Demorest, Jean-Jacques. 'Albert Béguin, le salut par les poètes.' *Modern Language Notes* 78 (1963): 453–70.
Esprit 268 (décembre 1958). On Albert Béguin.
Esprit 361 (juin 1967). On Albert Béguin.
Franck, Dorothée-Juliane. *La quête spirituelle d'Albert Béguin.* Neuchâtel: Baconnière, 1965.
Green, Julien, et al. *Albert Béguin: Étapes d'une pensée; Rencontres avec Albert Béguin.* Neuchâtel: Baconnière, 1957.
Grotzer, Béatrice, and Pierre Grotzer. *Les Archives Albert Béguin: Inventaire.* Neuchâtel: Baconnière, 1975.

Grotzer, Pierre. *Albert Béguin ou la passion des autres.* Paris: Seuil, 1977.
– *Les écrits d'Albert Béguin: Essai de bibliographie.* Neuchâtel: Baconnière, 1967.
– *Existence et destinée d'Albert Béguin: Essai de biographie.* Neuchâtel: Baconnière, 1977.
Grotzer, Pierre, ed. *Albert Béguin et Marcel Raymond: Colloque de Cartigny.* Paris: Corti, 1979.
Lawall, Sarah N. *Critics of Consciousness: The Existential Structures of Literature.* Cambridge, MA: Harvard University Press, 1968.
Lemke, Gerd. *Untersuchungen zu Zitat und Zitiermethode im Werk des Literaturkritikers Albert Béguin.* Frankfurt: Lang, 1973.
Michaud, Stéphane. 'Le moment Béguin.' *Œuvres et Critiques* 27:2 (2002): 91–104.
Miller, J. Hillis. 'The Geneva School: The Criticism of Marcel Raymond, Albert Béguin, Georges Poulet, Jean Rousset, Jean-Pierre Richard, and Jean Starobinski.' In *Theory Now and Then,* 13–29. New York: Harvester Wheatsheaf, 1991.
Mosci, Gastone. *Mounier e Béguin.* Urbino: QuattroVenti, 1983.
Mosci, Gastone, ed. *Albert Béguin: Letteratura e impegno.* Rome: Gruppo di Presenza Culturale, 1979.
Noirjean de Ceuninck, Martine, ed. *De l'amitié: Hommage à Albert Béguin (1901–1957).* Neuchâtel: Université de Neuchâtel, 2001.
Picon, Gaëtan. 'Balzac surnaturel.' *Esprit* 268 (décembre 1958): 841–52.
Pot, Olivier. 'Jalons pour une critique en mouvement (autour de l'École de Genève).' *Œuvres et Critiques* 27:2 (2002): 5–46.
Poulet, Georges. 'Albert Béguin.' In *La conscience critique,* 129–58. Paris: Corti, 1971.
– 'De l'identification critique chez Albert Béguin et Marcel Raymond.' In *Albert Béguin et Marcel Raymond,* ed. Grotzer, 13–39.
Puleio, Maria Teresa, et al., eds. *L'avventura intellettuale ed umana di Albert Béguin: Atti del Convegno internazionale … Catania 20–24 maggio 1981.* Rome: Bulzoni, 1984.
Raymond, Marcel. 'Albert Béguin.' In *Albert Béguin et Marcel Raymond,* ed. Grotzer, 269–74.
– 'Sur *L'âme romantique et le rêve.*' In *Être et dire: Études,* 209–16. Neuchâtel: Baconnière, 1970.
Rousset, Jean. 'Albert Béguin et l'Allemagne.' In Green et al., *Albert Béguin: Étapes d'une pensée,* 157–64.
Starobinski, Jean. 'Le rêve et l'inconscient: la contribution d'Albert Béguin et de Marcel Raymond.' In *Albert Béguin et Marcel Raymond,* ed. Grotzer, 41–63.
Wellek, René. *A History of Modern Criticism: 1750–1950.* Vol. 8: *French, Italian, and Spanish Criticism, 1900–1950.* New Haven: Yale University Press, 1992.

Zurowska, Joanna. 'Albert Béguin comparatiste: Une relecture de *L'âme romantique et le rêve*.' In *Bilan de l'École de Genève*, ed. Chudak and Grosrichard, 65–74.

Jean Rousset

Carrard, Philippe. 'L'École de Genève et la rhétorique de la circonspection.' *Stanford French Review* 13 (1989): 267–82.
– 'Starobinski, Rousset et la question du récit.' *Swiss-French Studies* 1:2 (November 1980): 24–61.
Derrida, Jacques. 'Forme et signification.' *Critique* 19 (1963): 483–99, 619–36.
Dubois, Claude-Gilbert. 'Le prospecteur et son suiveur: une promenade à pas rapprochés dans les labyrinthes du baroque.' *Œuvres et Critiques* 27:2 (2002): 169–78.
Francillon, Roger. *Jean Rousset ou la passion de la lecture*. Geneva: Zoé, 2001.
Jackson, John E. 'L'École de Genève.' In *Histoire de la littérature en Suisse romande*, ed. Roger Francillon, 3: 519–35. Lausanne: Payot, 1998.
Jeanneret, Michel. 'La forme et la force: Rousset, le baroque et les structures mobiles.' In *Bilan de l'École de Genève: Actes du colloque polono-suisse ... (Varsovie, mai 1992)*, ed. Henryk Chudak and Alain Grosrichard, 75–82. Warsaw: Éditions de l'Université de Varsovie, 1995.
Mathieu-Castellani, Gisèle. 'Marcel Raymond et Jean Rousset, maîtres-pilotes en baroquie: La critique séminale de Marcel Raymond; Portrait de Jean Rousset en critique amoureux.' *Œuvres et Critiques* 27:2 (2002): 153–68.
Miller, J. Hillis. 'The Geneva School: The Criticism of Marcel Raymond, Albert Béguin, Georges Poulet, Jean Rousset, Jean-Pierre Richard, and Jean Starobinski.' In *Theory Now and Then*, 13–29. New York: Harvester Wheatsheaf, 1991.
Poulet, Georges. *La conscience critique*. Paris: Corti, 1971.
Rousset, Jean. *Dernier regard sur le baroque*. Paris: Corti, 1998.
– *Forme et signification: Essais sur les structures littéraires de Corneille à Claudel*. Paris: Corti, 1962.
– *L'intérieur et l'extérieur: Essais sur la poésie et sur le théâtre au XVIIe siècle*. Paris: Corti, 1968.
– *Le lecteur intime, de Balzac au journal*. Paris: Corti, 1986.
– *Leurs yeux se rencontrèrent: La scène de première vue dans le roman*. Paris: Corti, 1981.
– *La littérature de l'âge baroque en France: Circé et le paon*. Paris: Corti, 1953.
– *Le mythe de Don Juan*. Paris: Colin, 1976.
– *Narcisse romancier: Essai sur la première personne dans le roman*. Paris: Corti, 1973.
– *Passages: Échanges et transpositions*. Paris: Corti, 1990.
Rousset, Jean, ed. *Anthologie de la poésie baroque française*. 2 vols. Paris: Colin, 1961.

C.S. Lewis

Adey, Lionel. *C.S. Lewis: Writer, Dreamer, and Mentor.* Grand Rapids, MI: Eerdmans, 1998.

Arnott, Anne. *The Secret Country of C.S. Lewis.* London: Hodder and Stoughton, 1974.

Barbour, Brian. 'Lewis and Cambridge.' *Modern Philology* 96 (1998–9): 439–84.

Barfield, Owen. *Light on C.S. Lewis.* Ed. Jocelyn Gibb. New York: Harcourt, Brace and World, 1965.

Bennett, J.A.W. *The Humane Medievalist: An Inaugural Lecture.* Cambridge: Cambridge University Press, 1965.

– *The Humane Medievalist and Other Essays in English Literature and Learning, from Chaucer to Eliot.* Rome: Edizioni di Storia e Letteratura, 1982.

Bennett, Joan. 'The Love Poetry of John Donne: A Reply to Mr. C.S. Lewis.' In *Seventeenth Century Studies Presented to Sir Herbert Grierson,* 85–104. Oxford: Oxford University, Clarendon Press, 1938.

Carpenter, Humphrey. *The Inklings: C.S. Lewis, J.R.R. Tolkien, Charles Williams, and Their Friends.* London: Allen and Unwin, 1978.

Coghill, Nevill. 'The Approach to English.' In *Light on C.S. Lewis,* ed. Jocelyn Gibb, 51–66. New York: Harcourt, Brace and World, 1965.

Coren, Michael. *The Man Who Created Narnia: The Story of C.S. Lewis.* Toronto: Lester, 1994.

Dorsett, Lyle W. *And God Came In.* New York: Macmillan, 1983.

Downing, David C. 'From Pillar to Postmodernism: C.S. Lewis and Current Critical Discourse.' *Christianity and Literature* 46 (1996–7): 169–78.

Edwards, Bruce L., Jr. *A Rhetoric of Reading: C.S. Lewis's Defense of Western Literature.* Provo, UT: Brigham Young University, 1986.

Edwards, Bruce L., ed. *The Taste of the Pineapple: Essays on C.S. Lewis as Reader, Critic, and Imaginative Writer.* Bowling Green: Bowling Green State University Popular Press, 1988.

Eliot, T.S. 'A Note on the Verse of John Milton.' *Essays and Studies* 21 (1936): 32–40.

Filmer, Kath. *The Fiction of C.S. Lewis: Mask and Mirror.* New York: St Martin's Press, 1993.

Fredrick, Candice, and Sam McBride. *Women among the Inklings: Gender, C.S. Lewis, J.R.R. Tolkien, and Charles Williams.* Westport, CT: Greenwood, 2001.

Gardner, Helen. 'Clive Staples Lewis: 1898–1963.' *Proceedings of the British Academy* 51 (1965): 417–28.

Glaspey, Terry W. *Not a Tame Lion: The Spiritual Legacy of C.S. Lewis.* Nashville: Cumberland House, 1996.

Goldberg, S.L. 'C.S. Lewis and the Study of English.' *Melbourne Critical Review* 5 (1962): 119–27.

Gormley, Beatrice. *C.S. Lewis: Christian and Storyteller.* Grand Rapids, MI: Eerdmans, 1998.

Green, Roger Lancelyn, and Walter Hooper. *C.S. Lewis: A Biography.* London: Collins, 1974. Rev. and expanded: London: Collins, 2002.

Gresham, Douglas H. *Lenten Lands.* New York: Macmillan, 1988.

Griffin, William. *Clive Staples Lewis: A Dramatic Life.* San Francisco: Harper and Row, 1986.

Hannay, Margaret Patterson. *C.S. Lewis.* New York: Ungar, 1981.

Hart, Dabney Adams. *Through the Open Door: A New Look at C.S. Lewis.* Tuscaloosa: University of Alabama Press, 1984.

Hartt, Walter F. 'Godly Influences: The Theology of J.R.R. Tolkien and C.S. Lewis.' *Studies in the Literary Imagination* 14:2 (Fall 1981): 21–9.

Hooper, Walter. *Through Joy and Beyond: A Pictorial Biography of C.S. Lewis.* New York: Macmillan, 1982.

Hough, Graham. 'Old Western Man.' In *Critical Essays on C.S. Lewis,* ed. Watson, 241.

Jeffrey, David Lyle. 'Medieval Literature.' In *Reading the Classics,* ed. Martin, 72–86.

Jones, Alan, and Edmund Fuller. 'An Affectionate and Muted Exchange anent Lewis.' *Studies in the Literary Imagination* 14:2 (Fall 1981): 7–11.

Kerby-Fulton, Kathryn. '"Standing on Lewis's Shoulders": C.S. Lewis as Critic of Medieval Literature.' *Studies in Medievalism* 3 (1990–1): 257–78.

Leavis, F.R. *Revaluation: Tradition and Development in English Poetry.* London: Chatto and Windus, 1936.

Lewis, Clive Staples. *The Allegory of Love: A Study in Medieval Tradition.* Oxford: Oxford University, Clarendon Press, 1936.

– *De Descriptione Temporum: An Inaugural Lecture.* Cambridge: Cambridge University Press, 1955. Repr. *Selected Literary Essays,* 1–14.

– *The Discarded Image: An Introduction to Medieval and Renaissance Literature.* Cambridge: Cambridge University Press, 1964.

– *English Literature in the Sixteenth Century (Excluding Drama).* Oxford: Oxford University, Clarendon Press, 1954.

– *An Experiment in Criticism.* Cambridge: Cambridge University Press, 1961.

– *The Personal Heresy: A Controversy.* See Tillyard.

– *A Preface to 'Paradise Lost.'* London: Oxford University Press, 1942.

– *Selected Literary Essays.* Ed. Walter Hooper. Cambridge: Cambridge University Press, 1969.

– *Spenser's Images of Life.* Ed. Alastair Fowler. Cambridge: Cambridge University Press, 1967.

– *Studies in Medieval and Renaissance Literature.* Ed. Walter Hooper. Cambridge: Cambridge University Press, 1966.
– *Studies in Words.* Cambridge: Cambridge University Press, 1960. 2nd expanded ed., 1967.
– 'What Chaucer Really Did to *Il Filostrato.*' *Essays and Studies* 19 (1934): 7–28. Repr. In *Selected Literary Essays,* 27–44.
– 'Williams and the Arthuriad.' In Charles Williams and C.S. Lewis, *Arthurian Torso,* 91–200. London: Oxford University Press, 1948.
Lewis, Clive Staples, ed. *George MacDonald: An Anthology.* London: Bles, 1946.
Loomis, Roger Sherman. 'Literary History and Literary Criticism: A Critique of C.S. Lewis.' *Modern Language Review* 60 (1965): 508–11.
Martin, Thomas L., ed. *Reading the Classics with C.S. Lewis.* Grand Rapids, MI: Baker, 2000.
McBride, Sam. 'C.S. Lewis's *A Preface to "Paradise Lost,"* the Milton Controversy, and Lewis Scholarship.' *Bulletin of Bibliography* 52 (1995): 317–31.
McGovern, Eugene. 'Reflections Provoked by *On Stories.*' *CSL: The Bulletin of the New York C.S. Lewis Society* 13:9 (July 1982): 3–6.
Milward, Peter, S.J. *A Challenge to C.S. Lewis.* Madison and Teaneck: Fairleigh Dickinson University Press, 1995.
– 'A Judgment Judged – Lewis on the More-Tyndale Controversy.' *Moreana* 64 (March 1980): 28–36.
Nicholson, William. *Shadowlands: A Play.* London: French, 1990.
Piehler, Paul. 'Visions and Revisions: C.S. Lewis's Contribution to the Theory of Allegory.' In *The Taste of the Pineapple,* ed. Edwards, 79–91.
Pittenger, Norman. 'C.S. Lewis: Combative in Defense.' *Studies in the Literary Imagination* 14:2 (Fall 1981): 13–20.
Sayer, George. *Jack: C.S. Lewis and His Times.* San Francisco: Harper and Row, 1988.
Schakel, Peter J. *Imagination and the Arts in C.S. Lewis: Journeying to Narnia and Other Worlds.* Columbia: University of Missouri Press, 2002.
– *Reason and Imagination in C.S. Lewis: A Study of 'Till We Have Faces.'* Grand Rapids, MI: Eerdmans, 1984.
Sharrock, Roger. 'Second Thoughts: C.S. Lewis on Chaucer's *Troilus.*' *Essays in Criticism* 8 (1958): 123–37.
Sibley, Brian. *Shadowlands: The Story of C.S. Lewis and Joy Davidman.* London: Hodder and Stoughton, 1985.
Stoll, Elmer Edgar. 'Give the Devil His Due: A Reply to Mr. Lewis.' *Review of English Studies* 20 (1944): 108–24.
Tillyard, E.M.W. *The Muse Unchained: An Intimate Account of the Revolution in English Studies at Cambridge.* London: Bowes and Bowes, 1958.
Tillyard, E.M.W., and C.S. Lewis. *The Personal Heresy: A Controversy.* London: Oxford University Press, 1939.

Tollefsen, Olaf. 'C.S. Lewis on Evaluative Judgments of Literature.' *Modern Schoolman* 56 (1978–9): 356–63.

Utley, Francis Lee. 'Anglicanism and Anthropology: C.S. Lewis and John Speirs.' *Southern Folklore Quarterly* 31 (1967): 1–11.

Vinaver, Eugene. 'On Art and Nature: A Letter to C.S. Lewis.' In *Essays on Malory*, ed. J.A.W. Bennett, 29–40. Oxford: Clarendon Press, 1963.

Watson, George, ed. *Critical Essays on C.S. Lewis*. Aldershot, Hants: Scolar Press, 1992.

Wilson, A.N. *C.S. Lewis: A Biography*. London: Collins, 1990.

F.O. Matthiessen

Arac, Jonathan. 'F.O. Matthiessen: Authorizing an American Renaissance.' In *The American Renaissance Reconsidered*, ed. Michaels and Peace, 90–112.

Bergman, David. 'F.O. Matthiessen: The Critic as Homosexual.' *Raritan* 9:4 (Spring 1990): 62–82.

Bowron, Bertrand. 'The Making of an American Scholar.' In *F.O. Matthiessen (1902–1950): A Collective Portrait*, ed. Paul M. Sweezy and Leo Huberman, 44–54. New York: Schuman, 1950.

Brooks, Van Wyck. *The Pilgrimage of Henry James*. New York: Dutton, 1925.

Cadden, Michael. 'Engendering F.O. Matthiessen: The Private Life of *American Renaissance*.' In *Engendering Men: The Question of Male Feminist Criticism*, ed. Joseph A. Boone and Michael Cadden, 26–35. New York: Routledge, 1990.

Cain, William E. *F.O. Matthiessen and the Politics of Criticism*. Madison: University of Wisconsin Press, 1988.

Caton, L. Freitas. 'The Old, the New, the American Canon: Reputation, History, Form.' *Interdisciplinary Literary Studies* 1:1 (Fall 1999): 60–80.

Cheyfitz, Eric. 'Matthiessen's *American Renaissance*: Circumscribing the Revolution.' *American Quarterly* 41 (1989): 341–61.

Grossman, Jay. 'The Canon in the Closet: Matthiessen's Whitman, Whitman's Matthiessen.' *American Literature* 70 (1998): 799–832.

Gunn, Giles B. *F.O. Matthiessen: The Critical Achievement*. Seattle: University of Washington Press, 1975.

Hicks, Granville. *The Great Tradition: An Interpretation of American Literature since the Civil War*. New York: Macmillan, 1933.

Marx, Leo. 'Double Consciousness and the Cultural Politics of F.O. Matthiessen.' *Monthly Review* 34:9 (February 1983): 34–56.

Matthiessen, Francis Otto. *The Achievement of T.S. Eliot: An Essay on the Nature of Poetry*. New York: Oxford University Press, 1935; 2nd ed. 1947; 3rd ed. 1958.

– *American Renaissance: Art and Expression in the Age of Emerson and Whitman*. London: Oxford University Press, 1941.

– *From the Heart of Europe*. New York: Oxford University Press, 1948.

– *Henry James: The Major Phase.* London: Oxford University Press, 1944.
– *The James Family, Including Selections from the Writings of Henry James, Senior, William, Henry, and Alice James.* New York: Knopf, 1947.
– 'Poetry.' In *Literary History of the United States,* ed. Robert E. Spiller et al., 2: 1335–57 New York: Macmillan, 1948.
– *The Responsibilities of the Critic: Essays and Reviews.* Ed. John Rackliffe. New York: Oxford University Press, 1952.
– *Sarah Orne Jewett.* Boston: Houghton Mifflin, 1929.
– *Theodore Dreiser.* The American Men of Letters Series; William Sloane Associates, 1951.
– *Translation: An Elizabethan Art.* Cambridge, MA: Harvard University Press, 1931.
Matthiessen, F.O., ed. *The Oxford Book of American Verse.* New York: Oxford University Press, 1950.
Matthiessen, F.O., and Kenneth B. Murdock, eds. *The Notebooks of Henry James.* New York: Oxford University Press, 1947.
Michaels, Walter Benn, and Donald Peace, eds. *The American Renaissance Reconsidered.* Baltimore: Johns Hopkins University Press, 1983.
Morris, Charles E. III. '"The Responsibility of the Critic": F.O. Matthiessen's Homosexual Palimpsest.' *Quarterly Journal of Speech* 84 (1998): 261–82.
Parrington, Vernon L. *Main Currents in American Thought: An Interpretation of American Literature from the Beginnings to 1920.* 3 vols. New York: Harcourt, Brace, 1927–30.
Ruland, Richard. 'F.O. Matthiessen, Christian Socialist: Literature and the Repossession of Our Cultural Past.' In *The Rediscovery of American Literature: Premises of Critical Taste, 1900–1940,* 209–73. Cambridge, MA: Harvard University Press, 1967.
Stern, Frederick C. *F.O. Matthiessen: Christian Socialist as Critic.* Chapel Hill: University of North Carolina Press, 1981.
Tompkins, Jane. 'The Other American Renaissance.' In *The American Renaissance Reconsidered,* ed. Michaels and Peace, 34–57.
Wellek, René. *A History of Modern Criticism: 1750–1950.* Vol. 6. *American Criticism, 1900–1950.* New Haven: Yale University Press, 1986.

Northrop Frye

Adamson, Joseph. *Northrop Frye: A Visionary Life.* Toronto: ECW, 1993.
– 'The Treason of the Clerks: Frye, Ideology, and the Authority of Imaginative Culture.' In *Rereading Frye,* ed. Boyd and Salusinszky, 72–102.
Alter, Robert. 'Northrop Frye between Archetype and Typology.' In *Northrop Frye and the Afterlife of the Word,* ed. Kee, 9–21. In *Frye and the Word,* ed. Donaldson and Mendelson, 137–50.

Atwood, Margaret. *Survival: A Thematic Guide to Canadian Literature.* Toronto: Anansi, 1972.

Ayre, John. *Northrop Frye: A Biography.* Toronto: Random House, 1989.

Balfour, Ian. *Northrop Frye.* Boston: Twayne, 1988.

Bates, Ronald. *Northrop Frye.* Toronto: McClelland and Stewart, 1971.

Bloom, Harold. '"Before Moses Was, I Am": The Original and Belated New Testaments.' In *Poetics of Influence,* ed. John Hollander. New Haven: Schwab, 1988.

Boyd, David, and Imre Salusinszky, eds. *Rereading Frye: The Published and Unpublished Works.* Toronto: University of Toronto Press, 1999.

Cook, David. *Northrop Frye: A Vision of the New World.* Montreal: New World Perspectives, 1985.

Cotrupi, Caterina Nella. *Northrop Frye and the Poetics of Process.* Toronto: University of Toronto Press, 2000.

Davey, Frank. 'Surviving the Paraphrase.' In *Surviving the Paraphrase: Eleven Essays on Canadian Literature,* 1–12. Winnipeg: Turnstone, 1983.

Denham, Robert D. *Northrop Frye and Critical Method.* University Park: Pennsylvania State University Press, 1978.

Djwa, Sandra. '"Canadian Angles of Vision": Northrop Frye, Carl Klinck, and the *Literary History of Canada.*' In *Northrop Frye: Eastern and Western Perspectives,* ed. O'Grady and Ning, 95–109.

Donaldson, Jeffery, and Alan Mendelson, eds. *Frye and the Word: Religious Contexts in the Writings of Northrop Frye.* Toronto: University of Toronto Press, 2004.

Elam, Keir. 'A Natural Perspectivism: Frye on Shakespearean Comedy.' In *Ritratto di Northrop Frye,* ed. Lombardo, 181–94.

Fekete, John. *The Critical Twilight: Explorations in the Ideology of Anglo-American Literary Theory from Eliot to McLuhan.* London: Routledge and Kegan Paul, 1977.

Findlay, L.M. 'Frye's Shakespeare, Frye's Canada.' In *Shakespeare in Canada: 'a world elsewhere'?,* ed. Diana Brydon and Irena R. Makaryk, 292–308. Toronto: University of Toronto Press, 2002.

Fletcher, Angus. 'Utopian History and the *Anatomy of Criticism.*' In *Northrop Frye in Modern Criticism,* ed. Krieger, 31–73.

Frye, Northrop. *Anatomy of Criticism: Four Essays.* Princeton: Princeton University Press, 1957.

– *The Bush Garden: Essays on the Canadian Imagination.* Toronto: Anansi, 1971.

– *Collected Works of Northrop Frye.* Vol. 4. *Northrop Frye on Religion.* Ed. Alvin A. Lee and Jean O'Grady. Toronto: University of Toronto Press, 2000.

– *Collected Works of Northrop Frye.* Vol. 7. *Northrop Frye's Writings on Education.* Ed. Goldwin French and Jean O'Grady. Toronto: University of Toronto Press, 2000.

– *Collected Works of Northrop Frye.* Vol. 10. *Northrop Frye on Literature and Society, 1936–1989: Unpublished Papers.* Ed. Robert D. Denham. Toronto: University of Toronto Press, 2002.

- *Collected Works of Northrop Frye.* Vol. 11. *Northrop Frye on Modern Culture.* Ed. Jan Gorak. Toronto: University of Toronto Press, 2003.
- *Collected Works of Northrop Frye.* Vol. 12. *Northrop Frye on Canada.* Ed. Jean O'Grady and David Staines. Toronto: University of Toronto Press, 2003.
- *Creation and Recreation.* Toronto: University of Toronto Press, 1980.
- *The Critical Path: An Essay on the Social Context of Literary Criticism.* Bloomington: Indiana University Press, 1971.
- *Divisions on a Ground: Essays on Canadian Culture.* Ed. James Polk. Toronto: Anansi, 1982.
- *The Double Vision: Language and Meaning in Religion.* Toronto: University of Toronto Press, 1991.
- *Fables of Identity: Studies in Poetic Mythology.* New York: Harcourt, Brace and World, 1963.
- *Fearful Symmetry: A Study of William Blake.* Princeton: Princeton University Press, 1947.
- *Fools of Time: Studies in Shakespearean Tragedy.* Toronto: University of Toronto Press, 1967.
- *The Great Code: The Bible and Literature.* New York: Harcourt, Brace, Jovanovich, 1982.
- 'Letter to the English Institute, 1965.' In *Northrop Frye in Modern Criticism*, ed. Krieger, 27–30.
- 'Literature as Context: Milton's *Lycidas*.' In *Fables of Identity*, 119–29.
- *The Modern Century.* Toronto: Oxford University Press, 1967.
- *The Myth of Deliverance: Reflections on Shakespeare's Problem Comedies.* Toronto: University of Toronto Press, 1983.
- *A Natural Perspective: The Development of Shakespearean Comedy and Romance.* New York: Columbia University Press, 1965.
- *Northrop Frye on Shakespeare.* Ed. Robert Sandler. New Haven: Yale University Press, 1986.
- *On Education.* Markham, ON: Fitzhenry and Whiteside, 1990.
- *The Return of Eden: Five Essays on Milton's Epics.* Toronto: University of Toronto Press, 1965.
- *The Secular Scripture: A Study of the Structure of Romance.* Cambridge, MA: Harvard University Press, 1976.
- 'The Structure of Imagery in the *Faerie Queene*.' In *Fables of Identity*, 69–87.
- *The Stubborn Structure: Essays on Criticism and Society.* Ithaca: Cornell University Press, 1970.
- *A Study of English Romanticism.* New York: Random House, 1968.
- *T.S. Eliot.* Edinburgh: Oliver and Boyd, 1963.
- *The Well-Tempered Critic.* Bloomington: Indiana University Press, 1963.

- *Words with Power: Being a Second Study of 'The Bible and Literature.'* New York: Harcourt, Brace, Jovanovich, 1990.
Gebbia, Alessandro. 'L'idea di letteratura canadese in Frye.' In *Ritratto di Northrop Frye*, ed. Lombardo, 313–19.
Hamilton, A.C. *Northrop Frye: Anatomy of His Criticism.* Toronto: University of Toronto Press, 1990.
- 'Northrop Frye as a Cultural Theorist.' In *Rereading Frye*, ed. Boyd and Salusinszky, 103–21.
- 'Northrop Frye on the Bible and Literature.' *Christianity and Literature* 41 (1991–2): 255–76.
Hart, Jonathan. *Northrop Frye: The Theoretical Imagination.* London: Routledge, 1994.
Hartman, Geoffrey H. 'Ghostlier Demarcations.' In *Northrop Frye in Modern Criticism* ed. Krieger, 109–31.
Hutcheon, Linda. 'Eruptions of Postmodernity: The Postcolonial and the Ecological.' *Essays on Canadian Writing* 51–2 (Winter 1993–Spring 1994): 146–63.
Jameson, Fredric. *The Political Unconscious: Narrative as a Socially Symbolic Act.* Ithaca: Cornell University Press, 1981.
Jones, D.G. *Butterfly on Rock: A Study of Themes and Images in Canadian Literature.* Toronto: University of Toronto Press, 1970.
Kee, James M., ed. *Northrop Frye and the Afterlife of the Word.* Semeia 89. Atlanta: Society of Biblical Literature, 2002.
Kenyeres, János. *Revolving around the Bible: A Study of Northrop Frye.* Budapest: Anonymus, 2003.
Kermode, Frank. 'Northrop Frye and the Bible.' In *Ritratto di Northrop Frye*, ed. Lombardo, 105–20.
Klinck, Carl F., ed. *Literary History of Canada.* 2 vols. Toronto: University of Toronto Press, 1965.
Kogan, Pauline. *Northrop Frye: The High Priest of Clerical Obscurantism.* Montreal: Progressive Books and Periodicals, 1969.
Krieger, Murray. 'Northrop Frye and Contemporary Criticism: Ariel and the Spirit of Gravity.' In *Northrop Frye in Modern Criticism,* 1–26.
Krieger, Murray, ed. *Northrop Frye in Modern Criticism: Selected Papers from the English Institute.* New York: Columbia University Press, 1966.
Kuchar, Gary. 'Typology and the Language of Concern in the Work of Northrop Frye.' *Canadian Review of Comparative Literature* 27 (2000): 159–80.
Lee, Alvin A. 'Sacred and Secular Scripture(s) in the Thought of Northrop Frye.' In *Frye and the Word*, ed. Donaldson and Mendelson, 23–42.
Lee, Alvin A., and Robert D. Denham, eds. *The Legacy of Northrop Frye.* Toronto: University of Toronto Press, 1994.

Lentricchia, Frank. 'The Place of Northrop Frye's *Anatomy of Criticism.*' In *After the New Criticism*, 2–26. Chicago: University of Chicago Press, 1980.

Lombardo, Agostino, ed. *Ritratto di Northrop Frye.* Rome: Bulzoni, 1989.

Mackey, Eva. 'Death by Landscape: Race, Nature, and Gender in Canadian Nationalist Mythology.' *Canadian Woman Studies* 20:2 (Summer 2000): 125–30.

Mandel, Eli. 'Northrop Frye and the Canadian Literary Imagination.' In *Centre and Labyrinth: Essays in Honour of Northrop Frye*, ed. Eleanor Cook et al., 284–97. Toronto: University of Toronto Press, 1983.

Manganaro, Marc. *Myth, Rhetoric, and the Voice of Authority: A Critique of Frazer, Eliot, Frye, and Campbell.* New Haven: Yale University Press, 1992.

Moss, John. *Patterns of Isolation in English Canadian Fiction.* Toronto: McClelland and Stewart, 1974.

O'Grady, Jean. 'Northrop Frye on Liberal Education.' In *Northrop Frye: Eastern and Western Perspectives*, 29–41.

O'Grady, Jean, and Wang Ning, eds. *Northrop Frye: Eastern and Western Perspectives.* Toronto: University of Toronto Press, 2003.

Russell, Ford. *Northrop Frye on Myth: An Introduction.* New York: Garland, 1998.

Salusinszky, Imre. 'Frye and Ideology.' In *The Legacy of Northrop Frye*, ed. Lee and Denham, 76–83.

– '"In the Climates of the Mind": Frye's Career as a Spiral Curriculum.' In *Frye and the Word*, ed. Donaldson and Mendelson, 43–56.

Sauerberg, Lars Ole. *Versions of the Past – Visions of the Future: The Canonical in the Criticism of T.S. Eliot, F.R. Leavis, Northrop Frye, and Harold Bloom.* London: Macmillan, 1997.

Staines, David. 'Frye: Canadian Critic/Writer.' In *The Legacy of Northrop Frye*, ed. Lee and Denham, 155–63.

– 'Northrop Frye in a Canadian Context.' In *Visionary Poetics: Essays on Northrop Frye's Criticism*, ed. Robert D. Denham and Thomas Willard, 47–56. New York: Lang, 1991.

Vendler, Helen. 'Frye's *Endymion*: Myth, Ethics, and Literary Description.' In *The Legacy of Northrop Frye*, ed. Lee and Denham, 201–12.

Willard, Thomas. 'Gone Primitive: The Critic in Canada.' In *Northrop Frye: Eastern and Western Perspectives*, ed. O'Grady and Ning, 110–20.

Willinsky, John. 'Frye among (Postcolonial) Schoolchildren: The Educated Imagination.' *Canadian Children's Literature* 79 (Fall 1995): 6–24.

Wimsatt, W.K. 'Northrop Frye: Criticism as Myth.' In *Northrop Frye in Modern Criticism*, ed. Krieger, 75–107.

Index

Adamson, Joseph, 138
Adorno, Theodor, 10, 162
Aeschylus, 169
aesthetics of reception, 23, 93, 193n5
Aiken, Conrad, 112
Alan of Lille, 97
Alberti, Rafael, 177
allegory: in American literature, 102,
  106; Christian practice of, 25, 46,
  48, 64, 120–1, 133–4; and courtly
  love, 87–8, 106, 172; in modern
  literature, 118
Alter, Robert, 137
American Humanist Association, 152
American literature and culture:
  American Renaissance (Matthiessen),
  4, 101–6, 108, 112–14, 142, 145,
  148, 166, 170; American studies,
  32, 101–2, 133; canon of, 4, 102,
  112–13, 114–15, 170; influence of
  seventeenth-century English literature on, 102–3, 104; poetry, 112;
  soap opera, 176; Sunkist advertisement, 21. *See also individual authors*
Amiel, Henri-Frédéric, 80
amor de lonh, 22–3
amour fou, 181

Anderson, Mark, 190n13
Anderson, Perry, 217n16
Andreas Capellanus, 90
Angelou, Maya, 180
Anglican Church, 144
Ansatzphänomen (Auerbach), 44, 46,
  146
Apollinaire, Guillaume, 67
Apter, Emily, 26, 27
Aragon, Louis, 64, 154, 171, 174, 177,
  184
archetypes (Frye's theory of), 120–1,
  125, 128–9, 137, 210n4; and topoi,
  38–9
Ariosto, Lodovico, 88, 182
Aristophanes, 169
Aristotle, 177
Arnim, Achim von, 58, 59, 67
Arnold, Matthew, 51, 161, 163
Artaud, Antonin, 160
Aspremont, 39
Atwood, Margaret, 136
Aubanel, Théodore, 48
Aubigné, Théodore Agrippa d', 73,
  194n15
Auerbach, Erich, 4, 5–6, 15, 43–56,
  141–50, 160–7; achievements,

book, 16, 146; as a Jew, 19, 26, 28,
52, 95, 144; as a linguist, 15–16;
methodology, 15–17; philological
circle, 16, 18, 19; as a philologist,
15–17, 30; as a polemicist, 17; practical criticism, 21, 22–6; response to
Nazi Third Reich, 3–4, 19, 143, 144
– general publications: *Classical and
Christian Ideas of World Harmony*, 22;
Leo Spitzer: Representative Essays, 26;
Linguistics and Literary History, 20;
MLA Bibliography of, 15, 20, 21,
28; 'Note on the Poetic and Empirical "I" in Medieval Authors,' 22;
Romanische Literaturstudien, 20;
*Romanische Stil- und Literaturstu-
dien*, 20; *Stilstudien*, 20; 'Le style
"circulaire,"' 22
– readings of specific authors and
fields: Dante, 24, 141, 144; French
literature, 19, 142; German litera-
ture, 19; Jaufre Rudel, 22–3; *Libro
de buen amor*, 24–5; Marie de
France's *Lais*, 23; Middle Ages, 21–
6, 170; Middle English lyrics, 25;
modern literary studies, 21; *Poema
del Cid*, 23–4; Spanish literature, 19,
20, 141; Sunkist advertisement, 21;
Villon, 25–6
Spivak, Gayatri Chakravorty, 176, 177
Staiger, Emil, 26
Stanzel, Franz, 77
Starobinski, Jean, 57, 64, 82
Statius, 36, 90
Stendhal (Henri Beyle), 47, 48, 65,
78, 149, 181
Sterne, Laurence, 122, 181
Stevens, Wallace, 112, 163
Stilforschung, 16, 27, 44
St-John Perse, 55, 64

Stowe, Harriet Beecher, 113, 114, 179
structuralism and structural analysis,
8, 145, 148, 180; French, 74–5, 135,
145; Matthiessen on James, 108–9;
Rousset's use of, 74–6
studia humanitatis, 152, 154
Studies in Medievalism, 176
Suarès, André, 31
Supervielle, Jules, 64, 67
surfiction, 175
surrealism, 57, 64, 65, 66, 67, 154,
155, 171
Surrey, Henry Howard, earl of, 89
Swift, Jonathan, 122
symbols (Frye's theory of), 120–1,
175

Tasso, Torquato, 71, 88, 96
Tate, Allen, 112
Taylor, Edward, 112
Tennyson, Alfred, 156
theatre of the absurd, 129
theatrical forms: of the French
baroque, 71–2; mystery plays, 172,
181, 182; Shakespeare's plays, 127
thematic criticism, 132–3, 135
theory, 6–8, 147, 175; and Curtius, 29;
and Frye, 119–24, 135–7, 138; and
Lewis, 92–5, 147; and Matthiessen,
115–16; and Spitzer, 18, 27
Thibaudet, Albert, 198n18
Thomas: *Tristan*, 50
Thoreau, Henry David, 101–6, 116,
170
Tieck, Ludwig, 58, 59
Tillyard, E.M.W., 92, 98
Tirso de Molina, 76, 83
Todorov, Tzvetan, 74
Tolkien, J.R.R., 99
Tollefsen, Olaf, 92

Tolstoy, Leo, 175, 181
Tompkins, Jane, 113, 179
topoi, 4, 20, 36–7, 38, 149
Toynbee, Arnold, 86, 217n16
tragedy, 106, 116, 121–2
tragicomedy, 71–2, 123
tragic realism, 155
Tristan, 50, 173, 181
troubadours, 22–3
Troxler, Ignaz-Paul-Vitalis, 58–9
Tyler, Royall, 104
Tyndale, William, 90, 95

umanisti, 5, 151, 152, 160
Unamumo, Miguel de, 38, 48
United Church of Canada, 133, 144
university, the: humanist critics' role
    in, 5, 28, 33, 54, 70–1, 98, 144, 167;
    public or political role of, 11, 28,
    35; in the United States, 3, 17–18,
    54, 168, 173–4
Urfé, Honoré d', 74

Valéry, Paul, 31, 32, 64, 163
value judgments, 97, 104, 114, 170;
    Frye's opposition to, 124, 137, 147,
    180
Vendler, Helen, 136
Verga, Giovanni, 17, 28
Verlaine, Paul, 67
Vian, Boris, 174
Viau, Théophile de, 74
Vico, Giambattista, 45, 49, 51, 142,
    147
Vigny, Alfred de, 34
Villon, François, 17, 25–6, 181
Virgil, 5, 47, 183; Curtius on, 38, 39,
    40, 100, 161, 162, 164; Lewis on, 88,
    89, 90–1, 161
Vittorini, Elio, 177

Voltaire, 48, 122, 171, 175, 177
Vossler, Karl, 15, 19, 20, 30, 44, 45

Walker, Alice, 180
Wallen, Jeffrey, 176
Wang, N.C., 27
Warburg, Aby, 36, 191n24
Warner, Susan, 113, 114, 179, 180
Warren, Robert Penn, 112
Watts, Alan, 205n29
Webster, John, 107
Wellek, René, 20; on Auerbach, 43,
    44, 50, 55; on Béguin, 57, 60, 64;
    on Curtius, 38; on Matthiessen,
    101, 103; on Spitzer, 20; on topoi,
    38
Westra, Haijo J., 29–30, 38
Whig literary history, 45, 51, 52
White, Hayden, 47
Whitman, Walt, 101–6, 116, 155, 169,
    170, 181
Williams, Charles, 91, 163
Williams, Raymond, 93
Williams, William Carlos, 112
Wilson, Edmund, 5, 61, 68, 74, 155,
    156
Winters, Yvor, 112
Woolf, Virginia, 163, 164
Wygant, Amy, 27

Year's Work in Medievalism, 176
Yeats, William Butler, 52, 112, 154

Zhirmunsky, Victor, 34
Ziolkowski, Jan M., 55
Zola, Émile, 47, 48, 111, 149, 155,
    158, 177
Zumthor, Paul, 30, 55, 180
Zurowska, Joanna, 67
Zweig, Stefan, 15, 55